INSIDE
HISTORIC KERN

INSIDE HISTORIC KERN

Selections from the
Kern County Historical Society's
Quarterly
1949-1981

Editors:

W. Harland Boyd
John Ludeke
Marjorie Rump

Kern County Historical Society, Inc.
Bakersfield, California
1982

Copyright © 1982
by the Kern County Historical Society, Inc.
All rights reserved.
Manufactured in the United States of America.
Pioneer Publishing Company
Fresno, California 93728
ISBN 0-943500-09-5

Table of Contents

Preface ix

The Kern County Historical Society xi

Presidents of the Historical Society, 1931 to 1982 xiii

I. Explorers and Pioneers 1
   Father Francisco Garces 2
   Edward F. Beale: Pioneer in the Path of Empire 3
   Thomas Baker Came to Kern Island in 1863 9
   Historic Willow Springs 15
   Granite Station 19
   Captain Elisha Stevens, 1803-87 21
   Early History and Reminiscences 23
   The Life of John McCray 28
   As I Recall 36
   California, Here I Come 41

II. Travel and Transportation 49
   Historic Routes and Passes 50
   When Camels Came to Kern 53
   Freighting Recollections 58
   From Trail to Rail 60
   The Street Car in Bakersfield 66
   Via Granite Station 68
   The Kern Canyon Road 70
   Early Flight and Autos in Kern 74
   Gossamer Condor Flight 79

III. Farming and Ranching 81
   The Historic Rio Bravo Ranch 82
   The Story of San Emigdio Ranch 83
   The Naming of San Emigdio 88
   The Hog Hunter of the Tules 90
   Kern River Flour Mill 93
   The Hospitality of Henry Miller 94
   Steam Tractor in Kern Debut 95
   The I.W.W in Kern County, 1911–22 96
   Sheep Industry in Kern County 99
   Rice Farming in 1915 102

IV. A Diverse People   105
    The Yokuts of the San Joaquin Valley   106
    Indian Attack   107
    The Keyesville Massacre of 1863   111
    Thomas Castro: A Founding Father   114
    The Chinese in Bakersfield   115
    Bakersfield Chinese Temple   119
    Early Negro Settlers   123
    Interview with William Henry Pinkney   125
    Russians in Kern County   131

V. Mining and Petroleum Industries   135
    Monolith Vital to History   136
    Red Rock Canyon   139
    Borax Mining in the Frazier Area   143
    Story of the Yellow Aster   148
    The Early Days in the Oil Fields   154

VI. Mountain and Desert Communities   159
    Havilah   160
    Recall Ballot Battle of 1873   162
    A Havilah School Teacher   164
    Kern County One Hundred Years Ago   169
    Claraville and Sageland   171
    Sageland: Its Rise and Fall, 1866–76   173
    On the South Fork   175
    Walker Basin   177
    S.P. Changes Names of Two Stations   185
    Woody Newest Kern County Town   185
    Saltdale   186

VII. Bakersfield and Sumner   187
    The Birth of Kern County   188
    Reminiscences of a Growing City   190
    Bishop's Narrative, November, 1881   194
    Bakersfield   196
    China Grade   197
    Sumner, A Place Almost Mythical   198
    East Bakersfield Vignette   200
    Virginia Colony   202
    Bakersfield's Public Utilities   202
    Southern Hotel   206

First Television Station West of the Mississippi River 207
Beale Clock Tower 209

VIII. **Valley Towns 211**
San Emigdio Indian Village 212
Delano: Random Notes 212
Caliente: Boom and Bust 217
"Joyful"—A Dream Rooted in Optimism 220
Kimberlina Dates from 1889 222
Gosford 223
Glenburn Becomes Jewetta 223
Survey for the Town of Edison 224
Will Call the Town McFarland 224
History of Arvin 225
The Beginnings of Taft 230

IX. **Flood, Fire, Flora and Fauna 237**
The Kern River Flood of 1893 238
The Bakersfield Fire of 1889 242
The Town of Kern Nearly Blotted out by Fire 245
Nineteen Fifty-two Earthquake Notes 248
Kern's Giant Grapevine 251
The Mighty Grizzly Bear 253
Pacific Coast Field Trials 254
A Wonderful Exhibition of Horse Breaking 256
Ostriches Unlimited 257
The Buena Vista Mouse Plague 261

Index 265

Illustrations

General Edward Fitzgerald Beale   5
Colonel Thomas Baker   11
Fort Tejon Hospital building, c. 1890   55
Tehachapi Loop, 1876   63
Bakersfield aviation meet, 1911   77
San Emigdio Ranch   87
Map of Kern River irrigation system, 1883   92
Hyde's steam tractor, 1875   97
Lakeside artesian well, 1889   103
Leong Yen Ming family in 1910   117
E. W. Winters' second hand store   127
Lakeview gusher near Maricopa, 1910   156
Kernville street scene, c. 1910   161
Havilah, 1880s   165
Walker Basin in the 1890s   179
Bakersfield parade, 1898   189
Bakersfield street scene before the Fire of 1889   203
Kern County Courthouse, 1896   205
Mack trucks on the Lion's Trail, c. 1914   219
Downtown Taft, 1928   233
Bakersfield after the Fire of 1889   243
Bakersfield under recontruction, 1889   249
Pacific Coast Field Trials   255

Preface

For more than thirty years, *Historic Kern* has served as the scholarly publication of the Kern County Historical Society. The contributors to this quarterly, with few exceptions, have been local authors interested in recording the history of this county. Some have written from personal experience, others out of professional interest. Certainly some of the most colorful articles have been authored by non-professional writers who, fortunately for us, recorded their experiences. This work is an effort by the Historical Society to make available to the interested reader a carefully edited selection of those articles, organized both by subject and chronology.

This collection represents perhaps one-third of the material available. Much time and thought were given to the selection process by the editors. Some topics, such as the mining town of Havilah, have received much attention over the years in *Historic Kern*, and it was possible to include here only representative pieces. Several articles were of some interest at the time of publication, but of less interest to today's reading public. The focus of other articles was outside the county and, therefore, inappropriate to this collection.

Unevenness in writing is to be expected in a publication of this sort. Over the years, authors of varying abilities ranging from professional to amateur have been published, and quite properly so. We have made minimal changes in style and syntax, excising material where tedious or repetitive and correcting gross errors in usage to achieve, we hope, a readable and informative book.

A mere glance at the topics covered in this collection reveals large gaps of information. No efforts have been made by past editors of *Historic Kern* to systematically explore Kern County history in all its aspects. Rather, as is the case with most local historical society publications, the editors have relied upon the talents and interests of writers as they have made themselves and their topics available. Important subjects have been ignored or barely touched: the 1952 earthquake, the fascinating story of water usage by valley farmers, the twists and turns of political history in Bakersfield and outlying communities, the more intimate tales of families and local businesses. All these subjects await the enterprising author who would contribute to *Historic Kern*. So if this collection is impressive in its variety, it is true that yet more topics remain to be explored and recorded.

This publication is in partial celebration of the fiftieth anniversary of the society's founding in 1931. It should remind us of the romance and color of a community that has progressed from something of a mining and agricultural backwater to a booming modern community in less than 100 years.

> W. Harland Boyd
> John Ludeke
> Marjorie Rump
>
> Bakersfield, California
> 1982

The Kern County Historical Society

The Kern County Historical Society was founded in April, 1931, by several civic-minded people interested in "collecting, preserving, and disseminating historical information" who met in the office of Alfred Harrell at the *Bakersfield Californian*. The historical society was a successor to the Society of Kern County Pioneers, which had been organized in April, 1895. Understandably, that pioneer society, comprised of an exclusive, non-renewing membership, could only "self-destruct" with the passage of time.

The Society of Kern Pioneers was waning in April, 1931, when Alfred Harrell and others of a history-minded group decided to replace it with the Kern County Historical Society. Among the founders of the new organization, in addition to Harrell, were Herman Spindt, Dwight Clark, William A. Howell, Jesse D. Stockton, Hugh S. Jewett, Roy W. Loudon, William V. Ewert, and Calvin V. Anderson. Alfred Harrell became the founding president, while Cora F. Bender served as financial secretary and Julia G. Babcock as recording secretary.

Over the half-century of its existence, the Kern County Historical Society has engaged in a variety of activities related to its stated purposes. Among these has been an outstanding publication program, starting with an article written by Professor Herbert E. Bolton of the University of California. In it he traced the route followed by Pedro Fages when he visited the southern San Joaquin Valley in 1772. This was the first of many pamphlets and books made available by the Kern County Historical Society. The organization has well merited its widespread reputation as a publishing society.

Members of the Kern County Historical Society were active in the founding of the Kern County Museum in 1946, and three years later they helped establish the Pioneer Village. Both of these have become unique historical institutions. In addition the historical society has maintained a continuing interest in the restoration of Fort Tejon in the Tehachapi Mountains.

With the placing of a plaque at Oak Creek Pass in 1927, the Kern County Historical Society undertook an extensive program of marking historical locations in Kern County. In doing this the organization often has worked in cooperation with other historically oriented groups, among them the Native Sons and Native Daughters of the Golden West. In recent years the historical society has undertaken an oral history project, recording the recollections of "old-timers." In retrospect, it is apparent that the past half-century has been an active one for the Kern County Historical Society.

Presidents of the Kern County Historical Society

Alfred Harrell	1931-1932
William Van Ewert	1932-1934
Herman A. Spindt	1934-1935
Jesse Stockton	1935-1936
Roy W. Loudon	1936-1938
Frank F. Latta	1938-1940
Ardis Walker	1940-1943
Clarence Cullimore	1943-1945
Peter N. Root	1945-1947
Orville Armstrong	1947-1948
Richard Bailey	1948-1949
Glendon J. Rodgers	1949-1950
W. Harland Boyd	1950-1951
Genevieve K. Magruder	1951-1952
J. Lee Mountain	1952-1953
Richard C. Bailey	1953-1954
Lester McDonald	1954-1956
Henry Raub	1956-1958
Ralph Kreiser	1958-1960
Georgia S. Sanders	1960-1961
Richard Hosking	1961-1962
Fred A. Miller	1962-1963
John B. Dowty	1963-1965
William G. Rea	1965-1966
Eva F. Granados	1966-1967
Eugene Burmeister	1967-1969
Louis Wakefield	1969-1970
Ted Freeland	1970-1971
Norman Berg	1971-1972
George Gray	1972-1973
Genevieve K. Magruder	1973-1975
Vicki Araujo	1975-1977
Trent C. Deverney	1977-1979
Mary Ming	1979-1980
Dorothy Bailey	1980-1981
Marje Rump	1981-1982
Curtis Darling	1982-1983

I

Explorers and Pioneers

Most of Kern County's pioneers were transplanted Americans from the eastern states, and more of them left the South than the North. Yet a substantial number came from outside the United States—France, Germany, Italy, China, and Mexico. The first comers were preponderantly men, whose typical social life involved drinking, gambling, and fighting at the local saloons. Offsetting this "rum shop" social life was the arrival of women and children, and a developing family life. In the early 1870s a journalist observed that "social, moral, and intellectual advancement" were developing more rapidly than "physical culture." The rougher pioneer life was being mellowed by the founding of schools and churches, as well as the increasing circulation of newspapers and magazines.

Father Francisco Garces
by W. Harland Boyd

Father Francisco Garces was a native of Spain, whose priestly career led him to the New World, where he was assigned responsibilities among the Indians along the northern frontier of Mexico. From a mission in what is now southern Arizona, he made several trips to the north and west in the interest of Spain and the Catholic Church. While on his most extensive trip he traveled some two thousand miles between October, 1775, and September, 1776. Besides seeking to spread the Christian faith, he also searched for an overland route between the Colorado River and San Francisco Bay. Fortunately for the historian, Father Garces kept a record of his travels.

In the course of his journeying Father Garces departed from San Gabriel Mission in April, 1776, and crossed the Sierra Madre and Tehachapi Mountains. At Indian rancherias he passed as he descended into the San Joaquin Valley he was well received, and then he went northward through the foothills of the Sierra Nevada, which he called the Sierra de San Marcos. Father Garces reached the Kern River in May, and he named it the Rio de San Felipe. The water made a "great noise" as it dashed from the narrow Kern River Canyon. He was not a swimmer, so friendly Indians led him downstream to a feasible crossing point, where four of them carried him across the river. His arrival was celebrated by natives living at a riverside rancheria.

As Father Garces made his way northward he reached Poso Creek, which he called the Rio de Santiago. Again hospitable Indians entertained him. In the vicinity of what was perhaps the White River, which he called the Rio de Santa Cruz, he encountered an Indian who spoke Spanish, and he presumed he had been at a coastal mission. At a rancheria Father Garces was told a little boy was dying, and he asked permission to baptize him, an opportunity he was granted. The Indians told him that Spaniards had come to live in the southern San Joaquin Valley. These he presumed were army deserters.

Although Father Garces was invited to visit Indian tribes living toward the north, he decided to retrace his route and then recross the Tehachapi Mountains. He reached the Kern River downstream from his previous crossing point, and he noticed that nearby the water followed two channels over the flat San Joaquin Valley. On some nearby foothills he felt there was a suitable site for a mission. He observed that the local Indians were trading deer skins for the products of others living on the seashore. After spending about two weeks in the southern San Joaquin Valley, Father Garces crossed the Tehachapi Mountains and journeyed toward the Mojave River.

(*Historic Kern*, March, 1976)

Edward F. Beale: Pioneer in the Path of Empire
by Richard C. Bailey

It is ironic that one of America's greatest adventurers should be practically unknown. Even in Kern County, his California home for many years, he is merely a name. His career was in the storybook tradition, and despite his having been born in our nation's capitol, Washington, D.C., he should probably be regarded as Kern County's most eminent "son."

Edward Fitzgerald Beale was born February 4, 1822, the son of George Beale, a naval hero of the War of 1812. His mother, Emily, was the youngest daughter of Commodore Truxtun, one of our navy's immortals. He was also related to the admirals Porter and Farragut.

With such a heritage and connections his appointment as Navy midshipman was not too surprising. In 1837 President Andrew Jackson became the 14-year-old boy's sponsor.

As a midshipman Edward was competent and pugnacious. He was, in fact, all that an Andy Jackson appointee should have been. In 1845 he was promoted to past-midshipman and ordered to the frigate *Porpoise* as acting master.

Hostilities were shaping up for the Mexican War, and young Beale was assigned to the Pacific Squadron under the command of Robert Stockton who had succeeded Commander Sloat.

In June, 1846, war became a reality. Colonel Kearney swung southward from Fort Leavenworth, and after raising the American flag over Santa Fe, he hurriedly pressed toward the Pacific Coast. Learning that Commodore Stockton and Fremont had already accomplished the conquest of California, he continued his march to the west after sending back part of his dragoons.

But the Californians, aware of the small American forces in California, soon took the offensive with such success that the gringo "conquerors" were in danger of being chased completely out of the southland.

This was the situation when Kearney led his travel-worn dragoons into Southern California. A superior force of mounted Californians worsted him, and a reinforcing group of sailors and volunteers from San Diego were quickly dispatched by Commodore Stockton, under the command of Captain Gillespie. In Gillespie's company was Midshipman Edward F. Beale, who was now destined to step into the spotlight of public acclaim.

Despite the reinforcements Kearney's entire command became surrounded on a barren hilltop by the superbly mounted Californian lancers who planned to starve the Americans into surrender. Young Beale, Kit Carson, and an Indian volunteered to steal through the enemy's multiple picket lines and seek further aid from the naval squadron at San Diego. All three succeeded, but each man arrived at the coast nearly dead of exhaustion.

Kearney was saved and this exploit spread the name of Beale before the country. Thomas Hart Benton in a speech before the U.S. Senate spoke highly of his conduct, and fellow officers presented him with a pair of epaulettes and a sword "in testimony of our admiration of your gallant conduct in the bold and hazardous enterprise."

In February Beale, with Kit Carson as his guide, and ten picked riflemen, set out for the East with urgent dispatches. Four hundred miles along near the Gila River they were "jumped" by hostile Indians who jumped right back when they discovered the Americans could hit what they shot at. But for the following 800 miles the little party was so shadowed by enemies that only eternal vigilance saved their scalps.

Beale and Carson were "lionized" by St. Louis and Washington society upon their arrival, much to the disgust of the modest

General Edward Fitzgerald Beale.

Carson. Beale's three months illness delayed their return to the west until August of 1847. Reaching Fort Leavenworth they struck out through the uncharted southwestern territory accompanied by seventeen raw troopers. Beyond Santa Fe the going became so rough that several of the men deserted, never to be heard of again. But the resolute Beale pushed onward into the wilderness of the Gila headwaters. Interminable river fordings, whirlpools, falls, and narrow gorges convinced him that here lay no sane man's wagon route. No matter; he was later destined to map the truly great path through the southwest to the Pacific.

Following the discovery of gold by Marshall at Sutter's Mill in 1848, the army and navy, rivals then as now, were both anxious to be the first bearers of the news to the unsuspecting East. Beale was selected by the navy to carry some gold specimens overland by way of Mexico, while his army rival took ship for the other shore of the continent by way of the isthmus of Panama. Beale made such good time that he had been in Washington two whole months when the army's messenger arrived.

Beale could therefore claim to have been the first man to bring east the actual proof that turned the eyes of the world toward California, and set off one of the greatest migrations in world history.

He was soon on his way back to California, this time with a wife, the former Mary Edwards. On March 5, 1851, he resigned from the navy and became the California business agent for Commodore Stockton and a New York steamship tycoon named Aspinwall. In nine months his astuteness netted his employers $100,000. Out of this Beale received $13,000 as his agreed percentage of the profits. This money became the foundation for the considerable fortune he later amassed.

A trip to Washington the next year resulted in his appointment as Superintendent of Indian Affairs for California and Nevada. $250,000 was appropriated by Congress "for the purpose of carrying into effect the plan which Beale had proposed for the better protection, subsistence, and colonization of the Indian tribes within his superintendency."

A rapid census indicated there were around 70,000 Indians under his care. In the southern San Joaquin Valley reservations were established on the Kings River, the Tule River, and at the Tejon. The last named was the Sebastian Indian Reservation in honor of William King Sebastian, chairman of the U.S. Senate Committee on Indian Affairs. Superintendent Beale, now raised to brigadier general, was chiefly instrumental in 1854 for the construction of Fort Tejon in Canyon de las Uvas, the present day Grapevine Canyon. The fort's chief purposes were to protect the Indians from encroachments of white settlers and to check horse thieving in the southern San Joaquin Valley.

Beale was an excellent administrator and a staunch champion of his Indian charges. He would not tolerate dishonesty among his Indian agents, and this policy soon built him a sizable list of vindictive enemies. Through connections in Washington these enemies succeeded in bringing Beale to trial for the misuse of government funds during his superintendency. However, the general had kept a meticulous record of all his dealings, and the trial resulted only in the disgrace of his accusers and the complete clearing of his name.

In 1857 he resigned this office and turned his attention again to the problem of roads. Wagon routes were sorely needed in the newly acquired American Southwest. President Buchanan selected General Beale as the man best qualified to survey a wagon road from Fort Defiance, New Mexico, to the Colorado River. It was on this trip that he commanded the famous U.S. Army Camel Corps, for whose existence he was partly responsible. Under Beale's care the camels were a huge success, but future caretakers of the African beasts cared nothing for them and seized every opportunity to place them in a poor light. This, and the rapid expansion of the transcontinental railroads, made the American camel corps a short-lived experiment.

During 1859–60 Beale was engaged in further wagon road construction on the central plains. The following year one of Lincoln's first acts as president was the appointment of General Beale to the post of surveyor-general of California and Nevada.

But surveying was the least of his duties at this critical period in our country's history. Southern sympathizers were a minority in California, but they were well organized. Moreover, they fully expected to bring this state into the Confederate fold within a few weeks of the outbreak of Civil War. It became Beale's concern to help organize Unionist sentiment on the west coast, and history indicates how well he succeeded.

At the conclusion of the war, Beale acted as a secret intermediary between our country and the Juarez forces seeking to oust the Maximilian government from Mexico. The surplus munitions channeled into the Liberals' hands at this juncture probably did much to bring about the downfall of the Austrian puppet. At least Beale's biographer, Bonsal, was of this opinion. Bonsal states that twenty years later President Diaz at a dinner where Beale was present "hailed him as a friend of Mexico in her hour of trial, and as one who had contributed mightily to the restoration of her liberties."

With the foregoing "business" concluded, the general resigned as surveyor-general and retired to his great rancho in California. This was the famous Tejon Ranch which Nordhoff, the noted traveler and writer, described as "what seems to me the most magnificent estate in a single hand in America." Here the general spent much of his time during the next eleven years developing his land and enjoying the unaccustomed life of a private citizen.

Then in 1876 President Grant appointed his old friend to the diplomatic post of envoy-extraordinary and minister plenipotentiary at the court of Austria-Hungary. After acquitting himself creditably for a year Beale resigned due to the press of personal affairs.

U.S. Grant, as ex-president, later requested President Arthur to appoint General Beale as secretary of the navy. But the president, swayed by contrary pressure groups, conferred the position on another man, an act that Grant never forgave.

In January, 1893, the general fell ill, but lingered on until April 22 when he died peacefully at his Washington home. He was seventy-one years old. The press of the entire nation mourned the passing of "the last of the pathfinders."

According to Bonsal, when Raimundo, one of Beale's old Indian scouts, heard of his beloved leader's death, "he said simply, 'I do not care to live any longer'; dressed himself in his fete-day clothes, in the sunshine outside his adobe hut, soon passed from sleep to death."

The Tejon Ranch still exists as part of the 300,000 acre Tejon Ranch Company. Its best known areas today border U.S. Highway 99 from Wheeler Ridge to Lebec on the road from Bakersfield to Los Angeles. The Beale family is no longer in Kern, but the name endures in Bakersfield's Beale Park and Beale Avenue in East Bakersfield. Not generally known is the fact that Truxtun Avenue is also named for Truxtun Beale, his son, and donor of Beale Park and Clock Tower.

Surveyor, explorer, traveler, rancher, and public servant, Edward Fitzgerald Beale was the personification of American daring, determination and altruism. He was, as his friend Bayard Taylor termed him, truly "a pioneer in the path of empire."

(*Historic Kern*, March, 1955)

Thomas Baker Came to Kern Island in 1863
by Eugene Burmeister

Thomas Baker, the founder of Bakersfield, was born at Zanesville, Muskingum County, Ohio, November 5, 1810, the second son of a farm family of five children. His grandfather, Colonel Thomas Baker, had fought in the Revolutionary War. His father, Thomas, who had come to the Ohio country, then still a part of the state of Virginia, was a soldier in the War of 1812.

Although his formal education was limited, Baker read widely, specializing in land law in which he came to be regarded as an authority. When he was only nineteen he was admitted to the Ohio bar and also appointed a colonel in the Ohio State Militia.

In 1830 he moved to Illinois, crossing the Mississippi River a few years later to become one of the first settlers in eastern Iowa. In 1838 he settled at Washington, Iowa, and was soon appointed clerk of the district court. He became a member of the fourth and sixth Iowa territorial assemblies and was appointed the first United States attorney of Iowa Territory. When Iowa was admitted to the Union in 1846, with the state capital at Iowa City, he was elected a member of the first legislature. He suggested and drafted many of the laws of the original code and was chosen president of the senate, thus becoming ex officio the first lieutenant governor of Iowa.

Baker married Mary Featherstone, an English girl, and she had four children by him. While still living in Iowa his wife died. Gold fever prompted him to head for California in 1850 and he settled for a few months that fall at Benicia before moving on to Stockton. In 1852 he moved to the newly-formed Tulare County where he became the co-founder with Nathaniel Vise of the town of Visalia. In 1855 Baker was chosen assemblyman from Tulare County and in 1856 was named receiver for the United States Land Office.

On September 12, 1857, he married Ellen M. Whalen, twenty-year-old daughter of Dr. Labon and Charlotte (Graves) Alverson, at Visalia. Alverson, a noted physician, surgeon and lecturer at the University of Michigan medical school at Ann Arbor, where his daughter was born, came to California from Iowa in 1870 and to Bakersfield in 1872 where he practiced before moving his practice to Tehachapi where he died in 1879. The Bakers had four children: Mary (Mrs. Henry A. Jastro), Thomas A., later a Kern County sheriff, Nellie (Mrs. C. C. Cowgill), and Charlotte E. (Mrs. John M. Jameson.)

In 1861 Baker was elected state senator from Tulare and Fresno counties and served in the sessions of 1861-62. In 1862, in partnership with Harvey Brown, he purchased the huge swamp franchise owned by the Montgomery brothers, including land along the Kern River and reaching north to Fresno Slough. After moving his family to a crude Kern Island house built by Christian Bohna on September 10, 1863, he hired thirty Indians from the Sebastian Reservation and set to work reclaiming some 400,000 acres of swamp and overflow lands. Under the terms of reclamation he acquired a total of 87,120 acres, much of it in what was to become Kern County.

While Baker was completing his reclamation project along the lower Kern River, Kern County was created in 1866. His selection as county surveyor was described as "a tribute to the abilities of a remarkably active and versatile man," and indicated a "realization

Colonel Thomas Baker, founder of Bakersfield.

that Kern Delta inhabitants were not to be overlooked." At that time Baker began to survey the site of the proposed city of Bakersfield.

Baker grew corn, beans, potatoes and other crops, and fenced off a field and planted ten acres of alfalfa just east of the present civic center, the boundaries today being between Fourteenth and Seventeenth streets and between K and P streets. Travelers enroute to San Francisco, Sacramento and Los Angeles were advised to stop at "Baker's field" to graze their animals. Baker said to all travelers, "Help yourself, but don't waste anything." The city's name was suggested by Philo D. Jewett, early sheepman in the county.

The Baker home was located at the corner of Nineteenth and N streets. It was here that Mrs. Baker opened a school in her home for her own children and those of neighbors, the first school in Bakersfield. Lacking textbooks, she cut letters from paper and made other ingenious devices for the eight children attending classes in order that her community "might have educated young people."

Baker had foresight in laying out the city. His experience in surveying together with what he had gleaned from observations in other cities made the selection and surveying of a site for the city ideal. He predicted that due to its geographical location the town would soon be the most important in the San Joaquin Valley south of Stockton. He mapped the city with streets 82½ feet wide and avenues 115 feet wide. He had observed that in cities with streets 66 feet wide horses and buggies of that early day hardly had room to meet or pass. From the land acquired following his land reclamation project he kept eighty acres for the Baker homestead. The rest he sold or gave to the city. Later his widow, who married Ferdinand A. Tracy on January 19, 1875, divided the land into lots and sold it.

To connect the growing valley settlement with the county seat of Havilah, Baker built Baker Grade, or Baker Toll Road, in 1867. Following the devastating flood at Christmas in 1867, he quickly made plans for helping rebuild the homes lost in the flood by building a sawmill. He also built a do-it-yourself grist mill a block and a half north of the location of the Kern River Mills on Truxtun Avenue, destroyed by the earthquake of 1952, where farmers could grind their corn and wheat without charge. The set of granite burrs used in the mill was given to Baker by General Edward F. Beale.

Within three years after Baker began surveying the town, the settlement was described as "quite a thriving village" and "bids fair to be a place of importance at no distant day." By April, 1869, Bakersfield's population had grown to 600. The town's two stores were operated by Livermore and Chester and Jacoby and Company. The town also had a church, a schoolhouse, and telegraphic communication with the rest of the world. Two months later a photographic gallery and a blacksmith shop were in operation and construction of a saloon was underway. The town still had no hotel, a fact much lamented by visitors to the "Island."

The April 20, 1869, issue of *The Havilah Weekly Courier* announced that "Colonel Thomas Baker has established a real estate agency at Bakersfield, the center of the agricultural lands." Baker was then serving his second term as county surveyor. He did a thriving business as a real estate agent and the *Courier* commented in its May 25 issue that "the demand for farming land is rapidly extending to Kern County. Bakersfield on the lower Kern River is visited daily by persons from the northern counties in pursuit of farms. There seems to be a strong impression that, whether the Southern Pacific railroad takes the east or the west side of the Great Lake [Tulare Lake], there will be a concentration of many roads in the midst of that rapidly growing settlement."

The election of 1869 saw a highly spirited race over the tri-county senate seat in the state legislature. In July, 1869, Baker entered politics again in the race for senator from the district including the counties of Kern, Tulare, and Fresno. Although a Democrat, he entered the race as an Independent, opposed by another Democrat, Thomas Fowler. Baker's reentrance into active politics was prompted by what he considered "dirty politics" at the Visalia convention. When the Democratic convention had met July 24 to nominate candidates for the offices of senator and assemblyman, the nominations of Fowler and Edward W. Doss, Kern County superintendent of schools, were rushed through at a speed seldom witnessed in political conventions. Baker charged that a previous arrangement had been made whereby Tulare County was to have the senator and Kern County the assemblyman, with Fresno County being left out entirely.

Shortly after Baker announced his intentions to run for the senate, with Thomas R. Davidson joining him in the race as an Independent for the assembly, the *Tulare Times* published accusations against Baker charging him with radicalism, dating back to his arrest in 1862 at Sacramento while a senator. At that time Baker had been accused of being a secessionist and was suspected of treason because of his vote with the "Peace Party" of the senate, charges which were eventually dropped.

The *Courier* in an August 24 editorial supported Baker and predicted he would receive a "three hundred vote majority in Fresno and a sure win in Tulare and Kern counties." The editorial added that "the contest for senator is between two Democrats, one of which will be elected, and that one will most likely be Colonel Baker." In a speech at Havilah, Baker "applied no soothing ointment to the already smarting wounds of the opposition," ". . . handled the Visalia Convention without gloves," declared himself in favor of the "fence law," opposed the Fifteenth Amendment, defended himself against the accusations made by the *Times*, and "all the while he was in good humor and kept his audience so by humorous touches in his speech."

Baker and Davidson displayed the usual confidence the day before the election, but when the results were announced, Fowler and Doss had won. The *Courier* stated that whereas in the June primary sixty-six Democratic votes had been cast, only sixty-six Democrats had voted in the general election for senator and fifty-two for assemblyman. The editor added that this was "suggestive of great apathy among the masses of the party," adding that he "suspected a lack of interest in the matter."

One of Baker's favorite mottoes was: "Time will justify a man who means to do right."

After his defeat Baker turned all his interest to building Bakersfield into a city of which he could be justly proud. The *Courier* had moved to Bakersfield under Augustus D. Jones where it was first published as the *Kern County Courier* and later as the *Bakersfield*

Weekly Courier. A blacksmith and carriage shop was established by Fred Macking, and a harness shop was opened by Phillip Reinstein. Littlefield and Philan founded a livery stable, and John B. Tungate opened a saloon. There were also a carpenter shop, a school of fifty pupils, and two boarding houses, and Dr. Lewis S. Rogers cared for the needs of his patients. Attorney C. H. Veeder had hung out his shingle, and a hotel and grist mill were planned.

By March 1871, Bakersfield had a postoffice with George B. Chester as postmaster. On January 4, 1872, J. S. Brittain arrived in Bakersfield "to found a democratic paper—*The Southern Californian*"—but was soon forced into bankruptcy and the paper was consolidated with the *Courier*. By June, 1872, the town had three saloons, and a brewery run by Baker's son-in-law, Henry A. Jastro. The big event in the town's growth was the announcement July 6 of the construction of the $20,000 Beale Hotel. There was talk of the railroad which was then laying track down the valley.

Baker did not live to see the arrival of the railroad nor the county seat moved to Bakersfield. He was stricken with typhoid and pneumonia and died November 24, 1872, attended by his father-in-law, Dr. Labon Alverson. He was buried in Union Cemetery. Naomi E. Bain in *The Story of Colonel Thomas Baker and the Founding of Bakersfield* wrote: "The remains were quite fittingly interred in the cemetery, the location of which had been chosen by the Colonel little more than a year previously. From the site of the grave one's view of the great treeless plain and the majestic mountains in the background was unobstructed. The Colonel's body now lay almost directly south from where he had set foot on the land in 1863 when he arrived with his family and, viewing the country, remarked to his wife: 'Here at last I have found a resting place, and here I expect to lay my bones.'"

(*Historic Kern*, September, 1967)

Historic Willow Springs
by L. Burr Belden

Along a main road of the last century, a few miles west of the San Bernardino-Kern County line is a cluster of stone buildings, the slowly-disintegrating walls of an even older adobe, and a large masonry horse trough—all set in a grove of venerable cottonwood trees. The place is Willow Springs, a community started over a century ago which attained its peak population of several hundred shortly after 1900.

Today Willow Springs, shrunk to four or five families, clings to life by a slender thread, refusing to accept the label of a ghost town. Four children regularly board the school bus there. East and north are some large gold mines, mines that produced fortunes in years before the economic squeeze made gold mining an all but dead industry.

Willow Springs is proud of a heritage that goes far back of gold mining. It was in 1772 that Pedro Fages, military commander of the California forces, left San Diego hunting a band of deserting soldiers. Fages chased the deserters up into the Descanso Mountains and found they had headed for the Colorado Desert. He sent some of his small command in pursuit of the decamping soldiers while he, intrigued with the unexplored province, headed north.

Fages kept a diary on his trip. It is none too plain in spots for the simple fact that no place names had been given any part of California away from the coast. It is known that the military leader, later named governor, crossed Riverside County somewhere around the Morongo Valley. Some historians think he came into the San Bernardino Valley via Reche Canyon and left up Lytle Creek. At least he reached the Mojave River in the vicinity of Victorville and turned west.

He was the first white man to see and describe the joshua trees. Fages, however, was no botanist. He called the giant lilies "palms," camped at a fine spring of sweet water with a flow more than ample for both men and horses. It was surrounded by willow trees with the mountains rising high to the north. A check of the caravan's time places Fages at Willow Springs.

Four years later another Spanish traveler, Fr. Francisco Garces, headed north from San Gabriel Mission. He too stopped at the fine Antelope Valley oasis.

After Garces the next visitors of record were in the 1830s, visitors of a far different stamp. A band of some fifty Ute Indians headed by the war chief, Walkara, stopped at Willow Springs with a band of some 200 horses stolen from the San Luis Obispo area. Walkara had taken as his personal piece of loot a high backed saddle found at San Luis Obispo Mission, a richly embroidered article formerly the property of a Franciscan priest. It is doubtful if the Indian enjoyed riding in the high Spanish contrivance but it is recorded he used it the rest of his life. Apparently the old saddle had a prestige value with the Indian who in summer was habitually attired only in a breech cloth.

Walkara was the scourge of the California ranches and conducted several raids. He may be credited with the initial use of Tejon Pass into Antelope Valley. The lost Death Valley party of 1849 was simply trying to follow Walkara's description of his horsethief trail, but unfortunately when the Ute's description reached a map second hand it bore but slight resemblance to the true track.

Once they had struggled through southern Nevada, the Amargosa Desert, Death Valley and the Panamints, these ill-guided 49ers eventually reached Willow Spring and pushed on to find food and friendship at the del Valle family's San Francisco Rancho near Saugus. Their passing served to write another colorful episode in the oasis' history.

After Walkara came John Charles Fremont with his party of topographical engineers skirting and mapping the north face of the San Gabriel Range and the San Bernardino Mountains. Before Fremont, however, the first Anglo Saxon visitor had been none other than Jedediah Smith, who passed through with his buckskin garbed trappers en route to beaver streams in the San Joaquin Valley.

After the 1848 gold discovery at Coloma the gold rush fanned out both north and south with new diggings being discovered on stream after stream to either side of the American River. By the mid-1850s, the upper Kern River and its tributaries supported several roaring camps at places such as Keyesville, Whiskey Flat and Havilah.

The Kern River gold rush was not just a flash in the pan. It resulted in the building of sizable towns and roads of sorts. One used by the bull team freighters came over Greenhorn Mountain from the San Joaquin Valley. Another headed south over Breckenridge to Havilah and Walker Basin, then via Old Town Tehachapi and Oak Creek Canyon to Willow Springs and on south to Saugus via Soledad Canyon.

Stage lines were soon traveling over the rough steep road to Havilah linking what became the first county seat of Kern County with Los Angeles. Willow Springs was a station on the Havilah line and the old adobe still standing near the historic spring dates from the days of the stagecoaches.

After the Kern River excitement had settled down to steady mining, Cerro Gordo, Coso, Panamint and Darwin came along as new bonanzas. A Los Angeles freighter with a genius for organization, Remi Nadeau, built a corral at Willow Springs. Nadeau ran his long teams by timetable much like a railroad and held the lion's share of the Cerro Gordo trade. He had a rival to the east in San Bernardino named Caesar Myerstein who ran the San Bernardino-Panamint stage and also freighters to the same silver camp, but Nadeau had a corner on the rich Cerro Gordo and Darwin trade.

When the Southern Pacific built south to the present Bakersfield, Nadeau switched his line terminal to the railhead. As the SP toiled up Tehachapi Pass Nadeau changed terminals and Willow Springs entered its second step. The railroad started the new town of Mojave and the old pass up Oak Creek fell into disuse while farther north Old Tehachapi dwindled away as business moved over to the new town of the name on the railroad.

The main road from Los Angeles north to Mojave and on to Owens Valley continued to run via Willow Springs, however, with a diagonal from that oasis northeast to Mojave. There was not much road travel, however, in the years after the railroad came until the advent of the automobile.

In 1900 Willow Springs had its big boom. Ezra Hamilton discovered gold paying good nearby. Three large mining centers sprang up. One was only a couple miles east of Willow Springs on the road to Rosamond where an ambitious developer built a two-story hotel with rock from the mine dump. Years later it was discovered the hotel walls contained plenty of valuable ore and there were recurrent stories of tearing down the hostelry and milling the walls. When the upper floor was actually demolished after the earthquake of the early 1950s gold prices were such that it was no longer an attractive venture.

Hamilton's discoveries resulted in the expanding of Willow Springs. Twelve or fourteen stone buildings were erected, bunkhouses, residences, stores and a hotel. The stages came back loaded with inbound crowds eager to share in the wealth. At one end of the hotel, a structure built like a fort, was the saloon with those swinging half doors that were the trademark of saloons from the Atlantic to the Pacific. The doors are still in place and a faded sign above proclaims some long forgotten brand of brew.

(*Historic Kern*, February, 1960)

Granite Station
from the Bakersfield *Morning Echo*, August 11, 1918

(In 1873 Julius Chester, a Bakersfield businessman, placed a twice-a-week stage in service between Bakersfield and Glennville, which was an eight hour trip each way. The running time was reduced to five hours after John Eldon built a station at Five Dogs Creek, and fresh horses could be obtained at this mid-point stopping place. The station was called Five Dogs until 1875, when the postal department established a post office there which it named Granite. The original post office was discontinued within a year, but another one was established in 1890 and called Elmer, but travelers continued to call the place Granite Station. Although Granite Station's heyday was over, its old charm remained when in August, 1918, a reporter for the Bakersfield *Morning Echo* visited Alex Bego, who reminisced about the by-gone days at the station. The following excerpts are from the article written by the reporter after the visit with the old-timer.)

Far in the mountains northeast of Bakersfield over an ascending, winding, rough road, surrounded by layer upon layer of small hills upon which giant boulders cling and against which the blue sky seems the bluer by contrast and the oak trees the greener, in the great outdoors, where the peace of solitude reigns, there is tucked away in the tiny valley at an unexpected turn of the rambling road, a picturesque, quaint roadhouse of the strictly Californian style of bygone days.

It is long, low, wooden, with a wide porch stretched across the front, a porch with a sloping roof, with innumerable doors opening from it to the large bare rooms within; a porch with high wooden sink, wooden soap dish, cracked looking glass, roller towel, all the comforts of a primitive wash room at one end, and at the other, boxes and old chairs to sit on and view the ever-lasting, silent hills and muse upon the days that are gone, and wish that the silence of the roadhouse might be broken and tell the secrets of its past period. How interesting if these walls could speak and picture those early days that seem almost fantastic to us now.

But there is someone who can tell of stories if he will and who by degrees one warm day recently told some of the milder ones, and with many chuckles of delight divulged a secret or two which really must never be told and declared emphatically again and again that "them was the days, yes them was the days, when you'd get to bed at night and not know if you'd awaken in the morning alive or not." And the whole place had that air of romance that carried with it the cold realization indeed "that them was the days" without a doubt.

As we listened to his tales we were in a large front room that was formerly the bar. The "bar" part was there, but not the where-with-all, the large rough room had no furniture, with the exception of an old stove and a bench in the farther corner, a pile of wood, unnecessary reminder, was beside the stove, and doors opened in each end of the room. From one half-open door the remains of what was once a general store, now furnished with a few tin cans and cobwebs knitting the odds and ends together in their filmy, silver-grey mesh, carried the suggestion of total desertion. The other door was closed and remained so—there was no clue as to what was beyond it.

And still today the roadhouse stands, a monument of recollections, a peaceful, quiet spot for it is not on the main, now traveled road. It resembles a farmyard, casting aside its traditions and closing your eyes to the historic side. Little pigs grunting and running around, numbers of sleepy dogs and cats eye travelers with wonder, and well they may, so few pass. Chickens and ducks find plenty of space at their disposal, and cattle roam the hills. Across the road from the house is a large barn, a flourishing garden and a large forsaken pigeon house standing high in the air with its empty doors gazing forlornly on the hills and sky.

So there [Alex] Bego lives, quite content to have his highway deserted, quite content to have his store closed, quite content to listen to the grunting of his pigs and the barking of his friendly dogs. Such companionship to those who know how to appreciate it in so beautiful a place is quiet joy and delight. And Bego is happy. He was asked if he longed for the frivolous happy-go-lucky days of the past; the days so full of life and uncertainty of life, too. "Oh no," he said, shifting his weight from one foot to the other, "now I know I will wake up in the morning safe and well."

(*Historic Kern*, February, 1975)

Captain Elisha Stevens
by W. Harland Boyd

"Captain" Elisha Stevens, as was the case with many Americans who found their way to the frontier West, must be characterized by many occupations During his long life he was a blacksmith, trapper, hunter, Indian agent, guide, soldier, farmer, and explorer. Born in South Carolina in about 1803, he probably lived in his native state until early adulthood, but most of his life was spent in the West. One can safely speculate that his early fur trapping pursuits led him as far west as the upper Missouri River, but sometime during the early 1840s he became a resident of New Orleans.

In 1844 Stevens helped guide the Stevens-Murphy train of wagons that made the overland trip from the Missouri frontier to the Sacramento Valley, in California. The route the travelers followed soon became known as the California trail, and the Stevens-Murphy party was the first that successfully brought wagons over the Sierra Nevada. Their route over these mountains was the same as that used later by the ill-fated Donner Party.

After staying for a time at Sutter's Fort, Stevens began to explore various parts of California, which at the time was still a province of Mexico. Lured by reports of a rich silver mine, he visited the San Joaquin Valley and the surrounding mountains. While he did not find the mine, he encountered a large Indian population and an abundance of game and wild horses. This was only the first of many trips he made into the San Joaquin Valley, including one in 1853, when he spent four months traveling by canoe on rivers and lakes in the pursuit of otter.

Meanwhile, when war between the United States and Mexico had begun in 1846, Stevens joined the volunteer American forces in the province that helped bring California to the United States. He was a resident of Los Angeles when the gold rush began, and he was one of the first to leave for the mines. While he was successful as a miner, he lost much of the gold he had mined in an unfortunate business venture.

In 1850, Stevens settled on a farm on the outskirts of San Jose, where he planted many varieties of vines and fruit trees, and then at a time when his success as a farmer was assured, he tired of "a mode of life so different from that to which he had previously been accustomed." While his decade of residence near San Jose endures in the name of Stevens Creek, he preferred to watch the advance of civilization from a distance, and this led him to the southern San Joaquin Valley.

Several times Stevens' earlier travels had brought him through the Kern River country, which because of its remoteness continued well into the American period to be "almost a wilderness, comparatively unknown," reached by few settlers. In 1860, Stevens settled near the site of the future Bakersfield, and except for a year or so that he spent with friends in San Diego, he lived the remainder of a long life at Bakersfield. Differing from the proverbial hunter, trapper and pathfinder, Stevens was described by contemporaries as "a man of strictly temperate habits" and "a generous, upright, and brave man."

Unfortunately, Stevens by the early 1870s was suffering from advanced age and some injuries that somewhat incapacitated him. Nonetheless, he lived until he was about eighty-four years of age, although prior to his death at Bakersfield he had long been an inmate of Kern County Hospital. He had been partially paralyzed for several years before his death in 1887.

(Historic Kern, September, 1964)

Early History and Reminiscences
by Benjamin Brundage

The Legislature of this state at its session of 1865–66 passed an act providing for the creation of the County of Kern out of a portion of Tulare and Los Angeles counties. Havilah, then a prosperous mining town, was named as the county seat of the proposed county, and in July, 1866, the county was duly organized by the election of county officers provided for by the act. Directly after the passage of the act above mentioned, I came from San Francisco to Havilah and took part in the organization of the county. Early in June, 1866, a Democratic convention assembled at Havilah for the purpose of nominating the officers of the new county, and as at least 90 percent of the voters within the territory of the new county were Democrats, it is needless to say all of the nominees were elected.

At that time Havilah was the most populous precinct in the county. Most of them were miners, the mines were productive, money was plentiful, and Havilah was the liveliest mining town in the state. The town had but one street, about a mile in length, and seven mills were running most of the time during 1866–67. The quartz veins were small and some of them rich in gold, but the ore below the decomposed rock was too rebellious to work in the kind of quartz mills then at Havilah, and during the years of '68 and '69, most of the mills were abandoned and early in the year 1868 most of the miners went to the new mining town of White Pine, Nevada.

In 1866, when I arrived at Havilah, there was only one church (Catholic) there, and no school house or public school. But on the side of the mountain about a half mile above Havilah, Col. A. A. Rand of Boston was engaged in mining and had about fifty men working his mines and running a ten-stamp quartz mill. He was a gentleman in every respect, and very much interested in the spiritual welfare of the men in his employ. So in 1867 he purchased and had sent a Mason and Hamlin organ from San Francisco to his mine and gave his men Episcopal prayer books and held sermons regularly every Sunday.

At the solicitation of some of the good people of Havilah, the colonel was induced to bring his organ and prayer books into town. The saloon men promised to close their saloons during service, a choir was organized, and services were held every Sunday morning during a period of about six months. At our first service we proceeded to organize by electing wardens and vestrymen. No person nominated for the office of vestryman or warden was permitted to decline office. We declined to accept excuses; each man named for office was duly and morally qualified for the position. I well recollect one genial pious gentleman, Ed Bigler, son of ex-Governor Bigler of Pennsylvania. He had charge of the N.Y. & C.C. Mining Co. When named for one of the vestrymen he attempted to decline, and excused himself by saying he "thought he was not a proper man for such a position, that he sometimes played pitch-seven-up for the whisky, that he played poker and other games, and that he attended horse races on Sunday and he did not wish any position that would interfere with his pleasure." But we all said he was a proper person for the office and he was unanimously elected vestryman. I had charge of the choir and the late George McCuen was the organist. It was composed of the following persons: Mrs. H. T. Reed, soprano; Mrs. V. G. Thompson, alto; McCuen, tenor and organist, and I tried to sing bass. The two ladies were then recently from Boston, and had come via Panama to join their husbands who were merchants in Havilah under the firm name of Reed and Thompson. Prior to that Reed was in the same business at Little Lake, Inyo County, and while at Havilah he was generally called Little Lake Reed.

Most of the early settlers of the county have crossed the divide. Those remaining are: J. W. Sumner of Kernville; John Nicoll, N. P. Peterson and L. B. Smith of the South Fork; Monroe Minter of Linn's Valley, now of Bakersfield; George Ritz, Frank Reynolds and A. T. Lightner of this city; and Mrs. F. A. Tracy. The latter was the wife of Col. Thomas Baker and one of the earliest settlers of this valley.

Early in the year 1868, Havilah began to rapidly decline in importance as a mining town and the greater portion of its inhabitants moved away. In October, 1868, I visited what was then known as Kern Island, at the locality where the city of Bakersfield now stands. At that time Col. Baker and family resided here at a place near where the King Lumber Company's yard now is. R. Hudnut and family then resided near where the Agricultural Park is. W. Shirley and family had their home in an adobe building at or near what is now Chester Avenue, and about three blocks south of where the Santa Fe railroad crosses Chester Avenue. Chester and Livermore had a small store just north of where the Southern Hotel now is, and across Chester Avenue near where the Grand Hotel is situated was a Mexican dwelling constructed of brush and tules. Those were all the houses within the limits of what is now known as Bakersfield. The area was then covered with trees and brush except a few acres, under cultivation by Col. Baker.

There was quite a number of settlers then on what is known as Kern Island whose names I do not now remember. There were no hotels or restaurants there within forty miles of what now is Bakersfield, and had it not been for the genial hospitality of Colonel Baker and wife we would have suffered for want of lodging and something to eat. The latch-string of their dwelling was always out, ready to be pulled by stranger or friend who never failed to find a kindly welcome from each and all of the family. The colonel was the pioneer and did all that was in his power to induce immigrants to settle on the rich alluvial lands of this part of the San Joaquin valley. He was a surveyor and had knowledge of the government surveys and by his personal services located most of the settlers on the choicest lands in the Kern valley.

Early in the spring of 1869 I again visited Kern Island—where Bakersfield now is was then called Kern Island—then traveled over portions of townships 30-28, 30-27 and 29-28, and from the cursory examination I then gave it, concluded that the future of Kern County laid in the Kern river valley; and that its rich alluvial soil would prove very productive, and soon would be populated. Out of what was designated as swamp and overflowed land there were a number of townships of government land subject to pre-emption and homestead entry. The best portions of the latter were within a short period settled on even numbered sections, the odd sections being within the limits of the Southern Pacific railroad grant.

In June, 1870, I made a more extended tour of Kern Island and found I had not seen in 1869 but a small portion of the fertile lands of the valley. The delta streams were then full of water and the grass in the Ellis, Lundy, Barnes and Canfield vicinities were three and four feet high, green growing and with the groups of cottonwood and willow trees, made it appear like a beautiful park inducing man to make that place his home. As a result of that visit I concluded to make my home at Bakersfield.

During that year Colonel Baker laid out the town and at the earnest request of his friends it was named Bakersfield. It was located on the west half and the west half of the east half of section 30 in T. 29 S., Range 28 E., and the east half of the SE ¼ of section 25 in T. 29 S., R. 27 E. The most of the described land was covered with brush and cottonwood and willow trees, and the main wagon road to the plains meandered through the trees and brush from the Chester and Livermore store out to and across the south fork of Kern River where the Kern River flour mill now stands. Prior to the flood in 1861 and '62, the main volume of the waters of Kern River flowed down that channel, and after that and up to the flood of 1867–68, only about half of the water flowed in that direction.

Directly after the town was laid out settlers commenced coming in from Havilah and elsewhere. Of those who came from Havilah were Joe Smith, the blacksmith, and E. H. Dumble, tinsmith, and started in business here.

The town soon grew to be the most important place in the county, and in the winter of 1869–70 an effort was made to obtain an act from the Legislature then in session, enabling the citizens to vote on the question of changing the county seat from Havilah to Bakersfield. I drew up the desired act, had it presented, and passed at the close of the session, but Governor Haight failed to approve the bill, and we were compelled to wait until the next session of the Legislature. That session passed what is known as the codes of this state, which contained a provision for county seat removals, and soon thereafter an election was held in this county for that purpose. It was a very bitter contest. The result was a small majority in favor of Bakersfield. But the Board of Supervisors, then composed of three members, a majority of whom were decidedly against Bakersfield, and determined to defeat the will of the majority, and in order to do so they refused to count the returns from two precincts, Bear Valley and Cummings Valley, that had voted for Bakersfield, and by rejecting the returns from those precincts, Havilah had a majority. I applied for and obtained a writ of mandate compelling the board to count the returns from those precincts, but the matter was pending in the courts for about a year before a final decision was obtained in our favor. Within thirty hours after I obtained the writ I had all of the county records on wheels rolling over the Baker road toward Bakersfield. The town hall, erected in 1871–72 was occupied as a court house. It was located where the Beale Memorial Library now is, and a log jail was erected where Stoner's store is situated. The second story of the town hall was occupied as an Odd Fellows' lodge room. As D.G.M., I instituted the lodge, on April 26, 1872. Members of the order from Havilah and other distant places were present on the occasion and on that and the four subsequent nights the festivities were enlivened by dancing in the town hall. The late N. R. Wilkinson furnished the music. The following year I instituted Bakersfield Lodge No. 224, F. & A.M., which also held its meetings in the same hall used by the Odd Fellows.

From that time on the town continued to grow in importance, although in the years of 1874 and 1875 strenuous attempts were made by its enemies to injure if not destroy the town. The Baker title to the land on which it was situated was contested, which delayed investment in town lots and contemplated improvements, until the Supreme Court of the state decided in favor of the Baker title. In the meantime a new Board of Supervisors had been chosen, a majority of whom were antagonistic to Bakersfield. A court house was in process of erection and when the basement story was about completed the majority of the board brought suit in the District Court to enjoin the erection of the court house on the ground that the election for a change of county seat from Havilah to Bakersfield was fraudulent and void. This was in 1875. The District Court decided against us, but on appeal Bakersfield again won the contest. The Southern Pacific railroad was an active participant in the last fight against Bakersfield, as they had constructed their road past Bakersfield and had laid out a town, called it Sumner, and wanted it established as the county seat of the county. Their town of Sumner was afterward called Kern and now it is added to Bakersfield and the two places merged into one city.

(Historic Kern, December, 1956)

The Life of John McCray
by Della McCray Campbell

John McCray was a covered wagon baby. He was born at Donner Lake, August 5, 1853. His family had just completed a long overland journey from Indiana, as members of a large emigrant train, California bound.

John's father, Alexander McCray, was a native of Nova Scotia. He married Margaret Learn, a Pennsylvania Dutch girl, and they moved into Indiana. When they came to California, a few years later, Alexander brought the first purebred Durham cattle into the state. They settled near Crow's Landing, later moving to Squaw Valley, east of Fresno. They were soon compelled to move again, as the grizzly bears were killing and devouring the young calves from their herd of purebreds. Their next location was at the foot of China Grade, near Kern River. They lived in an old adobe house. Wild game was plentiful, and Charley, John's older brother, who had a good mare, was able to rope antelope for the family's meat supply.

There was a shallow hole along the river, above the China Grade crossing, where people came to get oil to grease their machinery. No one dreamed of the possibilities of this "black gold" at that time. Alexander McCray had the oil analyzed, but it was considered of no commercial value.

At that time Bakersfield was a very small village. Houses were tule shacks. The water supply was a ditch running through town and everyone dipped water from the stream and carried it to their homes. There were many sloughs, and stagnant water was everywhere. People in this area went south of Buena Vista Lake for their salt. At the time, the lake extended east of what is now Highway 99.

After a few years in Bakersfield, the family was sick with malaria, so they moved to Poso Creek. This was a healthy location, but the bear trouble came up again, so another move was necessary. From Poso Creek the McCrays moved to Farmersville, near Visalia. Young John was about thirteen years old at this time. At Farmersville, his father homesteaded 160 acres of land. He went into the mountains and whip-sawed lumber by man power with which to build a home. Today the little house still stands in the middle of a big cotton field. John's father had no more than finished building the house, when he became ill with pneumonia and died.

John went to school briefly in the little log cabin school house in Farmersville. He said that he never got to go beyond the third grade. However, he never stopped reading and learning. He read history, geography and biographies, and when a young man could speak and write Spanish fluently. He could also speak the local Indian tongue. At community spelling bees he was always the last one to stand, and in mental arithmetic he was a natural mathematician. He could guess the weight and figure the selling price of a large herd of cattle without ever using a pencil.

The death of Alexander McCray left to Charley and John the duty of taking care of their mother, two sisters, Sarah and Marilla, and a younger brother, Alexander. John went to work for the Mehrten Brothers, a German family who raised cattle and also many horses. Their home was near Exeter. The Overland stages bought hundreds of horses from the Merhtens, and John helped to break and deliver them. Other stages went from Visalia over Greenhorn Mountain to Kernville; then through Walker's Pass to Coyote Holes—a junction where the Visalia stage met the Los Angeles stage—then on to Independence. Freight for Kernville and the South Fork Valley came from Visalia over Greenhorn. Later on the Caliente-Kernville road was opened.

When John was eighteen years old, he was working for Mince and Murray, a big cattle outfit, with headquarters at Porterville. Before long, he was made foreman, ranging cattle from Lemon Cove to

Buena Vista Lake. William Landers, another cattleman, ran cattle on the same range with Mince and Murray. A dry year came along, range feed was poor, so Mr. Landers moved his cattle and headquarters to South Fork Valley. He offered John the job of foreman of his outfit. It being a better deal than the one he had, John accepted and went with Mr. Landers to South Fork Valley.

The new range used by Mr. Landers included Kelso Valley, Piute and Scodie mountains, Walker's Pass, and much of the desert between Mojave and Little Lake. Mr. Landers owned 28,000 acres of land outright, so he controlled vast range lands, a custom still practiced in the arid western states.

Before leaving Mince and Murray, John recommended a young Mexican by the name of Jose Perez to take his place as foreman. The company gave Jose the job, and at the next roundup, near Bodfish, John and Jose, with their cowboys, made camp near each other. The following is a little story as told to John's son in later years by Mr. Perez:

"When I saw John and his boys, I really felt sorry for my old friend. His cowboys were Indians, poorly dressed and their outfits were shabby. They didn't look smart enough to work cattle. My men were Mexicans and white men, who wore good clothes and had fine saddles, bridles and riatas. But when it came to rounding up the strays and renegade cattle, it was the Indian cowboys who brought them in every time. My boys couldn't do the work in the rough mountainous country."

Mr. McCray found the Indians very good cow hands. They could tell by the tracks, the number and size of the cattle that had strayed from the herd. They were adept at predicting weather and could tell time at night by looking at the Big Dipper, not missing the hour by more than five minutes.

Kernville was a lively little town at this period—1860 to 1880—due to the gold mining in the Big Blue and other mines in the area. It was here that the cowboys, miners and ranchers came for business and recreation. It was in the year 1876 that John rode into Kernville for a little fun. He was six foot two, red headed and so bashful that he choked every time a girl looked at him. On this particular trip, he was espied by the pretty and vivacious Ellen Cummings. Ellen was sixteen at the time and with her black eyes, black hair and love for fun and gaiety, was easily the belle of the town. When she saw the handsome red headed cowboy, she immediately decided that he was her man. One year later, on November 5, 1877, they were married. Ellen was the daughter of a family who had crossed the plains in a covered wagon from Missouri. She was born at White River, August 11, 1860, but soon after her birth, the family moved to Kernville.

Soon after getting married, John quit his job with Mr. Landers and started a butcher shop in Kernville. Business was good, but most of his customers bought on credit. Many failed to pay, so the business was not very prosperous. While living in Kernville, a little daughter was born to Ellen and John, whom they named May.

After two years in the butcher business, John went back to work for Mr. Landers. He and Ellen loved Kelso Valley, about twenty-eight miles east of Weldon, the nearest post office. Kelso Valley was a central location to the mountain and desert range lands. It was at this time that the first government survey of the valley was made. The surveyors stayed at the McCray home.

While John was out on the range, Ellen and her little daughter lived quite a lonely life. The nearest neighbor was six miles away, and the trip to Kernville, with a team of horses, was an all day trip each way. Once in a while the Indian squaws would come to visit, but since they spoke no English, there was no conversation. They sat on the ground and worked on their blankets until time to go home. Ellen busied herself with the household duties, caring for May, sewing and tending to the vegetable and flower gardens. She also milked a cow or two and made butter with the cream. In later years, she enjoyed telling her grandchildren about using the stacks of butter to make soap. Little May amused herself with a pet calf, which she soon learned to ride. When she was five years old, her parents began teaching her the ABC's and numbers, and it was not long before she could read and write.

When May was eight years old, John moved his family to the "Mac Ranch" near Weldon so that his daughter could go to school. The ranch belonged to Mr. Landers and was well located, being one mile from the post office at Weldon and a half mile from the school.

Miss Ella Merriam was May's first teacher and the Sunday School teacher of the McCray children. Miss Merriam married Thomas Smith, another cattleman of the area. She became and still is the best loved spiritual leader of that community. She is now nearing her ninetieth birthday, and still is active in her church work.

There was a good orchard on the "Mac Ranch" and a much larger orchard on Mr. Landers' home ranch, which was also the headquarters for his outfit. Mr. Landers purchased all those fine fruit trees in Georgia and had them shipped across the continent by railroad during the first few years of railroad transportation. There were no peaches or pears in that area that could compare with Mr. Landers' fruit. Everyone in the valley was welcome to come and pick all the fruit they needed.

John McCray worked for Mr. Landers and lived on the "Mac Ranch" until 1892. There was no baby beef marketed in those days. When sold, the three and four year old steers had to be driven over Greenhorn Mountain, through Glennville, and on to Visalia. A man by the name of Bliss bought these range cattle, paying eighteen and twenty dollars per head. Mr. Landers sold about a thousand head at a time. John collected the money, which was around $20,000 in gold coins, and delivered it to Mr. Landers. The money was kept in a satchel and carried on the chuck wagon. There were never any holdups. If anything of that nature was sensed, Ned Conner, a cattleman near Glennville, alerted the officers and cattlemen in the vicinity, and some of them rode along with Mr. McCray until the money was safely delivered to Mr. Landers. Mr. Landers never kept his money in a bank. It was kept in a barrel in the storeroom alongside of the potatoes, beans, flour and other grocery supplies. He always paid his help in gold coins. There was no cattle rustling in those days. Once in a while, a hungry miner would kill a steer for meat, but that was all.

Mr. Landers had a herd of horses which ranged in the Coso Hot Springs country. Every year the cowboys would go there to gather about thirty geldings. They were as wild as deer. The horses were never brought in younger than four years old. It was John's theory that horses had longer endurance if they were allowed to mature before being broken for the saddle. After about eight years at the

"Mac Ranch," John wanted to buy a ranch of his own. He left Johnnie Johnson, a reliable cowman, in charge of Mr. Landers' outfit and bought the "Bill Garden" ranch, located six miles west of Weldon. When the family moved to their new home there were three children, two boys, John and Clinton, having been born at the "Mac Ranch."

Mr. McCray was proud of his new ranch and worked very hard to improve it. He raised alfalfa, grain, hogs and cattle. The surplus grain was sold to the A. Brown Company for seventy-five cents per hundred. In the summer his cattle ranged in the Monache Meadow country, south of Mount Whitney. Hogs ready for the market were driven on foot to Caliente, which took eight days. At Caliente they were loaded into stock cars and shipped to Los Angeles. They brought one and a half cents per pound, delivered in Los Angeles, averaging about three dollars per head.

While in Los Angeles, John bought a year's supply of groceries, also shoes and clothes for the entire family. He was always happy to provide well for his family and on these trips brought home many treats such as bologna, cheese, oranges, and candy, and also gifts of jewelry for his wife and daughter.

Things went well on the ranch for a few years. Two more children were born, both being girls and named Della and Gladys. However, in 1898 there was a severe drought, and John was forced to sell one hundred of his best steers for ten dollars per head. That year sheep marketed for twenty-five cents per head. John had no sheep. He was a cattleman and cattlemen allowed no sheep on their range. During this disastrous year, nearly all of Mr. Landers' 20,000 cattle died. The range was literally covered with dead cattle. After six months, when the count was completed, only about two thousand head were left. He asked John to come back to build up his herd again. John could not refuse his old employer, so he rented his own ranch to his son-in-law, Cecil H. Hanning, and in the fall moved the family back to the "Mac Ranch."

While the family was living on the "Mac Ranch" this second time, a little church was built across the road from the McCray home. Mr. Livingston, the minister, lived with the McCrays and worked with the carpenters on the construction of the church. John also worked on it whenever possible, and Mrs. McCray cooked for all who gave their services. After the church was completed, the women of the community worked to pay off the debt. Many church socials were held. Homemade ice cream and cakes were sold and everyone had a wonderful time. The big event of the year was the Christmas party. A beautiful fir tree was brought down from the mountains and set up in the church. It was beautifully decorated with long strings of popcorn and cranberries, and there were gifts for all the children.

Before a recreation hall was built, dances were held in the school house. These people worked hard, but they played just as hard. Dancing started about eight o'clock in the evening and lasted until daylight. Dances were held only on special holidays, such as Christmas and the Fourth of July, but when they had one, everyone came and brought the children. The Fourth of July was an all day and all night celebration. A community picnic was held in a grove of cottonwoods and willows. Long tables were loaded with fried chicken and every conceivable good thing to eat. There were swings for the children and games and races throughout the day. A large platform was erected for dancing.

There were no telephones in the mountain valley at that time and doctors were few and far between. Occasionally a doctor would travel through the country with his little satchel of medicine. He would prescribe for the ailing and do what he could, but usually it was the older women who took care of the sick and officiated at childbirth. Ellen McCray was always ready to assist her neighbors in time of sickness and childbirth. If the doctor failed to arrive in time, the little one and its mother were taken care of to the best of her ability. If there was no transportation, she would walk a mile or two each day to bathe the infant, care for the mother and cook for the other members of the family.

If someone was very sick and a good doctor was needed, a rider was sent to Caliente, the nearest telephone, to call a doctor from Bakersfield. The doctor caught a passenger train or light engine, if one were available, and rode to Caliente. The Southern Pacific would furnish an engine free in such an emergency. The doctor was transported the remainder of the journey in a relay of buggies pulled by the fastest teams of horses, similar to the pony express. Mr.

Charles Bennett of Caliente furnished the first team and driver, which carried the doctor up the steep and winding canyon road to Walker Basin. Here Mr. Walker Rankin, Sr. had a fresh team and driver ready, which went as far as the Nick Williams place. Changes were made at the Charles Rankin ranch, the John Neill place in Hot Springs Valley, and so on until the doctor reached the patient. Drivers had orders to use the whip and not spare the horses. They were driven on the run, hence the frequent changes.

Dr. Shafer, one of the fine doctors then practicing in Bakersfield, was called most often to the South Fork Valley. On the occasion of one of these calls, one driver told how he almost turned the buggy and the doctor over on a sharp downhill turn. Consequently, he slowed down. Dr. Shafer called out, "Hell, man! Why are you slowing down? Don't you know that I'm needed at the Powers' place?" Whereupon he grabbed the lines and whip, gave an Indian war whoop, and in no time at all was down the crooked mountain grade, with a very frightened ex-driver holding on for dear life. At that time it took from twelve to eighteen hours to get a doctor from Bakersfield to the South Fork Valley, twenty-two miles by rail and about seventy-five miles over steep and narrow winding mountain roads.

Everyone would care for the sick. It didn't matter if the sick one was Indian or white. Even the men helped. They would work all day and then ride perhaps twenty miles to sit with the sick at night. Mr. McCray was highly respected in the community and served as health officer whenever smallpox or other contagious diseases broke out. He believed in vaccination and used every effort to effect immunization in the valley. He was very successful at setting broken bones and often did this for his neighbors while waiting for a doctor to arrive. He was also a practical veterinarian and was quite successful in doctoring sick animals.

Mr. McCray stayed with Mr. Landers about four years the third time he was in his employ, and succeeded in putting his cattle business on a prosperous basis. Again he moved back to his home ranch. However, the children were all in school now, so in 1904 he moved his family to Bakersfield so that they might have the benefit of better schools. Two years later he sold his livestock, rented the ranch and came to Bakersfield to be with his family. He soon went to work for the Kern County Land Company as superintendent of cattle. On his buying trips for the company, he traveled extensively throughout the west and midwest and also into Mexico. He knew all phases of the cattle business and was considered an authority on the subject throughout the areas in which he traveled.

At this time Henry A. Jastro was general manager of the Kern County Land Company. He was a prominent leader in the Democratic party, both in the county and state. John McCray was a Republican. Shortly after John went to work for the company, Mr. Jastro was campaigning for a certain candidate in a current election. He asked John to vote for the man. John replied that he had been hired to take care of the company's cattle, but would vote for the man he considered best fitted for the office. Rather than losing his job, he always held Mr. Jastro's high esteem and confidence.

John McCray worked for the Land Company until his death in 1925. He was a kind, unassuming man, but possessed those traits of character that commend a man to the good opinion of his fellow men. He was ever alert in political affairs and believed in community, national, and world progress. In all relations of life he was actuated by honorable motives, and thus won the confidence, respect, and love of all who knew him.

(Historic Kern, November, 1952)

As I Recall
by Louise A. Renfro

When Rosedale began to be settled in 1891 it was the hope of many people from England, eastern United States and a few from New Zealand. The land agents had painted a glowing picture of the wealth to be gained by setting out fruit trees and vineyards and waiting for the riches to roll in. The land was irrigated from the Calloway Canal and everyone had to learn how to handle the water so that the low places would not turn into swamps as the water level was not far below the surface. Most of the farms were fenced against rabbits and some of the farmers planted fig trees along the boundary lines. I do not know the variety of these figs but they were delicious.

Contrary to the popular idea that the Englishmen were a dissipated breed of remittance men, there were actually very few in the Rosedale area. There were many young English bachelors but they supported themselves. In the main the settlers were families intent upon learning to farm. The American settlers knew how to farm but I am quite sure that none of the English people had ever farmed before they came to Rosedale.

The colonists must have suffered terribly from homesickness, especially the women. They had left friends and relatives in a green and familiar land to establish homes in a flat, sandy, hot country so far away. Living conditions were on the primitive side but they made things as convenient as possible. Many had a hand pump and a redwood sink on the back porch near the kitchen, and the bathroom was near enough to the pump for a trough to be put through the wall and water pumped into the tub. There was no ice, of course, so the next best thing was a desert cooler—a frame containing shelves over which was tacked wire netting and over this, burlap. On top was a zinc container for water with absorbent material such as old underwear or old cotton stockings used to siphon the water to the sacking. The legs of the cooler were placed in cans of water on account of ants. The wire netting was only necessary when the cooler had to sit outside where stray dogs and other animals were a menace. Milk was kept in the coolers and many a fine scum of cream was ruined by a sandstorm, to say nothing of our tempers, as everything in the house would be covered with sand. In a really bad storm the pattern on the floor covering would be hidden, which meant literally taking the dirt out in shovels.

Coyotes were a great nuisance and depleted many flocks of chickens. The dreary sound of the coyote's howl in the night is something that has disappeared with the changed times.

Our roads were plain dirt; through sandy soil it was hard going but on firmer ground they weren't so bad excepting for the dust. On the very sandy roads the county paid men to put straw on the surface; this in time was ground in and had to be replaced. Men with teams were paid one dollar per day for this work.

There were a few nice homes—nice by pioneer standards, that

is—built by the more affluent members of the colony, but in general the houses were built as cheaply as possible. They were the box type house with one-by-twelve siding and one-by-four bats to cover the cracks. Inside, the walls were covered with a sort of cheese cloth and then papered. The ceilings were usually high. Every house had a porch which was a life saver in summer, especially the kind that went all around the house. My home is the last of the original houses still habitable. There is not a straight line in it but it has withstood earthquakes and bad storms very successfully since it was built in 1892 by a man named Russell, who, after two years of bad breaks, went back to England. The place was planted in muscat grapes and one year the entire crop of raisins was ruined by sandstorms.

People who now depend upon the passive absorption of canned material for entertainment would be at a complete loss if they suddenly found themselves in the days when Rosedale began. Although there were no cars, radios, televisions or movies and no electricity or gas, we still enjoyed life and looked forward to the social events that took place fairly often. One of the most enjoyable of these affairs was the musicale. Everyone who was asked to perform did so, talent being no requisite; it would have been rude to refuse. We listened to "The Little Tin Geegee" sung with a slight lisp. The words were clever but the melody, if there ever was one, was somewhat obscured by the rendition. The singer of this popular song was Lowell Peters and his accompanist was always Jessie Burnett, now Mrs. T. A. Butterworth and living in Los Gatos. It was the only song that Lowell knew and he always obliged very cheerfully when asked to sing. One evening, I recall, we heard the song about the devoted couple Darby and Joan, sung by a shy, sweet voiced lady who suffered so much from stage fright that breathing was difficult and the tempo became slower and slower until the tale was finally told. Mr. George Wright accompanied her on a lovely little upright piano that had been brought from England. Mr. Wright was an excellent musician and taught piano, violin and organ. Other colonists were also well educated in music and they were always a pleasure to hear. One man whose last name was George and who was called Energetic for the same reason that a black cat is named Snowball, played the banjo. He seemed to know but one tune and when he played he had a hard time stopping—the performance was always quite prolonged.

Most of the Englishmen were young and they could think of lots of things to do; they took endless pains in putting on an entertainment. One memorable occasion was a minstrel show staged in the jam factory—the relic of a dream to supply the world with jam made from the fruit that was to be harvested from the newly planted orchards which died from lack of water before any fortunes were made. To the Americans present, many of whom were from the South, the dialogue being spoken with an English accent was the funniest part of the show. The music was all good. For this affair, only the ones who could put a song across performed.

This jam factory was located in the Rosedale townsite which was south of the present Rosedale grocery store. There was a one-story hotel nearby which failed to prosper and was moved away. A blacksmith, "Uncle" Johnnie Baker, operated a shop on the location of the present Rosedale Blacksmith Shop. Our first grocery store was owned by A. B. Adams. He sold out to W. R. Shephard, an Englishman. He, in turn, sold out to Amos Weller who eventually tore down the building and put up a much larger one. The post office was located in the old store but I do not know when it was established but I think it was when Mr. Adams ran the store. A George Bacon, brother of Mrs. Adams and Mrs. Amos Weller, was the mail carrier who made a trip to Bakersfield every day driving a team hitched to a light springwagon.

Cricket matches were held in a big open field south of the highway and west of what is now called Renfro Road. There were about eight hundred acres in this field which extended south to the river. It made a fine starting place for the rugged game of Hare and Hounds, or paper chase. Horses were used for this. Two riders, the hares, were each supplied with a sack of paper torn into bits which they scattered over a tortuous route. They were later followed by the hounds (the rest of the riders) in full cry who had to find the hares by following the paper trail. Horses were not spared and many a tumble was taken because of gopher holes in the uncultivated fields. The women all rode sidesaddles and the men used either English or western saddles.

I remember attending some saddle races but the only one that sticks in my memory was the umbrella race where each rider carried an open umbrella. Miss Julia Bedinger, later married to Herbert Underwood, owned a blue roan named Girlie. She was very fast and was ridden in this race by Frank Burnett.

One of the most appealing of the colonist families was that of brothers Robert and Thomas Grosvenor and their niece Charlotte Grosvenor. The two men, well past middle age, had taught in a school for "gentlemen's sons" in St. Johns Woods, London, and with this for an agricultural background, they came to Rosedale to make their fortune raising fruit. As a result, Miss Grosvenor had to do housework by the day to keep them all fed and sometimes food wasn't too plentiful. Knowing nothing about horses, the old gentlemen bought a good looking brown mare called Dolly, but she was a poor choice as she would run away at the slightest provocation. Robert and Thomas were great walkers. I expect they felt more secure on the ground. They always strode along at a good clip and in summertime a white cloth floated out behind their hats to keep off the tropical heat. They spoke beautiful English with never a trace of a colloquialism and seldom used a short word when a long one would do.

The Easter Monday picnics were always most enjoyable. They were held in the woods toward the river. We ate supper before dark then sat around a bonfire until late. I don't remember, but I imagine we slapped mosquitoes as we sang.

It was impossible to have grass in the yard unless it could be watered from the ditch that irrigated the farm and this was seldom possible. However, there was often an ornamental planting in front of the house and the entrance road circled around it. In calling on the Russells one drove up an avenue of palms, small at that time, and on leaving drove around a circle of cypress in the middle of which was an almond tree. The Burnetts had a circle of orange trees in front of their home and a lot of locust trees in other parts of the yard. Mr. Burnett was a real gardener and could make anything grow. The family moved to Bakersfield and after a time went to live in Santa Cruz.

As times became increasingly hard, the colonists gradually left

Rosedale. A few stayed in Bakersfield but others went to Los Angeles and vicinity and to the northern part of the state.

Our fuel for cooking and for heat in winter came from the woods near the river (Kern). Every year before the cold weather started people took their teams and hay wagons and brought back huge loads of cottonwood and willow logs to be worked over by hand to fit the cook stoves, the heating stoves or fireplaces. Oil for our kerosene lamps came in two five-gallon tin cans in a wooden box and on the outside was the trade name, "Pearl Oil." It was a Standard Oil product. The boxes were very useful for making cupboards, etc. A handy and ornamental container was made by putting a lid on a box and covering the whole with bright cotton material. This type of furniture could be called "early Rosedale" but it is not to be found in any antique shop, for after serving its purpose, it made excellent kindling.

(*Historic Kern*, December, 1959)

California, Here I Come
by Alfred Siemon

It was early in 1902. I had reached the age of twenty-one years, and was free of family ties. In that day a young man was deemed to be subject to parental control and his earnings were regarded as family property until he was twenty-one years old, and I had previously been subject to that idea. My brother Pro and I came to California via Santa Fe. Our first stop was at Monrovia, where Aunt Eliza and Cousin Charles Anson lived. We then went to Whittier where Aunt Grace Buckmaster, then widowed by the accidental death of Uncle Wilse Buckmaster, was living with her three children, Emma, who now resides and who for many years has taught school in Bakersfield, Joe, who is now and for many years has been a teacher in Ventura High School, and Eva.

I stayed there only a few days as I had a "job" as a farm-hand with my cousin "Gus" Rehkopf in Imperial Valley, which had only recently come under development by irrigation from the Colorado River. I went to work for him early in January, 1902; and most of my work was in leveling land for irrigation with a four horse team and a Fresno scraper. I was paid forty dollars per month and board. As the season progressed we planted crops, and later on harvested them. The summer was frightfully hot, and sometimes reached 120 degrees in the shade, where there was any, shade being quite scarce. Most ranchers lived, as Gus did, in tents boarded up on the sides with open kitchens in front covered with arrow-weed brush to provide shelter from sun. We worked through the warmest days, as it was actually more comfortable moving around than it was sitting under one of the brush shelters in front of the tents.

In the fall of 1902 I "came out," as the expression was, to Whittier and entered the Preparatory Department of Whittier College in what would correspond to about the third year in high school. By that time, the family had followed Pro and me to California, and had settled in Whittier; and I was able to board at home for a time, but later joined a boarding club of students and supported myself by doing janitor work at the college. I cleaned great expanse of halls and class rooms before and after classes; and during vacations I worked on ranches in Imperial Valley and sawmills in Riverside County. While in Whittier College I was a member of the college debating team and financed the college annual "Acropolis" by soliciting advertisements from the local merchants. One of my classmates was a young lady named Inez Bennett with whom I promptly fell in love. She was a couple of years ahead of me, but I was in some of her classes, and, on one occasion, she and I were on the same side in a college debate.

I do not remember the reason, but I soon decided that I could not wait out a full college course. I then secured a night watchman's position in the Whittier Reform School, which required that I stay (awake) all night in a dormitory full of spoiled kids to see that the little scoundrels did not set the place afire, escape or commit some other deviltry. I read everything in the public library during those long nights; and finally commenced to read law books and to study shorthand. I got an old Remington typewriter, and during day times when I wasn't sleeping, practiced typing. By the end of a year I had read Blackstone and several other law texts, and had become fairly proficient as a stenographer. My first position as a steno was in a Whittier law office; and in that connection I got appointed and acted as justice of the peace for about six months during 1905.

I then got a position in a Los Angeles law office as stenographer, working during office hours and attending U.S.C. law school, which was then held in night sessions. This was during 1906, 1907 and 1908; and I took the bar examination and was admitted to the bar on July 22, 1908. By that time I was doing strictly law work writing briefs in a first-class law office, where I worked until the fall of 1909. In the meantime I had married Inez, who had graduated from Whittier College, on the prospect of continued employment; but around October, 1909, a fellow student at U.S.C. got my job by agreeing to work for about one-third of what I was being paid, and I was out on the street, so to speak.

It then became necessary to look for a location to enter practice on my own, and I looked over several towns, including Hanford, Visalia, and Coalinga. None of them seemed to offer an impecunious young lawyer an opportunity to make a living; and I finally started back to Whittier where Inez was, thinking that I would see what Arizona had to offer. On the return from Coalinga, I stopped to spend Christmas at Wasco with John Britton, who was an uncle by marriage to my Aunt Henrietta.

Of course, I discussed my problem with them and they gave me no encouragement about locating in Bakersfield, saying there was no room for any more lawyers here. However, I was compelled to pass through Bakersfield, as I was traveling by Southern Pacific; and I thought I had just as well look the place over. My uncle had given me the name of W. W. Kaye, a lawyer then practicing here, whom he knew, and of whom he had high regard. I got off the Southern Pacific at the old depot in Kern, followed the streets north, south, and west, and soon found myself out in the country in each direction. I had about given up the matter of locating in Bakersfield and decided to go on, as it seemed the place was just a little burg with nothing at all doing. At the time I had reached the point about two blocks east of the present Union Avenue on Nineteenth Street, which was then out in the country except for the old car barns, when I met a fellow and stated to him that I had thought that Bakersfield was a larger place than this. He replied, "Hell, this ain't Bakersfield, this is Kern. Bakersfield's over there about a mile."

I accordingly came over to Bakersfield by the old street car then operating, went into Mr. Kaye's office in the old Hopkins Building, told him who I was and what I wanted; and without any formality whatever he told me: "See that table over there? Sit down and go to work," and that was that; and I have been here ever since. My location in Bakersfield, as will be seen from the above, was a pure matter of chance, because if I hadn't seen the fellow that told me Kern was not Bakersfield, I would have gone back to the S.P. depot, boarded the train, returned to Whittier and perhaps gone to Arizona or some other place to look for a location.

At that time I arrived in Bakersfield, which was the twenty-seventh day of December, 1909, it was a wide-open, rip-roaring, frontier town, with sixty-five saloons, a population of about 8,500, and a red light district that was a wonder. The population was typical of that which inhabited boom towns, free and easy in their morals, liberal in their attitudes, and all-around good sports. Everybody knew everybody else, and everyone was very friendly.

Having found something to do, the next thing was to set up a domestic establishment. The place was crowded by reason of an oil boom, and it was impossible to find a house to rent. I "roomed" for a month or so, and finally found an apartment in a basement where we lived for a few months, after which we obtained an apartment in a duplex on California Avenue.

A great oil boom developed in 1910. Perhaps a dozen new lawyers came here from Goldfield, Rhyolite, and other Nevada towns where a gold mining boom was rapidly deflating. Most of them came during 1910, and we had a very colorful bar made up of some very interesting characters. There were two Superior Court judges, and another was added two or three years later. Business of all kinds, good and bad, was flourishing. People were flocking in (by railroad train), and rushing to the west side to locate oil lands. Hotels, where the boomers put up for the night on the day of their arrival, were packed; and the few automobiles available were used by local people to take loads of boomers to locate oil claims. They were "taken up" as placer mine locations, which I believed could not legally be done for the reason that a mineral location cannot ordinarily be made until there has been a discovery of mineral; but the possessory rights of the first locator to take possession had to be respected as long as he was making an effort to discover mineral (oil); and much valuable oil land was acquired on that theory, as the locator promptly moved material and equipment onto his location and many oil wells were "brought in."

I have said that business of all kinds flourished. Maricopa and McKittrick began to grow; Taft and Fellows were established; and the concomitants of the boom went along. Each little place was over-populated with saloons, gambling joints and disreputable houses. All of that has now disappeared and these little towns shrunken from their former boom conditions. The oil development brought a lot of litigation to the law offices in the nature of disputes over possession of claims. There were a lot of criminal cases for lawyers who went in for that kind of business, as a boom is always accompanied by a floating criminal element compelled, at times, to resort to "stick-up," burglary, larceny and other things to avoid going to work.

The City of Bakersfield was organized as a Sixth Class City under general laws, with every officer elected at large; the majority votes of the entire city controlled; and was dominated by the saloon and red-light elements. Consequently, there was considerable graft and corruption in local elections and politics; and the residential elements were practically without a voice in local political affairs. On election days the saloon element rolled out their big automobiles with mufflers wide open and rushed about hauling their voters to the polls. There were many fake registrations of non-residents whose registration addresses were local rooming houses, and most of them voted at the "Old Bloody Third" precinct in the old fire station at Twentieth and K streets, the only fire station the city then had. The good government element, of which I was a member, kept a group of five or six precinct watchers at that voting precinct all day at every election to challenge voters who appeared to be fraudulently registered as residing in the precinct. The big autos of the saloon element would bring in the voters from the oilfields and elsewhere, and our group would challenge each voter who appeared to be fraudulently registered. The other party had its watchers there, also, to contest our challenges, and to raise a storm of protest. On each challenge the person challenged would be sworn by the precinct officers, and we would question him regarding his residence. He would then "swear in" his vote. The other crowd would be abusing us violently. Since the election officers had been hand-picked by the political machine, it was quite seldom that we were able to make good on our challenges; but they did not like to stand up and be sworn, and we doubtless kept many floaters from voting. After the polls were closed we would stay through the count and watch the ballots and the tally to see that the election officers read and reported the ballots correctly, as the officers would frequently try to misread and/or mistally the ballots; but when the returns were made the result was always strongly against our faction. A heavy majority in the "Old Bloody Third" precinct was usually enough to determine the result of the entire city in each election. As may be surmised, our activities just described always created a condition of high tension with dangerous explosive possibilities. Many of the "gang" would have gladly murdered us; but there were several determined, fearless and husky looking members in our group; we were merely acting in the interest of good government and beating us up would have been bad publicity. While it looked like a "close thing" on many occasions, we suffered nothing worse than rather violent heckling abuse.

County elections were dominated in much the same way; but the small towns were not able to put up the same sort of opposition. The "Old Guard," as we called the dominating political crowd, was led and headed by the Kern County Land Company interests, and the superintendent (Jastro) was the "boss." His henchmen were the keepers of the saloons, houses of prostitution and the city machine then controlled as shown. There were two daily newspapers then— the *Morning Echo* and the evening *Bakersfield Californian*. The former was aligned with the reform element, while the latter was definitely "Old Guard." Each had a fictitious character alleged to be in the "know" of the opposite faction, and who would be interviewed by and report to the editor whose creation he was. The Echo's character was "Colonel Blood," and the Californian's "Bos'n Big Mit." Each was represented as reporting and making public the private views and activities of the faction of which he was alleged to be a member, of course in the opposing newspaper. They were marvelous and fantastic pieces of fake reports and served to keep the factions in good humor, at least for some time.

On the advice of a certain individual I allied myself with what was then known as the anti-old guard political faction and for many years I was involved in various reform movements, which resulted in the election of a reform district attorney, Barkley McCowan, in 1914. He called me into his office as chief deputy, which office I held until the middle of 1917. I was then discharged along with the rest of the office force on account of our carrying on a prosecution of a man who had contributed to the downfall of a young girl. The thing created so much adverse criticism of the D.A. that a recall was promoted, and he was recalled. I re-entered private practice in a number of successive partnerships, and continued to carry on a good deal of reform activities.

In the early fall of 1932 I was elected to the Board of Bar Governors, where I served one four-year term and about two years in the second term. In the meantime along about 1934 I was elected to the City Council where I served for sixteen years, during which World War II was being waged; and I was mayor of the city during practically the entire period of the duration of the war.

As George Ade would say in closing one of his old Fables in Stang: "Little remains to be told."

(*Historic Kern*, December, 1977)

II

Travel and Transportation

The story of transportation in Kern County is a varied one, involving lumbering prairie schooners, the plodding "Camel Corps," phenomenal railroad engineering, and the man-powered Gossamer Condor. Yet in its early period, Kern County was little more than a thoroughfare, a place to get through as one passed from one destination to another. That's how Father Garces, the camel drivers, and the early teamsters saw it. But as Bakersfield grew into an agricultural and shipping center, it increasingly became the hub of a network of land and air routes that would have amazed the pioneers. The transportation story, perhaps more than any other, illustrates the shift in the San Joaquin Valley from a cattle grazing frontier to an industrial and agricultural center.

Historic Routes and Passes
by Goldie B. Ingles

Lt. R. S. Williamson, in 1853, acting on orders from the United States War Department, began an examination of the southern Sierra Nevada and the Tehachapi Mountains for the purpose of finding the most practical route for a railroad. He chose as guide for the expedition Alexis Godey, who was well acquainted with that part of the state and later settled in Kern County. Charles Preuss, a German scientist and map-maker, served as draughtsman, and Isaac W. Smith served the party as civil engineer. The expedition was escorted by a corporal and nine men. Six passes were found to be more or less available, and these will be described in the order in which Lt. Williamson dealt with them in his report of the findings of the expedition.

Through Walker's Pass extended a pioneer trail to the west, a pass discovered by Joseph R. Walker in 1834 and reported by him to be a feasible route through the Sierra Nevada to the San Joaquin Valley. Walker led several parties through this pass, most notably the Chiles-Walker party in 1844. Walker also guided John C. Fremont's expedition of 1845 through this area. While Fremont led a small contingency across the mountains from Walker's Lake to Sutter's Fort in search of provisions, Walker and the main group moved southward and westward through Walker's Pass, it being the intention of the two groups to rendezvous on the Kern River. Fremont mistook the Kings for the Kern River, however, and Walker's group spent some three weeks waiting on the latter river before journeying northward to rejoin Fremont in the Santa Clara Valley.

The discovery of Walker's Pass afforded an important route into the San Joaquin Valley, although this pass was not used as much as the others of the general area. Lt. Williamson deemed it impractical for a railroad since the region to the east was mountainous and desert, as well as almost destitute of wood, water and grass. He noted that the canyon of the Kern River on the western side of the mountains was narrow and obstructed with projecting rocks, features which made it too difficult for railroad construction. Lt.

Williamson reported that this route was feasible for a wagon road.

Tehachapi Pass, in the Sierra Nevada between the southeast corner of the San Joaquin Valley and the Mojave Desert, Lt. Williamson found to be the most practical in the general area for a railroad. The fact was accepted later by the railroad, and a line was completed through this pass in 1876. A century earlier, Father Franciso Garces traversed this area. Leaving Yuma in 1775 with two Indian guides, he crossed the Mojave Desert to San Gabriel, and then he passed northward to the San Joaquin Valley by way of either Tejon or Grapevine Pass. Garces then crossed the Sierra Nevada by way of Tehachapi Pass (or perhaps Oak Creek Pass, as will be noted subsequently), and he recrossed the desert on his return to Yuma.

Among those who searched for wealth and opportunity in this area were the trapper-explorers. Jedediah S. Smith, in search of beaver, probably crossed the mountains by way of Tehachapi Pass in 1827, although historians have not decided between it and Tejon Pass. In 1844 Fremont, on one of his several expeditions, passed from the San Joaquin Valley to the Mojave Desert by way of Tehachapi and Oak Creek passes. During the 1860s and early 1870s this became an important stage and freighting route between Los Angeles and Havilah.

Oak Creek Pass extends from the Tehachapi Valley to Willow Springs, and it is possible that Garces reached the desert by this rather than Tehachapi Pass. There has been confusion in name, since Oak Creek Pass was called Tehachapi until the building of the railroad, when the name was transferred to the present Tehachapi Pass. Fremont, on leaving the San Joaquin Valley in 1844, reached the Mojave Desert by way of Tehachapi Creek and Oak Creek Pass. A pioneer trail was soon to follow much the same route. Fremont apparently thought that he was crossing by way of Walker's Pass rather than Oak Creek Pass. Lt. Williamson mentions it, but had little specifically to say about Oak Creek Pass.

Tejon and Grapevine passes are described together, for though these are some fifteen miles apart and differ in ascent and descent, they have been confused in identity from the beginning. After the founding of Fort Tejon in the early 1850s, the greater part of the travel through the mountains went by way of Grapevine Pass, while Tejon Pass was not used much by wagons but rather by horsemen and cattlemen.

Pedro Fages, in search of a party of deserters, entered the San Joaquin Valley in 1772. He makes mention of the Pass of Cortes and the Buena Vista Valley. From the meager details, it appears likely that he came through Tejon Pass, which is east of Grapevine. The approach by way of Tejon Pass affords a splendid view of the valley, one which is not equally as good from Grapevine. The panorama before him probably induced Fages to name the valley Buena Vista. Whether through Tejon Pass or Grapevine Pass, there is no doubt that Fages was the first white man to enter the San Joaquin Valley. Grapevine Pass derived its name from the grapevines growing there. (In 1830 and 1832 Ewing Young, a trapper known also as Joaquin Joon, entered the San Joaquin Valley probably by way of Tejon Pass.)

Lt. Williamson described Tejon Pass as having grades greater than he anticipated, and as being not too favorable for a railroad. Grapevine Pass, characterized by low, rounded hills cut up by ravines, also presented problems for railroad construction in that the gradients were steep. He noted that a wagon road there could be easily traveled, and he urged the building of an improved road.

Located west of Grapevine Pass, San Emigdio Pass extends through the Cuddy Valley along the course of San Emigdio Creek. Little is known of the early history of this pass, but it appears that an expedition led by Francisco Ruiz entered the San Joaquin Valley by this route in 1804. The plan was to take Indian children to the missions to be educated. A native chieftain defeated the plan, and the expedition probably left by way of Tejon Pass. The Old Los Angeles Trail, or El Camino Viejo, the oldest north and south trail in the San Joaquin Valley, extended through San Emigdio Pass.

Lt. Williamson reported in conclusion that of the passes described, there were two that were pre-eminently superior, the Tehachapi and the Grapevine. If the railroad came from Mojave or the mouth of the Gila River, neither would have the advantage, since the two routes were almost exactly of the same length. Water was equally abundant along each, and gradients would be the main point of comparison, in which regard Tehachapi Pass proved better than Grapevine Pass. Lt. Williamson would probably be gratified to know his report is still valid in that the only railroad into the San Joaquin Valley from the east and south enters by way of Tehachapi Pass, and that the road through Grapevine Pass has been made into, shall we say, a very good wagon road.

(Historic Kern, September, 1949)

When Camels Came to Kern
by Richard C. Bailey

Outside San Antonio, Texas, at Val Verde, is a commemorative plaque that reads, "Home of Camels." This is no romantic phrase from the Arabian Nights. It is true enough, for in the 1850s and 1860s the United States Army imported camels for transport service between isolated posts in the American Southwest.

However, these were not the first camels in the western Hemisphere, as a few were introduced during early Virginia days, and others had been tried in Peru in the sixteenth century with some success.

Fort Tejon, located about thirty miles south of Bakersfield in Kern County, California, is another home of camels. For several years a part of the original army group was stationed here until the abandonment of the fort.

After the Mexican War in 1848 the United States acquired a vast land area in the southwest. Much of this was arid and the army posts were far apart. Transportation problems arose and the use of camels was suggested as one solution.

In March, 1855, Jefferson Davis, while secretary of war in Pierce's cabinet, succeeded in getting Congress to pass a bill appropriating $30,000 for the purchase of camels. Major Henry Wayne and Lieutenant David Porter were dispatched to the Near East to secure a herd.

While Porter was fighting his way through red tape, Wayne (in June, 1855) left in advance on another ship. His orders were to visit the Zoological Gardens in London and study the camels there. From there he went to Paris where he was to meet a French officer who had had much experience with camels in North Africa. This officer was absent, so Major Wayne proceeded to Genoa, and then to Spezzia where he was rejoined by Porter who had arrived by this time with the ship *Supply*.

Together they then set sail for Tunis, in North Africa, where they succeeded in securing only three camels.

Then in succession they landed at Malta, Smyrna, Salonica and Constantinople, the last point being reached in October.

Hearing that they might buy camels in the Crimea, where England and Russia were conducting the hostilities of the Crimean War, Wayne and Porter plunged valiantly into the midst of the action. They got no camels but they did have a good sideline seat during the "Charge of the Light Brigade."

They next sailed for Egypt, a country they should have visited in the first place. But sad to relate, they now found a law in effect which forbade the exportation of camels. But American ingenuity triumphed; a special permit was granted and nine camels were secured.

To fill out the quota, they returned to Smyrna. Finally, on the fifteenth of February, 1856, the shipload of thirty-three camels started westward for the United States.

The trip was long and stormy. The camels had to be tied down for days at a time to prevent injury.

After three months the ship *Supply* landed the herd at Indianola, Texas, on May 14, 1856. The camels were overjoyed to reach dry land again, but the Texans thought them funny looking critters.

Porter was sent back to North Africa and returned a year later with forty-four additional camels.

A camp had been prepared for them at Camp Verde, about sixty miles northwest of San Antonio, so there they were marched. After several weeks of rest they were considered ready for a real test to prove their value.

Routes for projected wagon roads and railroads were an important topic at this time. Some persons were afraid California might set up an independent government if closer ties with the east were not soon fashioned. Southerners wanted a series of southern links over potential slave territories.

So on June 25, 1857, twenty-eight camels left San Antonio under

Fort Tejon Hospital building, c. 1890.

the command of General E. F. Beale, who had been commissioned to survey a wagon road from Fort Defiance, New Mexico to southern California.

Beale was already a celebrated man. He had been the official messenger who carried the first gold from California to Washington, D.C. At the battle of San Pasqual he was one of the scouts who secured relief for Kearney's dragoons. He had also been superintendent of Indian affairs in California and Nevada.

Some observers predicted the camels would never reach California but would founder on the way. The doubters were confounded when the camels came through magnificently. In nearly five months of slogging across some of the roughest and driest terrain in North America, eating thorny plants and drinking brackish water, the camels performed all tasks required of them. They demonstrated conclusively that with proper handling they were far more efficient and economical than the army mule for desert transportation. The expedition's mules would refuse to descend certain dangerous slopes until the camels had gone down to prove that it could be accomplished. The camels went from six to ten days without water on the journey and most of the time carried the feed and water that the mules required. In crossing the Colorado River they proved to be powerful swimmers and crossed safely, but ten mules and two horses were drowned in the operation. This last was quite surprising to Beale since he had read and been told that camels could not swim!

After crossing the Colorado, two of the camels were detached and sent to Los Angeles to indicate that the camels had arrived in California. The rest were driven to Fort Tejon where they spent some part of January, 1858, stationed at a 5,000-foot elevation in snow to test their resistance. The camels are said to have loved the snow.

General Beale was ordered to return to Texas to complete the camel experiment, by observing how they withstood the winter trip across the same bleak desert land.

They returned by way of Los Angeles, and Harris Newmark in his book, *Sixty Years in Southern California*, wrote, "Los Angeles has experienced many exciting street scenes, but it is doubtful if any exhibition here ever called to doors, windows and the dusty streets a greater percentage of the entire population than that of the Government camels driven through the town on January 8, 1858, under the martial and spectacular command of E. F. Beale."

After completing the return trip Beale reported, "I have tested the value of the camels, marked a new road to the Pacific, and traveled 4000 miles without an accident."

This would seem to have secured the future of the Camel Corps, and indeed, Secretary of War Floyd recommended that Congress authorize the purchase of 1,000 additional camels. But no action was taken in 1859 or 1860, and the Civil War pigeonholed the proposal.

At the outbreak of hostilities in 1861 those camels then in Texas were seized by the Confederacy and used with varying success. They were later sold to private individuals, circuses and menageries. Some, however, were turned loose, to wander over most of the southwest. It is from those beasts that the weird tall tales of the American camel have arisen.

When Fort Tejon in California was partially abandoned in 1861, the camels along with most of the equipment were taken to the Quartermaster's Depot in Los Angeles. For a while the camels were used to freight between Los Angeles, Camp Drum in Wilmington, and San Pedro, but this was short-lived. It seems that nearly all horses and mules become panic-stricken upon entering the sight or smell of a camel. Runaway teams and pack-trains became the rule rather than the exception. No matter that a strong camel could carry a load of up to 1,200 pounds; he had to go.

They were next tried on a mail route over the desert to Fort Mojave from Southern California. Probably due to poor management as much as any other reason, the experiment was termed a failure after a short trial. Succeeding experiments had no better luck.

The camels were then marched up the coast to the arsenal at Benicia where they were auctioned. A man named McLeneghan purchased the entire herd of thirty-five. He later sold all the camels, some of which were used for packing in the Sierra among the mining camps. A few returned into the hands of General Beale who kept them on his Tejon Ranch south of Bakersfield until they died.

It is likely that descendants of the original herd are still alive either in wild state in remote sections of the southwest, or in circuses and zoos. The last two survivors of the army camels that the writer has been able to trace died in the Los Angeles Griffith Park Zoo in 1927 and 1931, respectively. Both of these camels bore the brand of the U.S. Army on their flanks. Both were probably second or third generation American camels since the camel does not ordinarily achieve an age much over forty years even with the best of care.

But if the army and private industry had no use for the camel, General Beale, at least, was happy about a pair he had. According to his biographer, Bonsal, he used to drive the hundred or so miles through the mountains to Los Angeles behind a pair of trained camels hitched tandem fashion. Also, as far as we know, he never had to get out and push!

(*Historic Kern*, March, 1953)

Freighting Recollections
by Andrew A. Allen as told to Dick Bailey

I started handling a long line team in 1906, starting first with six and then with eight horses and mules. A long line team generally had horses in the wheel positions hitched in pairs. A single line was attached to the near leader. Wagons were loaded with 500 to 1500 pounds of freight per animal, depending on the type and condition of road. On the lumber wagons I drove in the employ of the A. Brown Company, up to 3,000 board feet of lumber was carried.

I hauled lumber out of the Greenhorn area from two mills. One of them was the A. Brown Mill on the south side of Greenhorn and the other the Charles Likely Mill on the north side of Greenhorn, at the head of Lumreau Creek. The south side mill produced lumber that was used locally, but that produced by Likely was freighted out to the railway station at Ducor.

Driving these mountain roads was pretty ticklish since the outside of the road was lower than the inner. Double brakes were used and great care had to be taken when coming down with a load. Another fellow named Rankin and myself were the only two who never had a wagon get away from them. I once met a Chinaman on this practically one-way road and had quite a time passing him, as he was afraid of going over the edge with his cart.

For the benefit of those who might be interested in tracing my freight route from the Lumreau Creek mill, I am giving the following details: I crossed Cedar Creek by Billy Bowen's place, up a steep hill and then down to Poso Creek to the Campground Bridge, then to Dave Lavers' place where I stayed all night. From here I drove to White River (old Tailholt) where I stayed all night at Mitchell's Hotel. At that time Mitchell owned the store in which the post office was located. John Dunlap ran the saloon. I guess there were fifty people there in 1905.

From here I took the Porterville road to Fountain Springs where there was a ranch and a school, then I drove straight west to Ducor and usually camped about one-half mile east at an old deserted ranch where there was water to take care of my team. I unloaded my lumber onto the ground at Ducor, leaving it in charge of the S.P. agent there and drove back to White River the same day. I always carried a grub box on the wagon and cooked my food over a fire on the ground when it wasn't possible to stop at some ranch or town. Occasionally I drove to Woody from the Likely Mill where I would trade lumber for barley hay. To get to Woody in those days, I would drive to the road fork at Linn's Valley and swing to the left.

My first job around the logging business was as a swamper for two seasons. The following two seasons I spent snaking logs for the mill with a team. At the Likely Mill there was a donkey engine that could be moved about to snake in logs. This mill had two steam-operated circular saws three to four feet in diameter. One was set above and slightly ahead of the other. This mill produced around ten thousand board feet per day.

The mill crew consisted of a sawyer, a screw-tender, an off-bearer, two edgers who took off the bark slabs, and two men who stacked lumber in the yard. Fir, pine and cedar were milled at this place.

Sometimes we worked at one mill for a while and then moved to the other. In moving from the A. Brown Mill to the one on the other side of Greenhorn, the men would walk over a trail about two or three miles, but I drove a wagon around the mountain with the crew's bedding, cables, chains, stretchers and other equipment. On a trip from the Brown Mill I drove northwest, then west to Evan's Flat, then west to Pettit place. Then I turned north over the hill to the Blue Chief Mine, using blocks and cable to work the wagon up the slope. I then used the Likely road into the mill on the creek. Sometimes it would be dark before I arrived and my swamper would walk ahead with a lantern to light the way. There were no ox teams operating in the area during my time.

During the winter, logging operations closed down and I graded roads north and west of Hanford in Kings County. It was here that I learned to smoke a pipe to keep warm. After a road had been plowed up, a seven-ton roll was run over it to smooth out the road bed. A fellow named Daggs had a prize team of twelve matched mules that he had assembled from all over the Pacific Coast. One of his skinners tried to budge one of these seven-ton rollers from a spot where it had been setting for some time but couldn't do it. I was then given the job and by pulling the roller at an angle I was able to get it in motion with my ten ordinary horses and mules. My bosses thought I was a pretty good skinner but it made Daggs' team look bad; in fact, it looked so bad that the skinner got fired. Daggs had paid up to $500 for a single mule for that matched team of his.

In 1910 I hauled lumber at Shaver Lake from a small mill to the flume at the large Shaver Mill. Lumber was then flumed from this point to Clovis, a distance of sixty-five miles. In the winter of 1910 I graded roads in Kings, Tulare and Fresno counties. On Christmas Day I sold my team, intending to go to Alaska. Instead I went to San Francisco and spent all my money. And that was the end of my teaming experience.

(Historic Kern, March, 1950)

From Trail to Rail
by Erle Heath

There remained by November, 1874, a gap of only 149 miles from Sumner, near Bakersfield, to San Fernando separating Los Angeles and San Francisco from their first railroad connection. But before this section was completed in September, 1876, the Southern Pacific

TRAVEL AND TRANSPORTATION 61

Engineers under Col. George Grey and William Hood had accomplished two of the most difficult construction jobs met in building the entire railroad in the West.

Rising from the floor of the San Joaquin Valley, the Tehachapi Pass was surmounted at an elevation of 4,025 feet by a line of track that swerved back and forth up a mountain side through eighteen tunnels, and looped over itself by a remarkable stroke of engineering genius to climb 2,734 feet in a distance of but twenty-eight miles around gradual curves on a 2.2 grade.

While more than three thousand men were working the hundreds of horses and dump carts on the road over the Tehachapi mountains, a force equally as large was piercing San Fernando mountains with a 6,975-foot tunnel that carried the railroad from San Fernando Valley to connection with the line from the north. This tunnel of more than a mile and a quarter was then the second longest railroad tunnel in the United States.

During the four years that the Central Pacific and Southern Pacific were building the railroad south through the San Joaquin Valley, Bakersfield had grown from a village to the proportions of a town with about six hundred population. Incorporation was voted at an election on May 24, 1873, and in February the following year, Bakersfield officially became the county seat of Kern County, displacing Havilah, a small mining town in the mountains about thirty miles away. Every advance of the railroad shortened the distance that had to be traveled by stage coaches and brought Bakersfield closer to its source of supplies from San Francisco.

It took four days to go by stage coach from Havilah to San Francisco in 1868. Three times a week Thoms' stages left the county seat for Visalia, where a change was made to Concord coaches bound for San Francisco. Twice a week stages left Havilah for Los Angeles and San Pedro, connecting with the steamers. Supplies were shipped from San Francisco to San Pedro and then hauled by freight teams through San Francisquito or Soledad canyons over steep mountain roads that were frequently made impassable by heavy rains and snow.

Four years later a combination rail and stage line carried a traveler from San Francisco to Los Angeles in forty-eight hours. A

Southern Pacific timetable published in September, 1872, announced train service three times a week from San Francisco to Tipton, where connection was made with stage coaches which covered the remaining distance of 252 miles to Los Angeles.

With the approach of the railroad, settlers began to locate on the fertile valley lands around Bakersfield. Farming took on larger proportions and ranked along with mining and stock raising as important industries. The people of Bakersfield were looking forward to a day when their city would be a metropolis of a large and prosperous region.

The railroad was opened for traffic to the north bank of Kern River on August 1, 1874. "From the town we can hear the locomotive whistles," reported the *Weekly Courier*, "and for all practical purposes the railroad has reached Bakersfield." This point on the river remained the terminus for a short time while a bridge was under construction. In the meantime, grading and track laying was completed south of the river. The bridge was ready about October 2 and a week later passengers and freight were handled at a temporary station on a projection of Second Street. A station building, offices, and side tracks were being built on the new townsite at Sumner, about a mile and a half from the business section of Bakersfield. Engineering requirements made it necessary to keep the railroad line on higher ground to the east of Bakersfield instead of going direct into the town.

Grading gangs had pushed on ahead and by January 2, 1875, the road bed was ready for more than twenty miles south of Bakersfield. Shipments of rail were delayed and it was April 26 before the track was laid and trains operated to Caliente. This station was established at a settlement known as Allen's Camp. Here the railroad terminus then at San Fernando, twenty-two miles from Los temporary "place in the sun" while the region swarmed with hundreds of American and Chinese railroad builders. Daily stages "bridged" the ninety-eight miles over the wagon road to the railroad terminus than at San Fernando, twenty-two miles from Los Angeles. By that time the rail and stage journey between San Francisco and Los Angeles had been cut to thirty-three hours.

It was from Caliente that the real climb started over the moun-

Tehachapi Loop, completed in 1876.

tains. Tehachapi pass had long been established as the most feasible outlet into southern California. As early as 1853 this divide was chosen by Lieutenant R. S. Williamson, a government engineer, in preference to Walker's Pass as the best route for a railroad. It was over this pass, called Tah-ee-chay-pah by the Indians, that Col. John C. Fremont took his troops in 1844.

Lieutenants R. S. Williamson, J. G. Parke and George G. Anderson constituted a party of engineers delegated by the government to explore and survey the most practicable route for a railroad from the Mississippi River to the Pacific Ocean. The work was carried on during 1853–54 under direction of Secretary of War Jefferson Davis. Starting from army headquarters at Benicia, the party set out in the spring of 1853 to examine the passes of the Sierra Nevada Mountains leading from the San Joaquin and Tulare valleys. Also to explore the country to the southeast of Tulare Lake to ascertain the best railroad route between Walker's Pass, or such other as might be preferable, and the mouth of the Gila River. It was specified that the engineers should have an escort of at least three noncommissioned officers and twenty-five privates and should have the best horses and packers available. The party was in the Tehachapi region during the summer of 1853 and then went south, selecting San Gorgonio Pass in San Bernardino Mountains as being the best route for a railroad south of Los Angeles to the Colorado River.

Preliminary surveys were made over the pass by Southern Pacific engineers in 1866 and during succeeding years several additional lines were run in an effort to establish the best possible grade and curvature. It was not until the winter of 1875, however, when construction work was actually under way, that Engineer Hood mapped out his famous "loop."

"It was just a common sense plan," he explained in later years. Yet the expedient he used to "make distance" was then the talk of the engineering world and travelers over the winding crooked road have never ceased to wonder how it was ever planned or built. Resembling two large circles drawn with a giant compass, the loop was tunnelled into the side of a ridge, twisted around the crest of the peak and back over the tunnel, gaining an elevation of seventy-seven feet and bringing the line into position for easy gradient to the summit. In the present day, with powerful locomotives that pull long trains of freight cars, it is an uncanny but not uncommon sight to see a double-header of locomotives puffing over the top of the loop while the caboose is just entering the tunnel seventy-seven feet below, the train making a complete loop of itself. On the grade up the mountain it is possible to see the track above and below five different times as it winds its way around the hills and through the canyons.

Starting from Caliente at an elevation of 1,291 feet, a "U" turn was made and a swerving ascent of the mountain begun instead of following up Tehachapi Creek canyon. After a six-mile climb the line rounded onto a slope at the head of the canyon, down which could be seen the town of Caliente little more than a mile away on an air line. Just above this point (Bealville) was bored tunnel No. 5, the longest and the most difficult to construct on "the hill," as the Tehachapi Mountain became known to railroad men. This tunnel was completed about March 10, 1876, and on April 6 track had been laid and the first locomotive passed through. The road was in operation to Keene (now Woodford) on May 26.

The first swing of the loop was started just beyond Woodford, and, in a distance of five miles to the present station of Marcel, an elevation of 587 feet was gained. Seven miles more of heavy climbing brought the railroad into the valley at the summit of the pass. About a mile beyond was located the station of Tehachapi and trains began operating that far on July 10, 1876. Residents in the pioneer town of that name, about four miles west, literally picked up their homes and moved them to the new station on the railroad. The site of the rollicking mountain town that had witnessed so many "wild and wooly" frontier days was soon deserted except for a few faithful souls, and the place became known just as "Old Town."

With the summit reached, construction moved along rapidly through the pass onto the Mojave Desert. Trains were run to Mojave on August 8 and from that point the track was laid in practically a straight line across Antelope Valley to the mouth of Soledad Canyon, where the last big drive was made to a connection with the railroad from the south, which had just been pushed through the long San Fernando tunnel.

(Historic Kern, January 1951)

The Street Car in Bakersfield
by Dean A. Gay

When the Southern Pacific Railroad Company, in 1874, located its Bakersfield station more than a mile and a half to the east at the newly founded town of Sumner, no end of consternation was caused the citizens of Bakersfield, who detected that their town had been deliberately left off the line. In order to offset this disadvantage, omnibus service was provided by an enterprising citizen and a telegraph line was constructed between the two towns, both services being afforded in 1875. Although late in 1874 a franchise was granted to A. R. and C. D. Jackson for the building of a street railroad between the two towns, nothing came of this early venture.

In 1887 a franchise for the construction and operation of a horse drawn street railroad between Bakersfield and Sumner (later known as Kern and now East Bakersfield) was granted to H. A. Blodget, H. H. Fish and others, who opened for business the Bakersfield and Sumner Street Railroad in 1888. Connecting the Court House, in Bakersfield, and the Southern Pacific Depot, in Sumner, the original line passed along Chester Avenue, Nineteenth Street, and Baker Street. However, the service rendered by the squeaky and rattly horse drawn cars was none too regular, and sometimes it was barely regular enough to hold the franchise. The quality of the service was often subject to the temperament of the driver, and beyond that the little cars carried a fascination for the town rowdies who sometimes tore them up or lifted them off the tracks. The cars were very light, carried only a dozen passengers, and the track was frequently in need of repair. While the horse drawn cars were far from something to brag about, they were the best the town possessed until the introduction of electric cars about a dozen years later.

In the 1890s, Bakersfield acquired a new public service with the provision of electricity, at first derived from steam driven generators in town and later from a hydroelectric plant built near the mouth of Kern Canyon, the latter operated by the Power, Transit, and Light Company. Joined by C. N. Beal, Blodget and his associates began adapting the street railroad line of the reorganized Bakersfield and Kern Electric Railway Company to electrical operation in 1900. Considerable expense was involved in the laying of heavier tracks to accommodate larger rolling stock and the installation of trolley lines. In 1901 four twenty-four passenger electric cars began operating between the Santa Fe Depot, in Bakersfield, and the Southern Pacific Depot, in Kern (formerly Sumner). On the day the electric cars were put in service, the company did a "land office business," some three thousand paying passengers are known to have ridden the cars, while perhaps a thousand more friends of the conductors were picked up as "courtesy" riders. Thriving business led the company to acquire three improved forty-passenger cars the following year, and the company began to expand its lines to outlying parts of Bakersfield and Kern in 1903.

While the cars often were laid up for hours because of derailings, spreading tracks, and sinking road beds, hoodlums also caused the management considerable concern. The beating up of the motormen and conductors, and the breaking of seats and windows were quite common. In 1906 all of the employees were deputized and given permission to carry blackjacks, For the time being, at least, the motormen and conductors were kings, and such niceties of service as controlled speed, smoothness of operation, and the minimizing of rattling and bumping were at the discretion of the operating personnel.

When in 1910 the street railroad company was acquired by the San Joaquin Light and Power Company, a new era began for this system under the management of Harry Jastro. Now the motormen and conductors were toppled from their thrones, and emphasis was placed upon service to the patrons. In line with the new ownership, an overall reconstruction program was undertaken. A rock crusher was built near the Kern River bluffs to provide rock for ballasting the tracks, new steel rails were provided, and redwood ties were substituted for the nondescript ones laid earlier. Six new forty-passenger cars, of an improved type, were acquired in 1912.

Little change took place in the company during the following three years, but in 1915 a new kind of trouble plagued the business when jitneys—a jumble of conveyors—were placed in service beyond the reaches of the tracks, but also in direct competition with the streetcars to points within the urban areas served by the company. The failure to extend the lines into the new residential districts was partly responsible for the entry of the jitneys, and soon after the passage of an ordinance restricting the operation of the jitneys the company itself placed in service its first buses, which operated beyond the end of the tracks in East Bakersfield. During 1921 still more buses were placed in service to accommodate outlying areas, which carried a significant portent for the future of the electric street railway. The era of the automobile was dawning in the 1920s, and this was destined further to eclipse the street railroad business by bringing losses in revenue that could not be easily offset by increased fares, one-man cars, and the abandonment of unprofitable lines. The company was well on its way toward becoming a bus operating concern exclusively when, in 1933, the San Joaquin Light and Power interests were acquired by the employees, and V. N. Mickelberry became the president of the new company. By that time, despite their differing origins, the two towns of Bakersfield and Sumner had long since grown together physically and economically with a common destiny, thus fulfilling the predictions of far-seeing prophets who had earlier envisaged such an eventual development. Undeniably the street railroad had done its part in bringing about this trend.

(Historic Kern, June, 1954)

Via Granite Station
by Kyle Austin

The iron tires on the stage coach wheels made a continuous and rhythmic sound as they rolled on the hard packed dirt of the road running from Bakersfield to Granite Station. The sound of the horses' feet mingled with the creaking of the stage coach and the echo of moving leather and trace chains. It was a good sound—the sound of the open road and the West in 1902.

TRAVEL AND TRANSPORTATION

Iris Beatty, married but a few short weeks, was on the four horse stage for the two day trip to Delonaga Hot Springs on the Kern River to visit her husband, Charles Beatty, who was employed at the early day popular resort. The stage was driven by Bill May, a friend of the family. The route from Bakersfield led north on Jewett Avenue, across the old wooden Kern River Bridge, Walt's Station (Oildale), Poso Station and to Granite Station for an over-night stop.

Bill May and his passenger arrived at Granite Station in the late afternoon. The young Mrs. Beatty was shown to her room in the main building and the horses were stabled and fed. The main building housed a dining room, saloon, card room, and a couple of bed rooms for travelers.

Granite Station was the stage stop where teams were rested or changed on the route from Bakersfield to Delonaga Hot Springs, Glennville, Woody, White River, Jack Ranch, Kernville and other mountain points. In addition it was the only social center for miles for the miners and cowboys who worked and lived in the area.

The evenings and nights often became noisy with the revelry of drinking and gambling men who found a measure of comfort and relaxation here from their isolated work.

The operators of the hotel and bar were somewhat concerned about having a beautiful young bride as their guest for the evening and in anticipation of the social atmosphere which would exist they politely suggested an early dinner and retirement for her.

She followed their advice and early in the evening, tired from the long ride from Bakersfield, was soon sleeping soundly in her room which was only a door or two from the saloon. Later in the evening she was awakened by the shouts and laughter of rough men at play.

Now, she was not exactly naive about her position and as the evening advanced and the revelry became noisier she grew apprehensive about her situation and decided to peek out the door. She slowly opened the door only to find that Bill May had unrolled his bed directly across her door step and was fast asleep! Any would-be Lothario would have to cross his body to enter her bedroom!

With this assurance of her safety she returned to her bed and slept soundly through the remainder of the night.

The next morning, after breakfast, the stage left for Delonaga via Poso Flat, Burke Grade, Little Poso, Eugene Grade and across lower Greenhorn to the Kern River.

The old Granite Station buildings are intact and well preserved due to the interest of Harry West (now deceased) and his widow, Ethel West who now owns the property.

(Historic Kern, June, 1970)

The Kern Canyon Road
by Kenneth D. Taylor and Bertha L. Taylor

Transportation is a prime factor in the development of any locality. Kern County, being peculiarly located with mountains on three sides, has found this problem to be paramount. No attempt is made herein to cover the total road program of Kern County but covers only the area known as Kern River Valley or Kern Canyon.

Historical accounts point to Joseph Reddeford Walker as probably the first man to travel from the San Joaquin Valley to the east across the Sierra Nevada mountains. He was one of a party of fur trappers that came west from Salt Lake City in 1833 to search for better trapping areas. This party crossed into California by way of the Sonora Pass, and Walker, taking his leave of the rest of the group, continued southward into the San Joaquin Valley. He made the return trip to Salt Lake City in 1834 via the mountain pass that now bears his name.

Many subsequent crossings were made in both directions, but none were noteworthy until January, 1846, when General John C. Fremont made a West to East crossing. He was leading a party of troops across the mountains to the Owens Valley, using the Walker Pass route. In his party was a young man, Edward M. Kern, who was serving as a topographer for the expedition. General Fremont is credited with the naming of the Kern River in honor of his topographer, and this name was later given to Kern County when it was formed.

It became apparent that travel gradually increased through the Kern River Valley area until the early 1850s when travel increased sharply with the discovery of gold in this area in 1854. The peak of the gold rush was not reached until 1857, and it may be assumed that poor transportation was one possibility for the slow development of the actual gold rush.

As the boom developed, satisfying this growing area with supplies, both personal and mining, became a major problem due to the poor transportation facilities into this area. Pack trains were used to transport most of these needed supplies during the early 1850s, with no record of wagon trains until almost ten years later. The wagon drivers needed to be of the most courageous nature as early roads were more like trails, with very steep ascents and descents and many treacherous turns. Teams had to be double-hitched and the block and tackle was used on many of the steeper grades.

As one recalls that much of the population in Central California at this time was found to the north of the Kern River, it is not surprising that the first stage route to serve the Kern River area was from Stockton. A second route soon followed with its beginning in Visalia. This route crossed the Poso mountains following the Poso Creek with the southern terminus at Keysville; soon this route was extended to Havilah. It was not until 1861 that the stages from Los Angeles were serving this area via a Tehachapi crossing.

In 1860 there was advertising that the Walker Pass route was "the most feasible route south of Sonora pass that afforded year around use." This was important at this time for there was much traffic from California to Nevada with the opening of the Comstock Lode in this year.

The Comstock Lode did not develop into a widespread mining area as had been anticipated and many miners got only as far as the Kern River area when their dreams of riches were shattered with this news. The Kern River mines were also declining and new discoveries were few and these were very poor. This led to a general trend of switching from mining to agriculture, as everyone had been too busy in their search for gold to develop the agricultural possibilities in this region. Practically all the food had been shipped into the mining area. Beef cattle were driven in on "the hoof" from the range land of Southern California and then sold to the residents of the area.

There had been some farm development in the San Joaquin

Valley at this time and much of the produce of the valley farms was sent to the upper River markets. Colonel Thomas Baker, a leading Valley citizen, opened the road that now carries the name of Baker Grade as the solution to transporting the Valley produce to the miners. This road started at Bena and terminated in the Walker Basin and was classed as an excellent road when compared to the other existing routes of that day. Traffic from the Visalia-Keysville-Havilah road soon began to use this new road because it was less treacherous and time consuming, although it was a greater distance. It has been noted that the heavy freight from Los Angeles was transported over Baker Grade in preference to the trip north from Caliente. The Baker Grade road had a great bearing on the eventual growth of the Bakersfield area for it was by this route that many of the travelers from the north were first introduced to the Bakersfield vicinity.

Kern County was established in 1866 from portions of Tulare and Los Angeles counties. During the years immediately preceding the formation of Kern County, the citizens of the upper Kern River area made repeated efforts to get the Tulare County administration to establish new roads and improve the existing routes. There are no records to indicate any official compliance with these requests so much of the early road building and development was done by the land owners along the routes.

The railroad reached south to Bakersfield in 1874 and was joined by a line from Los Angeles in 1876. The railroad crossing of the Tehachapi mountains followed the same general route that is in use today. Caliente became a major stopping point for it was here that all the freight that was destined to go to the upper Kern River area towns was transferred to the stages.

The stage, drawn by four horses, left Kernville about 8 a.m. and reached Havilah in time for an early lunch. After a short rest, and four fresh horses, the trip was continued to Caliente, arriving with time to spare before boarding the evening train for a one hour ride into Bakersfield. The return trip was more time consuming for the train left Bakersfield slightly before midnight thus necessitating a long layover in Caliente before starting the all day stage ride back to

Kernville. The one way fares for this trip were $3.50 for the stage and seventy-two cents for the train ride.

The horse drawn stages were partially replaced in about 1915 by two Mitchell automobiles which started at opposite ends of the Kernville-Caliente road and each made round trips daily. To cover the forty-one miles was about four hours each way if car troubles were not too serious. An interview with the Caliente station agent of these days reveals that hardly a day passed that there was not a shipment of parts from the Los Angeles agency for Mitchell cars. The horseless carriage demanded better roads and as they were improved, more and more cars began to arrive on the scene. In 1918, the mail was being carried by trucks to the upper river areas from Bakersfield.

Another route of lesser consequence, but one that played an important role in the general development of the Bakersfield area was the Breckenridge Road. This road is still passable today, but it is seldom used. This route for the most part is a one way dirt road that crosses the western slope of Breckenridge mountain before it terminates on the south bank of the Kern River about a mile upstream from the Democrat Hot Springs. This is the road over which the materials and equipment for the first Kern River electric plant were moved. This plant site was picked and building operations started in 1904 at which time the nearest available road was about eight or ten miles upstream. The materials and machinery were taken by wagon train over the Breckenridge road to a point that was nearest to the power site, then it was sledded over the country side to the rim of the canyon where it was lowered to the canyon floor by means of skids and block and tackle. This plant produced its first electricity in 1906 and operated for the next twenty years with no access except for the trail from Breckenridge Road. The power from this plant also contributed greatly in the early development of Bakersfield, for it was soon after the completion of the power plant that the first electric street car was seen on the Bakersfield streets.

As early as 1913 there was a concentrated effort on the part of the county residents to improve the local roads; however, the supervisors of that date were reluctant to spend money on the existing road system. They held that before improving the present system of highways, there should be a long-range plan for highway development.

In 1913, the Kern County Supervisors voted a bond issue of $2,500,000 for 316 miles of county roads of which 230.7 miles were to be paved. Bakersfield was to be the hub of this system, with the individual roads radiating to the extremities of the county much as the spokes of a wheel radiate from the hub. One of the proposed roads in this 1913 study was the Kern River road (it is now known as State Highway No. 178). However, this did not reach the real stage of actual development until 1920. This plan called for a road from Bakersfield, through Isabella, Walker Pass and on across the Sierra Nevada Mountains to the desert.

The most interesting and most difficult part of this construction adventure was at the westerly end of Kern Canyon where the walls rise almost perpendicular and the canyon is scarcely wider than the river bed. This part of the road was built by convicts that were brought in from Folsom Prison. The first men to arrive, on May 15, 1924, were to set up the camp that was to be used as headquarters. The first working crew of 100 men arrived on July 1, 1924 under the custody of ten prison guards. Guards were thought to be adequate in number. However, due to the rough terrain and inadequacy of compound facilities, escapes were numerous. Many articles in the *Bakersfield Californian* of this period refer to the escaping prisoners of the road crew.

(*Historic Kern*, September, 1958)

Early Flight and Autos in Kern
by Lester McDonald

From earliest times Kern County had had an interesting history with cowboys, bandits, explorers, etc. With mining came the railroads in 1874, followed by oil development which led further to a new field of mechanical contraptions. In 1903 the Wright brothers were experimenting and made a successful flight with a four-cylinder engine. Kern County, booming with oil, looked into its use.

In 1902 Joe Ferris of Caliente brought the first automobile into Kern County. It was a 1902 one-cylinder single-chain drive Oldsmobile with its engine under the body. Hillman Arms was manager and operator of the first garage in Bakersfield on Eighteenth Street, just off Chester Avenue, known as the Ben McLeod Cyclery. In 1904 Mr. Arms sold my father a Logan two-cylinder automobile made in Chillicothe, Ohio. This, the first car sold in Bakersfield, was a proverbial red two-seater with a rear door entrance. Shortly before this Mrs. Fred Linz drove a one-cylinder Rambler up the front Chester Avenue steps of the old court house, later known as the city hall. This was probably the first time in history that an automobile ever went into a court house.

Another local first was performed by Donald McGregor, a newspaper man. On July 5, 1909, wearing a pair of borrowed red tights, he made a parachute jump from a balloon at the Hudnut Park half-mile track, near the present county Agriculture Building on M Street. McGregor landed in the Chinese vegetable garden of Gee Dong.

The first aerial club was formed locally on December 17, 1909, when two fourteen-year-old boys, George Fourtier and Tom Murphy, Jr., sent aloft their tissue-paper and cheesecloth fabricated balloon. It was filled with gas by burning high gravity fuel oil, and sent into the air with a dummy, which was released by means of a slow-burning string. The balloon later burned in flight.

In January, 1910, Dominguez Field outside Los Angeles held a national meet of aircraft. The country's outstanding pilots performed there in gliders, balloons, dirigibles and airships.

A big event in Bakersfield took place April 15, 1911 at Recreation Park, off Oak Street, where the temporary P.G.&E. Building now stands. I was working in a local bank, and remember that $2500.00 was guaranteed Eugene Ely of the Curtiss Aviation Team for two flights by H. M. Hamilton who promoted the aerial show. All collected money was deposited in the bank, but due to more people staying outside the fence to see the airship than paid admission, the event ended up in the red. $500.00 was eventually put up by others.

Ely made two flights, one of nine miles and the other ten miles. As the field at Recreation Park was so small, part of the high board fence on the west was taken down. The airship was rolled to the top of the bank of the big ditch outside the park. It was then hand-pushed to give the plane more speed in starting down the ditch bank, from which it gained momentum crossing the ball field to clear the board fence on the east side. William Hoff, a mechanic, Dick Wells, a hard-rock miner, and George (Red) Peterson were all knocked down when they tried to stop the airplane after it landed.

Kern's first flight by a locally-built plane, flown by a local pilot, occurred on April 20, 1911. The builder and pilot was Henry McGregor, who still resides in Bakersfield where he operates an auto repair shop at 1904 South "M" Street. He constructed his Santos Dumont monoplane from plans and made two flights with it of a quarter-mile, east of Bakersfield, off Niles Street at a spot then known as Counterfeit Valley. McGregor was thrown out uninjured on his ill-fated second flight. This venture was backed by three local contractors: E. A. White, J. R. Rogers, and J. E. Yancey. McGregor was a mechanic at the Bakersfield Garage, at the corner of "G" and Twentieth streets at the time, and the plane was put together on the second floor of this structure. McGregor remembers the remains of his plane were burned in the fire of the Eastside Garage, Nineteenth and Baker streets, around 1914.

A Curtiss biplane was taken to the Bakersfield Garage by E. J. Erb and W. E. Drury to be assembled. It was then taken out to the Counterfeit Valley camp along with the Santos Dumont which had been purchased from Henry McGregor by Otto Wannock and L. F. Scott. On June 24, 1911, while preparing for the test flights a big wind came up, wrapped the canvas hanger around both ships and destroyed them.

Edith Emmons, a local woman, was probably the first woman passenger in aviation history when she paid my Uncle Conner's relative, Roy N. Francis, $100.00 for a twenty-second flight of 1100 feet. This event took place May 4, 1912 at Edison, eleven miles east of Bakersfield, and many local people paid to see the historical flight.

Another first in national aviation history was the flight taken by Silas Christopherson in a Curtiss biplane, when he flew from San Francisco to Bakersfield, He made the trip by following the rail-

An aviation meet was held at Bakersfield, April 15–16, 1911.

road track, and set a new American record for a single flight. He left San Francisco February 9 and finally reached Bakersfield February 10, 1914, landing at the race track of the Old Fairgrounds on Chester Avenue. Gassing up again, he took off before a large crowd and flew across the Tehachapi Mountains, by way of Tehachapi to Los Angeles. This is believed to be the first flight ever made over these mountains. The trip was not made without trouble. Christopherson was forced to land on the mesa south of Bakersfield. He later reported that when he reached an altitude of 4000 feet his carburetor began to freeze, and he recommended that later ships be constructed so their exhaust pipes could play heat on the carburetor to keep it warm at high altitudes. This was an important observation, and the suggestion was carried out in later plane construction. After adjusting his own exhaust pipe in this manner he finally made the flight into Los Angeles on February 16, 1914, taking four hours for the trip.

One of the greatest early day events was the air race from San Francisco to Bakersfield on February 25, 1914. One pilot, Charles Poulson, was unable to get off the ground. Another, George Sherman, crashed into San Francisco Bay. Silas Christopherson won the race, arriving at the Old Fairgrounds race track in a pouring rain where the crowd had nearly given up hope that anyone would arrive. Another pilot did not arrive until the next day. While in Bakersfield Christopherson raced his plane against the famous Barney Oldfield in his car, and beat him, covering the mile course in fifty-nine seconds, proving that aviation was here to stay.

Lincoln Beachy was the first pilot in Bakersfield to do acrobatics in a plane on November 16, 1914. Then on November 22, 1914 he again showed the superiority of the plane by beating both a motorcycle and automobile in a race, circling the track at a speed of eighty miles per hour. Beachy also flew his ship upside down for a further thrill.

On December 6, 1917 Katherine Stinson became the first woman pilot to fly over Kern County when she made an air trip from San Diego to San Francisco via Tehachapi at an altitude of 9000 feet.

In 1919 my father helped H. H. Holloway (Dutch) rent a piece of ground from Louis Olcese by a large pepper tree where Alta Vista and Pacific streets are today. Dutch took up passengers in an old Army Curtiss Jenny biplane, and gave them what they paid for in loop-the-loops, etc. He was our first barnstormer.

(Historic Kern, December, 1954)

Gossamer Condor Flight
by Chris Brewer

Among mankind's long-cherished aspirations has been that of flying by virtue of his own power. Aware of this aspiration, British industrialist Henry Kremer in 1959 offered a prize of 50,000 pounds to anyone who would selfpower a flight over a mile-long, figure-eight course. The prize was won on August 23, 1977, when the Gossamer Condor was self-propelled at Shafter Airport. The aircraft was designed by Dr. Paul MacCready, president of Aero-Vironment, Inc., and piloted by Bryan Allen. The accomplishment has achieved world-wide recognition as a significant event in aviation history, and it will be commemorated by the placing of a marker at Shafter Airport on February 24, 1979, at 2:00 p.m. The plaque will read:

Site of Gossamer Condor Flight

This plaque at Shafter Airport commemorates the world's first man-powered flight to complete the Kremer Circuit, August 23, 1977. The circuit, a figure eight around two pylons one-half mile apart, was completed in six minutes, twenty-two seconds. The plane was designed by Dr. Paul MacCready, Jr. and flown by Bryan Allen. A cash prize of 50,000 pounds was awarded by the Royal Aeronautical Society, London, England.

California Registered Historical Landmark No. 923
Plaque placed by the State Department of Parks and Recreation in cooperation with the Kern County Museum, Kern County Department of Airports, and Kern County Historical Society, February 24, 1979.

(Historic Kern, December, 1978)

III

Farming and Ranching

California's gold rush created in the minds of many people the impression that the state was only "a place for acquiring wealth" with which to return to the comforts of a home somewhere else in the world. Yet many wealth seekers, after "toiling for years to make a scanty living among the mines," according to one observer, found the fulfillment of "hopes, expectations, and wanderings" on the farms and ranches of the state. Some of those who formerly had pursued mining became the farmers and ranchers who assured an increasingly important agricultural production in Kern County.

The Historic Rio Bravo Ranch
by W. Harland Boyd

The Kern County Historical Society held its May, 1976, meeting at the historic Rio Bravo Ranch, on the banks of the Kern River. The pioneer settlers on the ranch were two brothers, Solomon and Philo D. Jewett, who in the early 1860s occupied a narrow strip of land on both sides of the river. From their headquarters they had control over a vast stock range which extended up and down the foothills and into the Sierra Nevada. The Jewett brothers were among Kern County's best known sheepmen. When they came to the southern San Joaquin Valley the sheepmen were raising a Mexican variety of sheep called the Churro, which was a hardy variety, but it did not produce mutton and wool in quantities and qualities desired by the Americans. The Jewett brothers, among others, improved their flocks by introducing blooded stock, notably the Merino.

After the editor of the *Havilah Miner* visited the Rio Bravo Ranch in the spring of 1874, he wrote of his good fortune in being a guest at the "beautiful home of the Jewett brothers," where he was "handsomely entertained." The ranch, he observed, was "conducted much on the style of the accomplished eastern farmer," being "complete in its appointments." In view was "charming mountain scenery," including "a fine growth of vegetation," and toward the east "the clear water of the Kern River" emerged from a deep chasm in the Sierra Nevada.

In the fall of 1874 the Jewett brothers sold the Rio Bravo Ranch, together with several of their flocks of valuable sheep. At that time they withdrew from wool growing on the natural grazing areas in the foothills and mountains in favor of farmlands planted with alfalfa on the flatlands near Bakersfield. Although they continued to raise Merino sheep, a variety for which they were famous as importers and breeders, they began to import Leicestershire, a long-wooled mutton sheep, which they expected to do well on their new ranch, but a variety that could not compete favorably for the scant pasturage on the open ranges with the Merino.

(*Historic Kern*, June, 1976)

The Story of San Emigdio Ranch
by Barbara G. Gray

San Emigdio, an area in the southern foothills of Kern County, San Joaquin Valley, California, probably received its name from Father Jose Maria Zalvidea, Franciscan, who explored the Valley with a body of soldiers and camped there on August 5, 1806. It was customary to name places according to the feast days of the saints, and this is the feast date of St. Emigdius. It appears only coincidental that the locality is in the vicinity of the San Andreas earthquake fault, and St. Emigdius is the saint invoked against earthquakes.

Before Commandante Pedro Fages in 1772-73, Father Juncosa from Mission San Luis in 1774, and Father Garces in 1776, probably the only white men to enter the San Joaquin Valley were deserters or renegades and the occasional military pursuit. The year 1806 started active, authorized exploration of the interior valleys of California under orders of Governor Arrillaga.

In 1824, coastal Indian neophytes at three missions revolted against the military who forced them to work without compensation. Seven Indians were executed for complicity in the death of four Spaniards while twelve others were imprisoned at the presidio at Santa Barbara for active participation in the revolt.

Father Ordaz, writing from Santa Inez Mission, reported that in 1824 "rebels were at San Emigdio where a Russian was instructing them in the use of firearms."

Buena Vista basin was accessible to the Santa Barbara channel, home of the Chumash Indians, via Cuyama or Santa Clara River in three days to a week. For this reason fugitive Indians would know of this place, for the earliest inhabitants of Canada or Arroyo de San Emigdio were a branch of the Chumash.

Eighty soldiers from Santa Barbara Mission were sent to bring the fugitives home Soldiers skirmished on April 9, at Buena Vista Lake, and on April 11, troops fought at or near San Emigdio. Here four Indians were killed and three Spaniards were wounded. Hindered by heavy winds and dust, the men returned to Santa Barbara.

Next the governor, urged by the padres to pardon all of the Indians because of the soldier brutalities committed at Santa

Barbara, granted full pardon. To advise the Indians of this pardon, sixty-three soldiers left Santa Barbara on June 2, 1824, with one field piece. Simultaneously from Monterey, fifty men with another cannon left San Miguel. The two forces combined on June 3 at San Emigdio, "far out in the plains of the Tulares."

Indian fugitives, camped at San Emigdio, were willing to return to the mission, but afraid of punishment if they gave up their weapons. Two padres with the soldiers "dispelled their fears while the Commander, too, assured them all should be forgotten." With the return of the fugitive Indian neophytes, the revolt of 1824 was ended.

Traders and trappers from Hudson's Bay Company were in San Emigdio Canyon in 1828. El Camino Viejo, earliest valley wagon route from Pueblo de Los Angeles to San Francisco, came through this canyon, first as a refugee trail for Spanish fugitives. Carreta drivers came with their oxen enroute to San Antonio (now East Oakland) before 1800. Don Jesus Lopez, for fifty years cattle boss of Tejon Rancho, was familiar with the road in 1840. In the area of San Emigdio grizzly bears were so numerous they resembled herds of cattle, and endangered travelers. Antelope, bear, elk, deer and wild fowl were abundant and provided excellent hunting grounds.

El Camino Viejo passed by the foundations of what was romantically believed to be an extendencia of the Santa Barbara Mission, but Fray Zephyrin Engelhardt, O.F.M. historian and scholar, stated: "No mission was ever located in Kern County nor anywhere east of San Juan Bautista."

The San Emigdio Grant, given by Governor Alvarado of Alta California in 1842 to Jose Antonio Dominguez, included four square leagues of 17,709 and 79/100 acres, "a tract of land in the Tulares, in or near the Tulare Valley in the County of Santa Barbara [sic]."

Pedro Fages, who came to San Diego as captain of the Portola Expedition in 1769, inaugurated the rancho system with the provision that the tracts in question did not encroach upon the four square leagues of "water and pastures, wood and timber" allotted to a pueblo; or upon the holdings of a mission; or upon any Indian rancheria (the word was the common name for a small Indian village). The recipient should also build a stone house upon the land, stock the ranch with at least 2,000 head of cattle, and provide enough vaqueros and sheepherders to prevent his stock from wandering.

Jose Antonio Dominguez left as widow, Francisca; a son, Francisco; three daughters, Ysabel, Marie Antonio who married one Cavalleri, and Maria Ygnacia who married one Olivera. These heirs at law sold for $2,000 an undivided one-half interest in this grant to John C. Fremont. In 1853, the Federal Board of Land Commissioners in San Francisco heard the petition of the Dominguez heirs and John C. Fremont, and granted favorable recommendations later approved by the District Court of the U.S. for the Southern District of California.

In the early 1860s Edward F. Beale, surveyor general for California, certified the survey of the San Emigdio Rancho boundaries under the original Mexican grant. A patent was issued by the federal government to the heirs of Dominguez and to Fremont in 1866.

San Emigdio Rancho during its history has been considered part of Santa Barbara, Buenaventura, Los Angeles, Tulare, and now Kern County. Various documents affecting the title are recorded in these counties and in no one county is a continuous series of documents to show transfers of interest which occurred from the 1850s to 1870s.

Even though a patent was not issued until 1866, Fremont deeded his undivided half interest to a trustee as early as 1860. This interest had several subsequent transfers, one involving Edward F. Beale. By 1877, Emory Charles Singletary of Colusa had acquired title through creditor sales, tax and sheriff sales.

The Dominguez half interest, meanwhile, was divided by various heirs selling their respective shares, with some sales occurring as early as 1852. The last sale by an original heir was in 1869 when Ysabel, oldest daughter, sold her share to Samuel Brinkerhoff. Beale acquired a portion of the Dominguez interest and so did Singletary, both of whom sold to one L. T. Fox. Another portion of the Dominguez interest came through a series of transfers to one

John Funk. Both the Fox and Funk interests were sold to satisfy creditors' claims on this and other property and Singletary ultimately acquired these interests, confirmed by a Kern County Sheriff's deed. Singletary was the first single person to own San Emigdio Rancho which he sold to J. B. Haggin in 1877, who sold to Kern County Land Company in 1890. Title of the Kern County Land Company was upheld in 1941 when some heirs of the Dominguez chain of title brought suit.

The grant is irregularly shaped, taking in most of the choice grazing land of the low foothills and many good springs. It is bisected from south to north by the large canyon cut out by San Emigdio Creek which flows north; the larger part of the grant being on the west side of the creek. This is the very heart, the central point for the cattle, for feed is good and it is well watered.

Original headquarters of the Rancho San Emigdio were on the grant, but present headquarters are one mile north at the mouth of the creek gorge, outside the grant boundaries. This section was subject to the School Lands Act of 1853, whereby Congress set aside Sections 16 and 36 of every township to provide funds for establishment of state universities. Chain of title passed from the federal government to the State of California.

In 1869, a George Thompson received a patent from California and conveyed the land to Alexis Godey, Fremont's guide and colorful Kern pioneer, for $960.00. Godey deeded the property to J. B. Haggin in 1883 for $2,000 and Haggin acquired the east half of section 36 by a patent from the State of California in 1878, and he conveyed the entire section or 640 acres to the Kern County Land Company in 1892.

(Historic Kern, September, 1957)

San Emigdio Ranch in the Tehachapi Mountains.

The Naming of San Emigdio

Franciscan Fathers,
Old Mission,
Santa Barbara, California
July 5, 1940

Miss Gretchen D. Knief,
Bakersfield, California

Dear Miss Knief:

I have gone through Engelhardt's works, his Missions and Missionaries and his local missions of Santa Barbara and I find that nowhere does he give the date or the circumstances of the giving of the name of San Emigdio. The references to that place are in connections with Indians from the coast going into the Tulares. I have also looked up the pertinent passage from Sanchez' book on place names. What she quotes there is from a letter which Father Engelhardt sent her in 1913 in response to a letter, still preserved in the Santa Barbara Archives, which Mrs. Sanchez sent to Fr. Engelhardt, November 1, 1913.

The fact that St. Emygdius is the patron to invoke against earthquakes (the Franciscans still pray to him daily in each monastery for preservation against earthquakes) appears to me a pure coincidence that the locality is near the San Andreas fault.

I have here in the archives the original diary of Father Zalvidea who made a journey from Santa Barbara to Kern County in 1806. It was made in July and August of that year. On August 5, he was about 15 miles from Buena Vista. Most probably it was he who named San Emigdio for it was customary to give names to places according to the feast of the saint which happened to be celebrated on the day.

However Father Zalvidea does not mention in his diary any names which he gave to places through which he passed. So that is the closest guess to which I can come. However, I can not prove it. There are many other places in California through which the San Andreas fault runs and any one of a hundred could have been called San Emigdio from the same reason. My strong suspicion is the

FARMING AND RANCHING 89

name may have been given by Fr. Zalvidea for he was in the vicinity in 1806 when the feast of St. Emygdius occurred. There are no other references in Engelhardt on San Emydio (*sic*) and so it would be impossible to probe the matter further.

In Rensch and Hoover Historic Spots in California it is stated that in San Emigdio Canyon there remain to this day the ruins of the San Emigdio Mission Station, a stone foundation for a church, 30 by 60 feet. It is known that the fathers intended to build a chain of missions in the San Joaquin Valley, but never got that far by reasons of the revolution in Mexico. The book is carefully written but I do not know the source whence the writers got the information.

Sincerely yours,
(Signed) Rev. Maynard Geiger, O.F.M.

Franciscan Scholar Refutes Existence of Mission at San Emigdio

Mission Santa Barbara
May 3, 1933

No Mission was ever located in Kern County, nor anywhere east of San Juan Bautista Mission. San Emigdio is right (spelling). There was one camp or temporary station somewhere east by north of Santa Ines; but the Franciscans had nothing to do with it, as it came into existence after the Mission Period, so far as I remember. There is nothing in the documents about it.

If you will look into the separately bound Index for volumes II–IV, you will find Kern mentioned, but in connection with Father Garces, chapter ix, volume ii.

Respectfully,
(Signed) Fr. Zephrin, O.F.M.

The above was in answer to an inquiry from R. W. Loudon relative to whether or not San Emigdio was ever used as a mission site. Father Zephrin, historian of the Franciscan Order of California, was eighty-two years old at the time of this letter. His death occurred in the following year (1934). (Letters referring to San Emigdio reprinted through courtesy of R. W. Loudon.)

(*Historic Kern*, June, 1957)

The Hog Hunter of the Tules
from the Bakersfield *Southern Californian,* May 6, 1875

Twenty miles to the southwest [of Bakersfield], just where the Coast Range sends out a hill sharpened to a point which threatens to cut off the waters of Buena Vista Lake from the slough that unites them to Tulare, lives Mr. Jesse Cole, whose reputation for tracking the wild hog among the tule and catching the otter that still claims its place in the wilderness of water, has ranked him among the famous trappers of the West.

His cabin is on a little rise of ground, most of the year surrounded by water. He moors his boat to the roof of brush which shelters his back door, and during the winter he paddles out among the ducks and geese which he kills for our town market. His hunting dogs, after a day's weary work catching wild hogs, share his blankets at night. They generally come in worn and wounded, for the hog makes a desperate fight.

Sitting in his cabin, waiting for the hunter's return, we had the pleasure of listening to the stories of an old settler in that section, whose sole subsistence in earlier days was the tule pork, which every fall he supplied himself with and made into bacon. He related the last encounter the trophy of which, in the shape of an ugly jaw, was slung by a piece of rawhide under the porch. A small band of hogs had managed to escape the vigilance of the hounds for two winters, and at last the forces were combined for their capture. They were protected by two fierce boars, whose tusks had reduced the number of dogs one-half in the two seasons.

The band was started about a mile from the cabin, and as they followed their trails through the tule and along the borders of the lake, often for a long distance, the hunters kept outside within hearing of the hounds, mounted on their horses. As the band reached each slough making up from the lake the boars would halt on the bank, and hold the dogs at bay while the band, little and big, swam the stream.

All the dogs had been trained to the business and seemed equal to any contest, but when the halt was made they paused and commenced maneuvering to seize the sentinels and avoid the tusks, which stood out like the horn of a rhinoceros on each side of their jaws.

When they made a dash at a dog if he failed to plunge by main strength through the tule out of the way, one of the tusks would separate his ribs, and nothing was left of him except the echo of his howl. Then the boars would wheel, rush across the stream and join the band which had waited to take breath, and on all would go, followed by such dogs as were left. After repeated contests, and when all had traveled several miles, the band emerged upon open ground, covered with high grass, which parted for half a mile the jungle of tule. The guns were brought to bear, and a number of the tired porkers were sent rolling in the grass before the two chieftains made their appearance, with the hogs close upon their heels. They hesitated when they saw the horses in the way, but for a moment, when a yell from the hunters sent the horses on a run out of their path. They were not quick enough, however. One of the boars with the violence of desperation, rushed for one of the horses, and, although the rider had urged him into a run, the boar passed under the horse and turning his head as he went, sent his tusk across the belly of the horse and let his bowels out upon the ground. The boar did not stop his headway. A large black dog, a cross of the hound and Scotch terrier, was close after him, and seized him by the ham before the horse had fairly fallen. As quick as light and with the strength of a panther, the boar slung the dog to one side and as he did so darted across his bow, cutting a gash from the shoulder on one side to the opposite ear, which left the dog panting his life blood out upon the soil. Five dogs were yet behind, the band had disappeared, and the boar—as if seeing no friend in sight and his strength well nigh spent—resolved to make a stand. The froth at his mouth hid all of his jaw but his dangerous tusks, and the dogs, panting with the race and heat, stood at a respectful distance waiting for breath to make another attack. Before they could resolve, however, one of the horsemen rode up, and cocking his shotgun, loaded with pistol balls at the head of the enemy made an end to the chase. The jaw was preserved, with its tusks the length of a finger, and are hung under the porch as a trophy.

(*Historic Kern*, December, 1963)

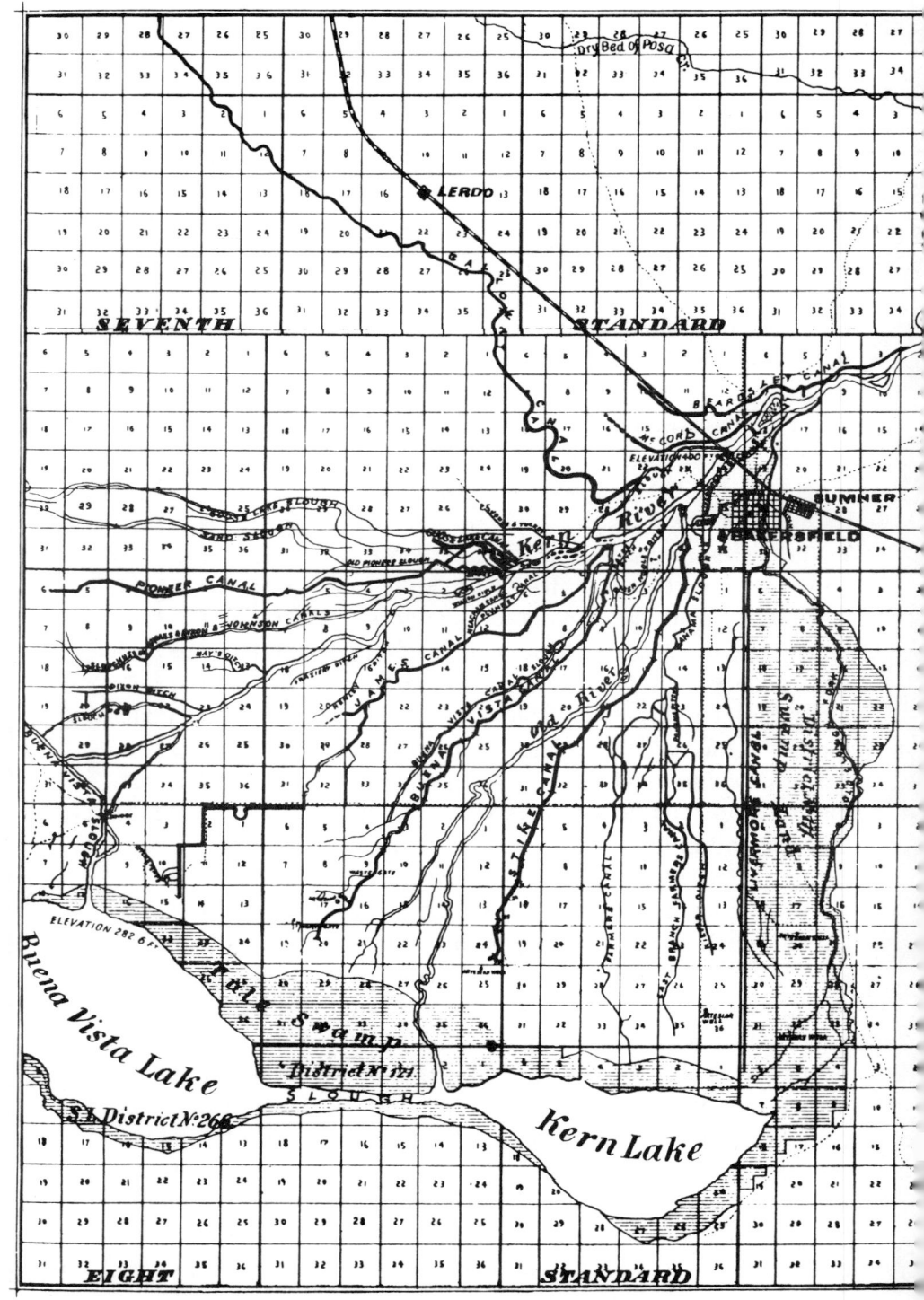

Kern River irrigation system, near Bakersfield, 1883.

Kern River Flour Mill
by W. Harland Boyd

Among Bakersfield's pioneer industries was the Kern River Flour Mill, which for more than eighty years was a familiar site on S Street, between Truxtun Avenue and Seventeenth Street. In 1871, soon after the Kern Island Canal was completed to a point east of town, the mill was placed in operation. Horatio P. Livermore, of San Francisco, who helped finance the canal project and was the owner of a large amount of land along its course, also helped build the flour mill, but its operation was the responsibility of his partner, William Muehe. The original milling equipment consisted of one set of burr stones for wheat and one for barley, and the water power needed to run the machinery was derived from the Kern Island Canal. In 1875 Muehe sold his interest in the mill to Fordyce Roper, and soon after another set of burr stones was added for the processing of middlings.

In 1879 Horatio P. Livermore's interests in the Kern Island Canal and the ranches he owned along the canal route, as well as his interest in the Kern River Flour Mill, were acquired by James B. Haggin, Lloyd Tevis, and William B. Carr, of San Francisco. They also acquired Roper's interest in the mill in 1884. In 1890 the Haggin-Tevis-Carr holdings in the southern San Joaquin Valley became the Kern County Land Company.

After the roller process for the milling of wheat became popular, it was adopted at the Kern River Flour Mill in 1891, when "a four break roller mill with six reductions," capable of producing sixty to seventy-five barrels of flour daily, was installed. The production of flour at the mill continued until 1923, and subsequently the machinery was used for the cleaning of seed grain and the rolling of barley. The building served as a warehouse for the storage of nonperishable staples used at the various ranches of the Kern County Land Company. An earthquake in 1952 led to the demolishing of the severely damaged brick building, and a long-familiar landmark was lost in Bakersfield.

Although there is no longer an historic structure to mark the site where the Kern River Flour Mill formerly stood, the Kern Island

Canal still flows through the property. The swift-moving water in the channel where the mill stood is an enduring reminder of the way in which power was developed to turn the flour-making machinery in the days prior to the use of electricity. The historic site is now occupied by the Hill House Vagabond Hotel.

(*Historic Kern*, December, 1976)

Hospitality of Henry Miller
from the Bakersfield *Morning Echo*, December 14, 1912

The Miller ranches, situated in Kern, Merced, San Benito, Monterey and other counties of Central California, are probably better known to the tramping fraternity than any other locality in this glorious golden state, says the McKittrick Clarion.

The weary wayfarer, when he reaches any of these ranches, is assured of a haven of rest. Supper is provided, a place furnished whereon to lay one's weary head, and supplied with a good breakfast in the morning, the rejuvenated traveler goes on his way rejoicing. This custom prevails at all the Miller ranches, and the bounty is given without money and without price.

Many good men, who during the summer months eke out an existence picking fruit and other light labor, and who in the winter time might otherwise become county charges, travel around from one of the Miller ranches to the other during the slack season of work and manage to live, if not luxuriously, at least free from the pangs of hunger. No attempt is made to keep a record of the meals given away each year, but the number must be many thousands. No questions are asked and no discrimination made among the unfortunates. All applicants stand on the same equality.

Whatever opinion one may entertain as to the effect on the donors of this indiscriminate giving, it must be admitted that Henry Miller, in his unostentatious and unobtrusive way, is one of California's greatest humanitarians. If charity is the greatest and most excellent of virtues, as it is said to be, and as the Clarion believes it is, then surely the Recording Angel has placed many credit marks opposite the name of Henry Miller.

(*Historic Kern*, December, 1976)

Steam Tractor in Kern Debut

Kern County Weekly Courier, January 2, 1875—The Hyde Steam Wagon that we had expected at an earlier date, steamed into town Thursday, December 31, and was for several hours an object of curiosity to our citizens. It has four wheels and the boiler and machinery are located centrally between them. The track is about three feet wider than that of a common wagon. The matter of friction, upon which its tractive power depends, seems well provided for in the wheels. It is easy to see that it can not only ascend a steep grade but drag a huge weight behind it.

Many years of labor, thought, and costly experiment have been expended in bringing it to its present state, which is believed to be a success. Attached to it was a track laden with plows, harrows, etc.

Its place of destination is the farm of W. B. Carr, about seven miles in a southwesterly direction from town, where its power, for a few months, will be applied to plowing and the cultivation of the soil. After that it will be put into the freighting business between the terminus of the railroad and the mines of Inyo County.

From the little we saw of it, while in motion, we would say that it can be guided quite as easily as a wagon drawn by a single pair of horses. It is thought that over such a road as that to Panamint, it can pull wagons loaded with fifty tons of freight, besides conveying its own supplies of fuel and water.

Kern County Weekly Courier, January 9, 1875—On Tuesday, January 5, of this week, we made one of a considerable concourse of people to assemble at the farm of W. B. Carr to witness the performance of the Hyde Steam Wagon as a plow propeller. The ground was a sandy loam, covered with weeds and filled with tenacious roots. Attached to the wagon was a gang of plows.

These were not of the proper description and set at the wrong angle for the work to be done. As might have been expected, they clogged up at every few yards distance and did not work in a manner at all satisfactory. But the trial was a success nevertheless. The machine was demonstrated to the satisfaction of all present to be perfectly manageable and manifested power enough for anything. With the proper plows, there is no doubt of its ability to plow, harrow and seed twenty-five or thirty acres per day. No doubt the inventors have discovered the true principles of the steam wagon and in a few years we may expect to see them in common use on every farm and running on all the roads. We were shown some excellent work it had done in the way of ditching. There are two ditching machines on the farm, of ingenious construction, and that work admirably. The wagon travels along with them without the least difficulty.

Kern County Weekly Courier, January 16, 1875—The Hyde Steam Wagon, now at the farm of W. B. Carr, is busy drawing a ditching machine that makes a ditch eight feet wide at the top and the work is done admirably. The amount of work accomplished is enormous. Carr is now almost ready to flood the vast tract he has seeded with water. He has wisely determined to place no dependence on rain.

Kern County Weekly Courier, March 20, 1875—Hyde's Steam Wagon that still continues at work at Carr's is attracting attention. Everybody that comes to see the country goes to see it work. That it may be successfully used for most purposes of the farm wherever a tractive force is required is sufficiently demonstrated. The work it has thus far been engaged in is ditching, clearing and plowing. Like all first attempts, Col. Hyde says, the machine is full of imperfections, all of which he is carefully noting as they manifest themselves, and that will be remedied in future construction.

(*Historic Kern*, September-December, 1972)

The I.W.W. in Kern County, 1911-1922
by William H. Boyd, Jr.

Although the Industrial Workers of the World, or "Wobblies," which sought to unionize western miners, farm workers, and lumber workers, never had a large following, this radically-oriented organization had a widespread impact in the far West. Three of its organizers gave speeches at the corner of Nineteenth Street and Chester Avenue, in the heart of Bakersfield, in July, 1911. Their activity was ended by the police, who didn't like "their way of expressing themselves." Again in December the three organizers were in town,

Colonel Oliver Hyde's steam tractor, 1875.

and they were identified as Clarence Hunt, Thomas Gray and Albert Dumont. They were granted permission to speak on Twentieth Street between L and M streets, in the red light district.

In the following week the organizers, unhappy with the restriction imposed on them, began to speak at the intersection of Sumner and Baker streets, in East Bakersfield. An audience of about eighty people had assembled when Hunt, Gray and Dumont were arrested and charged with blocking traffic. The men were released on bail. A few days later Hunt once more endeavored to speak at the intersection of Nineteenth Street and Chester Avenue, and again he was arrested and then bailed out of jail.

In the spring of 1912 there was a mass migration of I.W.W. members to San Diego to protest against the speech-making restriction imposed in that city. A vanguard of southbound protesters reached Bakersfield in March, and the main body arrived in April. About one hundred men were given permission to camp in the "jungle" along the Kern River, at a site north of Bakersfield. By May the migrating I.W.W. members had departed, leaving the town little the worse for their having been present. In the meantime they had been denied permission to use the local National Guard armory for a "protest-sympathy meeting" on behalf of the demonstrations at San Diego. Instead the meeting was held at the intersection of Twentieth and H streets. This time no arrests were made, for apparently the authorities had become more tolerant of the speech-making activity.

During 1917 and 1918 several acts of arson occurred in the West, when fires destroyed lumber mills, haystacks, and stored grain. In July, 1918, Kern County suffered the loss of fourteen haystacks at Rosedale and one at Rio Bravo. The Kern County arson was charged to Frank Elliott, the "Red Bicyclist," so named because of the color of his vehicle. He was one of nineteen indicted on federal charges of conspiracy to hamper the war effort, and all were found guilty when tried at Sacramento.

The political outlook in postwar California led to the adoption of a Criminal Syndicalism Law in 1919. Under the provisions of this law arrests were made during raids on the "jungle" along the Kern River, and during the next few years arrests were made at Delano and Taft. At a time when membership in the I.W.W. assertedly was growing in the United States, a score of presumed members were arrested in Taft in September, 1922. The arrests were a part of a "nation-wide war" against the organization. Some of those who were arrested were declared to be guilty of the charges, while others were found to be innocent. Their attorney argued that the I.W.W. had a right to exist and teach discontent in accordance with the American tradition.

The repressive national atmosphere of the early 1920s was very hard on the I.W.W. Public actions by the authorities during the "nation-wide war" and private actions by groups such as the Ku Klux Klan made it unpopular, and even unhealthy, to advocate radical or foreign philosophies during this period. As a result, the I.W.W. left the Kern County scene.

(*Historic Kern*, September, 1977)

Sheep Industry in Kern County: Experience of a Pioneer from *The Bakersfield Southern Californian*, June 3, 1875

During the last fifteen years, California has made a wonderful advancement in agriculture. This is especially true of sheep husbandry, and in no portion of the State during the period mentioned, have sheep increased more in numbers, or improved more in quality than in Kern County. From a few thousand Mexican mustang sheep, shearing about two and one-half or three pounds of wool, or rather, of hair, per year, our flocks have increased more than fifteen fold in number, and the average weight of fleece per head, has more than doubled. Kern is probably the best sheep growing county in the State. Sheepraisers of our neighboring counties on the coast are fully aware of our advantages, and it is to the hills and mountains of Kern that many bring their sheep to graze during the summer. During the dry years of '53 and '64, many sheep and cattle died of starvation in the coast counties, but Kern had not only food enough to keep her own flocks and herds in fine condition, but kept from starvation hundreds of thousands of stock driven here by our less favored neighbors.

Stock-raisers and tax-payers, with reason, complain that it is not right for stock that is taxed and shorn in other counties to be driven here, and subsist upon the feed that ought to be eaten by the flocks owned within the county. But our county will not long be deprived of the revenue that rightfully belongs to her, for our mountain valleys and mountain streams are fast being settled upon by the intelligent, industrious immigrants who are now flocking to and making their homes in all portions of our golden State, made so, more by the farmer's golden grain than by the miner's gold dust taken from the ground. Sheep raising is on the eve of a new departure in Kern County for successfully engaging in the sheep business without owning a foot of land. Without a person owns a large tract of land, the only way to raise sheep successfully from this time forward is to have a farm that will produce hay. The farm should be fenced and sown with alfalfa. Two or three crops of hay can be cut from it during the summer; then, in the fall, when the grass on the dry hills and plains has been consumed, the sheep owner can bring his flocks and graze them upon his alfalfa fields until the rains come and green feed is abundant upon the hills again. It has been estimated that an acre of alfalfa will keep from fifteen to twenty sheep the year round. Then if the hay is cut and fed to them, it will, with the pasturage, keep four times as many sheep three months, or by taking the average estimate, an acre will keep seventy head three months, and one hundred and sixty acres will keep 11,200. Now, all sheep men know from bitter experience that it is the three months that come between the old and new feed that cause them the greatest anxiety, for then it is impossible to find sufficient feed for his flocks. No other county in California can begin to compare with this in its facilities for raising alfalfa or any other crop that is grown by irrigation; for here we have the largest body of rich land to be found in California, and it seems as if nature wished to doubly bless us, for through the whole breadth of this land runs one of the largest and most beautiful rivers in the State.

There were many disadvantages that our pioneer sheep men had to encounter that our new settlers know nothing of. The cost and time consumed in getting our wool to market and of bringing our supplies from San Francisco was a great drawback. Our wool had to be taken to the ocean or to the San Joaquin on wagons, a distance of over one hundred and fifty miles, at a cost of about three cents a pound. Then, there was an additional cost to get it to San Francisco. Wool would often lay at the corrals for months before teams could be found to haul it, and notwithstanding all of this cost and delay, the highest price that gladdened the eyes of the sheep raiser was from ten to fourteen cents per pound, delivered in San Francisco. All our supplies had to be procured by the same way, at a heavy cost.

The flocks of the pioneers were very much troubled by wild animals. Fifteen years ago, there were probably ten times as many coyotes in this county as there were sheep, and wild cats, lions and bears were numerous. The herder could not let his sheep be out of sight a moment, and he had to sleep with one eye open, but with all the precaution that could be used, many sheep and lambs were killed from every flock. It is rather a singular fact that while provisions, clothing, building materials, etc., are much cheaper now than they were a few years ago, the price of common labor has greatly increased. At the time of which we speak, Indian herders received $15 per month, Mexicans from $18 to $20, white men from $20 to $25. Now none can be had for less than $30 to $35. Then Indian shearers received from 25 to 50 cents per day; now no better shearers command $2.50 to $4.00 per day. Then they sheared from one hundred to one hundred and twenty-five mustang sheep per day; now, from twelve to fifty, according to quality, the twelve thoroughbreds producing about as many pounds of fine wool as the one hundred mustangs did of hair. But in order to make wool-raising pay us its highest dividends, we must utilize the magnificent water-power that is at our very doors. It is folly to send our wool to San Francisco to be washed and scoured, then transported to Massachusetts to be made into cloth, then sent back for us to buy. The water of Kern river is as soft as rain water, and as clear as spring water, and is therefore just suited for scouring wool. Here is a fine opening for an enterprising man to erect scouring works on the banks of Kern river, and if he would erect a woolen mill by its side, so much the better, and greater the dividends. Sheep owners should take this business in their own hands, for they would not only enhance the price of their wool, but would be sure to reap a rich reward for their enterprise. (*Historic Kern*, March, 1978)

Rice Farming in 1915
by John W. Sward, as told to F. Hal Higgins

Kern County was a frontier for young men. It had plenty of open spaces for ideas in 1915 when I put in 2000 acres of rice not far from Wasco. I had an engineer from the Sacramento Valley tell me I had plenty of water available for a rice crop. Neither of us knew that it took a lot more water for a crop in the hotter Kern County than in the Sacramento Valley 300 to 400 miles farther north. We had to learn the hard way.

Those were the days of artesian, or flowing wells. With eight artesian wells, two of them delivering 200 miner's inches of water each, there seemed no reason to worry about that essential. A custom tractor owner-operator came in with his big steam Holt and a Yuba gas crawler to do the plowing and harrowing at one pass. The rice was seeded by a four-horse grain drill. No one had thought of using the airplane at this early date for seeding from the air in water as practically all rice crops are seeded today. My crop was coming along nicely when suddenly the super-heated cropless valley began to absorb the water needed for the rice—like a blotter.

I went to old man Jastro (general superintendent for the Kern County Land Company) since he had told me at the outset of my planning, "Come and see me if you get into trouble. We can't let this project fail." So he ran his own ditches down an extra three miles to get me enough water to make that rice crop. That's the kind of man Jastro was. He wanted to build up Kern County and this project was being watched by everybody in the county and over far areas outside.

Jastro was the man who raised what probably was the first big cotton crop way back in his early days in Kern County. He had brought in colored laborers from the old South to pick the cotton when a beautiful crop was ready for harvest. When he got up against government red tape on account of his imported labor, he solved his problems by setting fire to the cotton crop and burning it in the field.

A man named Peters had homesteaded in Kern County and raised ten acres of rice way back in 1913 or '14. It had a yield of forty bags to the acre. But we got forty-two bags per acre out of this 1,040

Lakeside artesian well, 1889.

acres that had me in a water crisis in 1915. It was cut by binder and threshed by steam thresher on belt power, as in the old way still seen in some Arkansas and Louisiana areas. There were no combine rice harvestings at this early stage.

    Well, I wound up the year broke and in debt $212,000. But I had a Danish geologist scouting for me in Texas and he had explored a lot of territory. He came back to me with 280,000 acres of oil leases on Texas lands. I went to Texas for two years and returned to pay off my debts. Oil was in the air, and by this time in my blood. With the aid of the local county recorder, I and my group had seventeen sections in the Elk Hills rounded up and in our names when President Taft signed the Elk Hills withdrawal order for the U.S. Naval Reserve. The oil rug was pulled out from under us after we had spent $50,000 developing the area. Such is the oil game! But that is the way the ball bounces. I am now engaged in Wyoming oil development and look ahead as eagerly to black gold from that area as I did to rice in Kern County in 1915.

(Historic Kern, June, 1962)

IV
A Diverse People

Kern County easily matches the remainder of California in the diversity of its population. The early mining industry attracted a great variety of people to mountain communities such as Keyesville, Kernville, and Havilah. In the San Joaquin Valley, Bakersfield's slow but steady growth has been largely the result of agricultural opportunities. Available land at modest prices lured, among others, Americans, Frenchmen, Basques, Portuguese, Italians, Englishmen, and Russians. The enterprising farmers required a continuous supply of farm labor that was both readily available and modestly paid. New sources of labor were sought as successive ethnic groups found their way into better paying jobs. This constant demand for field labor attracted a veritable parade of workers from around the world, starting with the native Indian, and followed by Chinese, Blacks, Japanese, Mexicans, East Indians, and Filipinos, as well as "Okies."

The Yokuts of the San Joaquin Valley
by Melissa Landis

The Yokuts once lived in the San Joaquin Valley from Stockton south to Grapevine Canyon and the Tehachapi Mountains, ranging from the west side of the valley to the foothills of the eastern slope. The name Yokuts came from a word in their language meaning "the people."

The Yokuts consisted of no less than 25,000 people closely related by blood and language. Probably at one time there were as many as fifty sub-tribes. Since they did not come in contact with white people and were not seriously disturbed by the westward movement until the 1860s, their language wasn't affected and remained very primitive. It consisted of wheezes, and coughing and blowing sounds deep in the throat, to name a few.

Each tribe had a definite boundary. One of the most interesting of all the tribes was the Yowlumne. It ranged in every direction from the central village of Woila, located about where the Santa Fe depot now stands in Bakersfield. According to aged Yowlumne tribesmen there were two villages within this area. Both villages were between the present railroad station at Sixteenth and F streets and Mercy Hospital at Sixteenth and C streets.

When the first white settlers arrived at Bakersfield there was a mound at the present Santa Fe station. The mound was removed when the depot was built. Many stone mortars, pestles and Indian skeletons were uncovered when the mound was removed.

Along the Kern River the Yowlumne's upstream limits were about where the second powerhouse stands. Their downstream limits were on the plains at about Pioneer Weir and Pioneer Bridge on the Kern River.

When Colonel Thomas Baker, for whom Bakersfield is named, arrived in 1863 a large group of Yowlumne lived in the two villages on the opposite banks of the Kern River. They were willing workers. They washed clothes, made gardens, scrubbed floors, mended clothes, cut firewood, cared for children and did all sorts of housework for the early settlers.

The Yokuts probably had developed the science of hunting with the bow and arrow further than most tribes. The Yowlumne of Kern County were foremost among the Yokuts. At least three types of bows were made, the most common being a bow of elderberry wood.

The Yokuts had at least five different kinds of homes. There was one permanent home which lasted ten to fifteen years before it had to be rebuilt. The rest were of a temporary nature. The permanent home was partially underground and looked somewhat like a burrow. The communal house held many families. Sometimes a whole village lived in one communal house. The older men slept in the sweat house during the winter. A fire was built in the center of the sweat house and stones were placed on it. When the stones were hot, water was poured over them which caused intense heat and perspiration. The men stayed in the house as long as they could, then they threw open the covering and ran and jumped into the river.

The Yokuts played many games. The most popular was called Shinny, a game similar to hockey. They also had a game similar to football. The women played a dice game, and there were many guessing games.

(*Historic Kern*, March, 1967)

Indian Attack
by L. Burr Belden

The eastern half of Kern County is little known between U.S. Highway 6 and the San Joaquin Valley. Highway 58 traverses the Tehachapi Pass, and several miles to the north California Highway 178 utilizes Walker Pass. In between these two paved arteries is a network of unsurfaced roads. The Sierra can be assailed and ascended by Jawbone Canyon, Butterbread Canyon and Bird Spring Canyon. If the traveler is not particularly concerned with taking a "through" route, there are also roads up Horse Spring, Sage and Cow Heaven canyons.

The Jawbone Canyon route continues from U.S. 6 all the way through the Sierra National Forest by multiple choice roads via such spots as Claraville, Piute Mountain, Kelso Valley and Sageland. An alternative and more rugged entrance is up Butterbread Canyon but it is deeply rutted in spots that are not suitable for low-slung automobiles.

The Jawbone, Kelso Valley route continues over a 5,000-foot summit to descend through scattered ranches to Weldon in Walker Pass. This is the historic route taken by the early freight teams that plied between Los Angeles and the rollicking gold camps of the Kern River in the 1850s and 1860s. Almost at the road summit are the extensive ore dumps of the St. John mine. This celebrated gold property was worked on a large scale. The miners lived down the steep grade to the north where a typical mining town grew up, stretching for a mile along the road and its parallel creek. This was the town of Sageland. Of the old buildings a couple of foundations are all that remain. A cloudburst made a clean job of eradicating Sageland.

High on the rocky hill west of Sageland is an ancient Indian burial ground. In a nearby side canyon a populous rancheria flourished a century ago. From the latter, in the 1860s, reckless young braves rode forth to attack the passing freight wagons.

The white-Indian relations in the Kern River area mirrored those in other regions throughout the Southwest. Soldier garrisons on the few frontier forts were, of necessity, withdrawn when the hard-pressed Washington government needed every available soldier to combat secession. There had been no troops in the Kern mines, but there had been soldiers as close as Fort Tejon and along a chain of little outposts in the Mojave.

The Indian was quick to sense that he could loot with less fear of punishment. In earlier years there had been little trouble in the Walker Pass area but now it flared up, some think because renegade Owens River Indians arrived to incite it. The cause of the inter-racial trouble has as many reasons offered as there are writers to describe it. It is known that it seemed to start simultaneously over a vast territory. In Walker Pass it was pioneer cattlemen who were the first victims in the winter of 1861–62. Thieving bands are said to have come from as far as Nevada.

Colonel George S. Evans, at the head of a column of California volunteers, arrived and negotiated a peace with the Indians. It lasted only a little while, however. Once the soldiers had gone, the Inyo War spread back over Walker Pass. An infiltrating Indian band incited Kern River tribes to strike again. Two packers, taking freight to the Coso-Cerro Gordo district, were attacked at Canebrake Creek and slain. Their supplies were stolen. These victims were John Lee and Jose Grijalva. Whole herds of cattle belonging to William B. Weldon and J. V. Roberts were stolen. The pioneer ranchers faced ruin. More California troops were sent to Camp Independence in the Owens Valley but trouble up in Walker Pass was not halted.

California had a military camp at Visalia, designated as Camp Babbitt. It had been established in the first year of the Civil War to keep watch on the secessionist hotbed which was the county seat at Tulare. It had been at Visalia that Assemblyman Dan Showalter had recruited his troop of Confederate cavalry and headed for Texas. Now the Indian uprising was considered a greater danger than any potential disloyalty in Visalia, so Captain Moses A. McLaughlin was sent with a company to restore quiet on the Kern River while en route to bolster the Owens Valley garrison.

It was Captain McLaughlin who struck an Indian rancheria on Kern River and killed thirty-five warriors who had been pointed out as disloyal by a friendly chief. Some Indians asserted that the friendly chief, Jose Chico, had designated as peaceable only his own relatives and friends.

Not even the severe lesson administered by McLaughlin and his twenty troopers brought peace to the area, however. Back in unprotected Jawbone and Kelso canyons the Indians could and did hide and pounce on freight outfits. In mid-1863 when peace was presumed established, five teamsters with heavy wagons halted and ate their lunch at the summit of the Kelso Valley grade, almost at the spot where the St. John Mine was later worked. During the lunch stop, or nooning, as it was known in the vernacular, conversation drifted around to the Indian question and possibilities of attack. All five had rifles and revolvers. One driver remarked about the good quality of his lunch and that if he had to die it would be in a happy frame of mind with his stomach full. An hour later he was dead.

As the heavy freight wagons descended the grade and passed a grove of willows where Sageland was later built, the attack materialized. Indians fired from ambush in the thicket. Martin Hart and Oliver Burke were slain. Moses Hart, William Dawson and James Hazlum escaped. The cargo of all the wagons fell into the attackers' hands, a band of thirty. Martin Hart did not die at once but he knew his wound was fatal. Sitting propped up against a wheel he continued to shoot at the attackers until he toppled dead.

Dawson fled and reached a safe haven at Scodie. His shoes were cut to ribbons on the sharp rocks over which he ran. Moses Hart, finding he could do nothing for his brother, was able to get away on horseback. He easily outdistanced his pursuers and reached Weldon. Hazlum fled on foot, taking the back trail and then going higher up into timber. He eventually reached Tehachapi with Indian arrows yet hanging from his shirt. It was said he never returned to the scene though he spent his lifetime in the Tehachapi Mountains.

The days of freighting from Los Angeles via Willow Springs and Jawbone Canyon closed when the Southern Pacific snaked a rail line over Tehachapi Pass. The pioneer freight route gave way to the road from Caliente to Havilah via Walker Basin, and from Havilah on to Keyesville and Whisky Flat. Freight for Owens Valley no longer used the Walker Pass route either. It went up Red Rock Canyon from Mojave.

As the colorful freight caravans passed from the scene, the road up Kelso Creek and into Kelso Valley was not forgotten however. Equally colorful lumber wagons with huge solid wheels were drawn over the steep grade by long ox teams. Sawmills were operated at several locations in the Piute Mountain area. Lumber for the Kern and Owens river valleys was brought out to Weldon down the Kelso Creek road. That consigned farther south was snaked down to Jawbone Canyon by way of a series of switchbacks known yet as Geringer Grade. A conventional low gear will not hold back a car on that grade today any more than brake skids and drags did eighty years ago. Heavy loads had to be snubbed down with hawsers.

High up in the Piute Mountains, Claraville was established early, a mining center and trading post for the lumber camps. Claraville's principal link with the outside was via the same Kelso Creek

Canyon. A trading post at the scene of the 1863 massacre became known as Sageland Station. Later when the St. John Mine was operating the settlement expanded with miners' cabins.

The mine closed as most mines do. Cabins were deserted except by one or two old-timers who clung on and prospected over nearby hills. The cloudburst all but obliterated the mine camp. Sageland passed from the scene. Today it is essentially the same clump of willows in which the thirty Indians lay in ambush back in 1863.

(*Historic Kern*, October, 1961)

Keysville Massacre, April 19, 1863
taken from military correspondence by Moses A. McLaughlin

The decision of the army to close down Fort Tejon in 1861 was wrong on two counts. Tactically, the fort was necessary to help contain the large segments of population in the San Joaquin Valley which were sympathetic to the Confederacy. The military could have prevented a great amount of traffic and correspondence which passed between Southern sympathizers in the Valley and the Confederate Army in Texas and the New Mexico Territory.

There was another threat, however, which was overlooked in the army's desire to consolidate its forces in the Department of the Pacific—the Indians.

The fort had been established to oversee the conduct of the Indians in the area. The Indians had been calm and peaceful in the few years of the fort's existence, and the Office of Indian Affairs, with its influence, gave all to feel that it could handle the situation without assistance. That his point of view was wrong can be attested by the two pieces of correspondence below:

Camp Babbit,
near Visalia, California
April 8, 1863

Col R. C. Drum, Asst. Adjt. Gen.
Dept. of the Pacific
San Francisco, California

Sir: I have the honor herewith to forward a petition from the citizens of Keysville and vicinity asking military protection from the Indian depredations. Capt. McLaughlin will leave this camp on the arrival of the detachment of Company E, which will accompany him to join their company at Owen's Valley. They are expected to arrive this evening, and will leave on Saturday or Sunday morning, passing by the way of Keysville through Kern River Valley. The captain will halt a few days in the upper end of the valley, where the difficulties are said to exist and investigate the matter, and if the position of the Indians should be found as favorable as represented, will give them battle. The captain will have about forty men, with arms to arm twenty more. This, with the number of citizens that will join him from Keysville, will give him a force sufficient to handle any number of Indians that he will be likely to meet at that place.

There is no doubt of an organized movement among the disloyal people of this part of the State, for what purpose I am unable to find out. I have information of thirty-seven of them being together near Kern Lake, with quite a number of government horses with them, which would be sufficient excuse for the military to take the matter in hand. I last heard of these men at or near Fort Tejon, and from a letter intercepted here they seem to be moving south toward Fort Yuma. Had I sufficient force I should send out in the direction of these parties and scour that part of the country and ascertain the meaning and intentions of those armed bodies of men, and recover, if possible, the government property. If there is any part of this state that should be patrolled, it is the southern tier of counties, for there is no county in the state that offers such facilities for the organization of lawless bands of thieves and outlaws, and there is no country on earth that can furnish more and better material, according to its inhabitants, than this tier of counties can for purposes of that kind. This would be a very good field for Company F to operate in if it could be spared from Camp Union.

I am, very respectfully, your obedient servant,

Wm. Jones,
Lt. Col.
Commanding Camp Babbitt
near Visalia, California

Report of Capt. Moses A. McLaughlin, Second California Cavalry

Camp Independence, Owen's River Valley
April 24, 1863

Colonel: I have the honor to report that in obedience to instructions dated Camp Babbit, near Visalia, Calif., April 10, 1863, and signed Lieut. Col. William Jones, Second Cavalry California Volunteers, I left Camp Babbitt on Sunday, the 12th instant, in command of twenty-four men of Company E, accompanied by Lts. French and Daley, one 12-pound howitzer, and four six-mule government teams, used for the transportation of rations, company property, ammunition, and forage, all of which arrived in good condition at Camp Independence, Owen's Valley, on the 24th of the same month. Distance traveled I suppose to be 250 or 275 miles. I had been instructed by Colonel Jones to investigate the Indian troubles on Kern River. On arriving at Keysville I was waited upon by several of the residents of the place, who represented that there was a large body of Indians encamped upon the North Fork of Kern River; that many of these Indians had doubtless been engaged in the war and in the depradations committed in Kern River Valley; that one man had been murdered in Kelsey Canyon; that Roberts and Waldron had lost about 150 head of stock; that many other citizens had lost cattle, horses, and other property; that the roads were unsafe, and finally, that the Indians there congregated were for the most part strangers in the valley, and were thought to be Tehachapi and Owen's River Indians, who after seeing so many troops pass had endeavored to shield themselves from punishment by seeking the more immediate vicinity of the white settlements. After having the above statements, and learning that Jose Chico was in the neighborhood, I sent for him and two other chiefs who were known to have been friendly.

Accordingly at 2 a.m. on the 19th, accompanied by a detail of twenty men of my company and Lt. Daley, with Jose Chico as guide, I left camp, and at dawn surrounded the camp of the Indians, which was situated about ten miles from Keysville, upon the right bank of the Kern River. I had the bucks collected together, and informed Jose Chico and the citizens who had arrived that they might choose out those whom they knew to have been friendly. This was soon done. The boys and old men I sent back to their camps, and the others, to the number of thirty-five, for whom no one could vouch, were either shot or sabered. Their only chance for life being their fleetness, but none escaped, though many of them fought well with knives, sticks, stones, and clubs. This extreme punishment, though I regret it, was necessary, and I feel certain that a few such examples will soon crush the Indians and finish the war in this and adjacent valleys. It is now a well-established fact that no treaty can be entered into with these Indians. They care nothing for pledges given, and have imagined that they could live better by war than peace. They will soon learn that they have been mistaken, as with the forces here they will soon either be killed off, or pushed so far in the surrounding deserts that they will perish by famine.

I have the honor to be, very respectfully, your obedient servant,
Capt. M. A. McLaughlin
Second Cav. California Volunteers
Comdg, Camp Independence

The events leading up to April 19, 1863 gave the army reason to appreciate the value of Fort Tejon. Accordingly, on July 9, Capt. McLaughlin was ordered to re-establish Fort Tejon as a precaution against further depredations. The fort was thus put back into active duty until August 1864, when, as a consequence of the removal of the Indians from the Tejon Reservation, it was abandoned for all time.

(*Historic Kern*, November, 1952)

Thomas Castro: A Founding Father
by Dr. Rodolfo G. Serrano

Among Kern County's early-day families was that of Thomas Castro, who came from Hermosillo, Sonora, Mexico. Castro arrived in 1867 and settled in the area called Rio Bravo (more recently known as Panama). Here he bought Sections 12, 27 and 30, which were adjacent to land occupied by Ventura Cuen and Dolores Montano, who had settled there in 1849. After a short stay in the Rio Bravo area, the Cuen and Montano families returned to Mexico.

With Thomas Castro when he arrived in Kern County were his wife Concepcion, together with his children Ramona, Leonides, Domatilio, Manuel, and Thomas, Jr. As the years passed the family grew to include Perfecto, Luciano, Epifanio, and Emilio. The family engaged in both farming and stock raising.

Among Castro's noteworthy accomplishments was the organization of a private school in the Rio Bravo area in 1869, for which he secured a lady teacher from Los Angeles at a pay of $25.00 per month! This school, together with another short-lived one, became a county school in 1875. From this county school eventually came the Panama School District.

Another of Thomas Castro's notable accomplishments was the excavation of an irrigation ditch. In order to assure an adequate supply of water for his farm lands, he, together with his sons and farm hands, plowed four and one-half miles of ditch through his property. This project enabled him to divert Kern River water to the Rio Bravo, or Panama Slough, area.

Even greater than Thomas Castro's significant economic and educational contributions to Kern County was his personal influence among the Mexican American population. The charisma of this kind-hearted and understanding pioneer attracted many Mexican nationals to the area.

(*Historic Kern*, March, 1976)

The Chinese in Bakersfield
by William Hoy

Near Bakersfield there is a section of a highway known as China Grade. If you should walk or motor up China Grade you will suddenly see the entire town of Bakersfield in the distance, see it as it sprawls for miles through this rich, fertile valley of the San Joaquin.

And behind the name China Grade lies an interesting story. It has to do with watercress. This humble little vegetable is much esteemed by the southern Chinese for it has the power of decreasing excessive heat in the general bodily system and restoring it to its proper level. More important still, to watercress has been attributed the power of helping to cure certain ailments of the lung. Watercress soup is much liked by the Cantonese, and even if it hasn't the curative power given to it by tradition, it is still a very tasty dish.

Well, not long after the first Chinese came into Bakersfield—which was in the early 1870s—some of the brethren found that watercress was growing in wild profusion on the slope of a hill a few miles from the town. This was good news indeed, so off they went to gather a supply of it. But the first ones found the way hard going for there was no road or trail into the section of the hill where the watercress grew. So they made a path around this hill and for years afterward this path was well trodden by the feet of hundreds of Chinese who went there to gather watercress. Years later, when a highway was built through this section it followed the course of the path made by the Chinese. As a result, therefore, this section of the highway came to be called China Grade.

In the early 1870s sections of the Southern Pacific railway were built through the San Joaquin Valley, and in this construction work many Chinese laborers were employed. When the railroad was built through Bakersfield some of the Chinese left this work to seek employment in other lines, mainly agricultural and domestic. These few Chinese formed the nucleus of the first Chinese community in Bakersfield. When Bakersfield became the seat of Kern County in 1874, taking this honor away from Havilah, a gold mining town fifty miles from it, the town already had quite a number of Chinese. This number grew until at one time there were at least a thousand permanent settlers, with several hundred transient seasonal farm workers.

For more than twenty-five years, until the early part of this century, there was but one Chinatown in Bakersfield. It was a Chinatown filled with provision stores, with association headquarters, including the powerful Chee Kung Tong, anti-Manchu Revolutionary Society, and with restaurants and homes.

Then, for some unknown reason, a dispute arose between members of the Sze Yup and members of the Sam Yup clans. The affair was brought before the elders of the community benevolent society, who attempted to arbitrate the matter and bring about a just and peaceful settlement. But for once reasonableness did not prevail

Leong Yen Ming family in 1910.

among those who sat at the council table. The dispute grew more heated than ever.

Then, to prevent further dispute and possible violence, the Sze Yup clans called their elders together and decided to move to another section of the town and establish another Chinese community of their own. This they did, and thus it came about that Bakersfield has two Chinatowns. In appearance little is left of the original and older Chinatown except a few stores and the headquarters of the Chee Kung Tong, the Six Companies and the Suey On Association. To show how prosperous the old Chinatown was, as late as 1899 there were more than thirty merchandise stores, herb stores, restaurants, and also two banks.

In the second Chinatown one finds the only Chinese temple in Bakersfield, a little brick structure built in 1902. Years ago many came to worship the five deities enshrined in this temple, but today the gods are left unattended. Only rarely does an old-timer come in to burn incense and the sound of the temple drum has not been heard for many moons.

Almost as unattended is the old Chinese cemetery, located only a short distance at the outskirts of the town. It covers an entire square block, and at one end stand two sacrificial paper burners. The remains of the dead buried in this cemetery are disinterred every ten years and transported back to China where they are given final burial in the proper villages where these dead originally came from. Thus the spirits of the old-timers are not left to wander in an alien land.

There is living in San Francisco's Chinatown today a gentle little lady who this year is sixty-four years of age. She was trained in the old tradition, both in her religion and in her manners. She worships the gods of her fathers and regularly burns incense to the spirits of her ancestors. She has lived in this city for half a century, but she knows nothing of the life of America for it has never touched her.

This woman, I am told, is the first Chinese born in Bakersfield, in the year 1876. Her father gave her away when she was four to another family in Bakersfield. Her foster father gave her away in marriage to a San Francisco Chinese when she was only fifteen. She has borne eighteen children, but only one, a son, still lives. This little lady left Bakersfield fifty years ago, and has never been back since.

Many famous men in modern China's history have paid short visits to the Chinese colony at Bakersfield. The first was Kang Yu-wei, leader of the ill-fated reformist party under the Manchu dynasty and a great scholar. Kang came from the same district of Canton as some of the Chinese at Bakersfield. Another famous visitor was Lin Sen, who was then a leader in the Chinese Nationalist Party at San Francisco. The last celebrated visitor was Dr. Sun Yat-sen, one of the greatest revolutionists of modern times and first president of the Chinese Republic. Dr. Sun came to Bakersfield to enlist the support of his countrymen to overthrow the effete Manchu dynasty. Since many of the Bakersfield Chinese came from the same provincial district as Sun Yat-Sen, the financial contributions to his revolutionary cause were very gratifying.

Today the Chinese in Bakersfield still number several hundred. They are mostly of the second or third generation, for the first generation—the pioneers, the old-timers—has practically vanished. With the going of the first generation, there will also follow, inevitably, the disintegration of the two Chinatowns there. When the final disintegration will come about no one can tell, but the process has been going on for more than two decades. When that day comes perhaps the only historical landmark that will be preserved will be the temple.

(Historic Kern, January, 1950)

Bakersfield Chinese Temple
by Mrs. Sing Lum

According to local Chinese tradition the original temple in Bakersfield was built during the 1870s on a spot across Kern Island Canal from where the Kern River Mill stood, about where Seventeenth Street runs today. The building faced south, and stood in the middle of a strawberry patch.

It was a one-story structure of unpainted rough lumber, sixteen feet wide and about twenty feet deep. A porch was built on the front, and the roof was peaked of typical Chinese design. There were two small single-pane windows. The cost of construction ran between two and three hundred dollars. Furnishings for the temple were brought from China.

The first sponsors and worshippers were former gold miners and railroad construction workers. A number of the miners had settled on the outskirts of town after gold became scarce in the Kern River area, and they were later joined by laborers from the Southern Pacific Railroad whose services were no longer required after completion of the line through the Tehachapis in 1876.

The wooden temple survived until the early 1890s when it was replaced by a new red brick building at the southwest corner of Eighteenth and R streets. The bricks were supplied by the Curran brick yard. Sponsors of this temple included Sam Yick, Jung Chuck, Leong Gee Ping, Jang Gee Fong, Yee Chong, and Din Toy. Mrs. Din Toy, of 912 Seventeenth Street, widow of the last-named, is the sole surviving member of this group.

This was one of the twenty temples built in California since 1855, most of which were erected by "District Associations" called Hui Kuon, according to Chingwah Lee, noted Chinese scholar. The word "joss" is a corruption of "Deus" or God. Hence, a joss house, as a Chinese temple is often known, is actually a "House of God."

On each side of the restored (1951) Bakersfield temple doorway is a wooden panel. On them are written poetical expressions voicing the sentiments of the founders.

Within, near the entrance, stands Men Kuan, guardian deity of the temple. His duty is to protect the temple from evil influences and to ward off thieves, fire and flood.

The golden hanging screen is elaborately carved by hand and depicts a pageantry enacted in front of the palace, with the emperor, the premier, and the high priest looking down on a mock battle between the prince of righteousness and the prince of evil—personified by a General P'o and a General Shih. Members of the court are looking on; and the lower section indicates that the prince of righteousness was victorious.

The screen was carved in Canton, famous for its wood and ivory carvers. It is called by many names, usually called ts'ai p'ing or fei ts'ai p'ing—flying floral screen.

The golden altar is also hand carved and is imported from Canton. In the center are five gods. The altar table is faced with a carved wooden gold panel which depicts the Court of Neptune, known to the Chinese as Hai Lung Huang—the Dragon Emperor of the Sea. In this panel are to be found the denizens of the deep—crabs, lobsters, giant clams, etc.

The five-piece pewter altar set consists of one large rectangular incense urn, two vases with floral tinsel bouquets, and two candlestick holders with two large artificial candlesticks of carved bamboo (which has an oil holder at the top so that it will burn just like candles).

The large bronze incense urn is cast of what is called tzu tung or purplish bronze. Flanking this urn are two candle holders. The incenses are placed in the urn three at a time or in multiples of threes, which represent the trinity of past, present and future. Candles are placed on the altar table two at a time or in multiples of twos to represent the dual principles of yin (negative) and yang (positive), components of the philosophical atom (ta chi).

Kuan Yin is the goddess of mercy, Kuan Yin meaning "one who hears prayers." She takes care of children, mothers and all those in need and so is the most popular goddess in the orient, being worshipped in China, Japan, Korea, Indo-China, Siam, and many other countries. By one account she was born when the spiritual Buddha cast his eyes on a lotus bud, and she vowed to remain on earth until every living creature has received salvation.

The great seal of Kuan Yin is usually wrapped in yellow cotton cloth and imprints are made with a red cinnabar paste on yellow squares of paper. The paper with the seal imprint is folded into a small triangle and then enclosed in a cloth sack and carried by children for good luck.

Kuan Yu is the god of valor (sometimes mis-called the god of war) and he was a historical character of the period of the Three Kingdoms (San Kuo). He fought many battles for his emporer and, while so engaged, became very friendly with two other generals, and later a third was added. The descendants of these four formed an organization known as the "Four Family Association" which is still going strong today.

Hua T'o is the god of medicine. When on earth he studied the "ten thousand herbs" and performed miraculous surgery. All the sick pray to him for rapid recovery. He is also known as Hua Kwong, or "Floral light that shines."

Pei Ti (Buk Dai) is the god of the north. He protects the country from enemies and from natural calamities, such as flood and earthquake. His companions are the tortoise and the snake. He carries a sword which guards against demons, diseases and depression.

Liang Ma is the goddess of mystic power. She can foretell events and gives a guiding hand to good marriages and easy childbirth. She is the goddess of black magic and weird incantations which results in all kinds of miracles.

Chung Kuo, or drum and bell of the temple, are placed on a wooden stand. They are struck repeatedly before worship so as to announce the worship period to the gods, and so that those about the temple will be quiet. It is of interest to know that the bell was borrowed by Europeans for their churches during the eighth century, as was the use of the rosary.

In 1947 the old temple was condemned as unsafe by the City of Bakersfield and torn down. It was replaced in 1951 by a fire-resistant brick structure erected on the same site. Rebuilding was brought about through voluntary donations. The Chinese association acting as custodian is headed by Sing Lum as president, with J. S. Joke treasurer, and Mrs. Lum as the secretary.

The new temple houses the original five gods. These gods, the altar decorations and other articles have been reinstalled in the new structure.

Many Chinese pioneers attended services in the old temple, and numerous descendants of those families still reside in the Bakersfield area. Notables from China also have visited the temple, among them the celebrated Dr. Sun Yat-Sen, first president of the Chinese Republic.

Data is now being gathered by the Kern County Historical Society in order that this historic site may receive recognition as an official State Landmark by the Landmarks Committee of the Division of Beaches and Parks.

(*Historic Kern*, December, 1953)

Early Negro Settlers
by Melton McClanahan

For the purpose of serving others is why the Negro came to Kern County. In 1884, Haggin and Carr, a land development company, decided to plant 1,000 acres of cotton. Looking for workers who knew how to raise cotton and do it cheaply, they turned to former Negro slaves of the South. Haggin went to South Carolina in hopes of luring 1,000 Negroes to plant and harvest the crop. They were promised transportation, a place to live, ten dollars a month for men, eight dollars a month for women and four to six dollars a month for children. Three trainloads of Negroes left South Carolina, and just how many came is unknown, but by cotton picking season, there were only about 130 families to gather the crops. Due to the lack of richness of the land, cotton raising in these early days was unsuccessful. Instead of yielding cotton, Haggin and Carr had nothing but stalks. Thus, the Negro turned to other methods of making a living.

The arrival of Negroes in the county created problems for the poor whites, who in the past had depended upon work from the various land companies for their living. They tried putting pressure on Haggin and Carr and when this did not work the Kern County White Citizens Committee convinced some of the Negroes that the wages they were receiving were too low, and others were frightened away.

By the end of the first cotton season, only twelve families remained to form the solid Negro citizenry. The leader of the group seems to have been Matt Stevens, a Baptist minister. Belton and Gideon Vessel, two brothers, opened a repair shop in Kern County. Will Walker established a tailor shop. The Pinckney brothers opened the famous Teddy Bear Saloon, which was well known throughout the San Joaquin Valley. Henry Caldwell was a well digger and gardener; Francis Campbell worked for the foreman of the Stockdale mule farm. What the other four families did for a living is unknown. Their names, however, were John Henry, Henry Simpson, Anderson Bowen and Pleasant Martin.

By 1894 the Negro population in Kern County had increased to about twenty-five families. The newer families were of the aggressive type, for they had been landowners in the South and when they came they had some capital with which to operate. Although some of them took jobs with land companies, they had a reserve to fall back on if necessary. B. G. Russell went to work for a lumber company, while his wife opened the first beauty shop for Negroes in Kern County. Malcolm Hall, Sr. became a blacksmith for the Kern County Land Company. George Reese was a horse trainer for the same company. E. W. Winters opened a second hand store which became the largest of its kind in the San Joaquin Valley. It was one block long, located at Eighteenth and K streets, where the old Sears Roebuck was located. When he died in 1928, he had assets worth some $80,000. Henry Houston opened a barber shop.

Social events which took place at this time were centered around the church. Under the leadership of the Reverend Matt Stevens, the Methodists and Baptists at first met together. However, in 1894, the Methodists pulled out to form a church of their own.

A notable event in Kern County in the year 1900 was the graduation of Henry Simpson, the first Negro to graduate from the Kern County Union High School. He was outstanding in a class of five students, four girls and himself, and he was the valedictorian. The first Negroes to play football for the high school were John Howard and Henry Fletcher in 1907. Jack Johnson, the first Negro heavyweight boxing champion, started fighting in Bakersfield about the same time. Another early fighter was Willie Buckner.

By 1908 the Negro population of Kern County had increased to approximately seventy-five families. The prominent newcomers were Henry Spencer, Pop Person and Romeo Fit Price, an entertainer. Frank Cumby was a "red cap" for the Santa Fe Railway. Boyce and Sherill Geary did odd jobs. Life for some of the Negroes was very lonely. They would often go to the train station to see if other Negroes were stopping off in Bakersfield.

In 1913 the Negroes of Kern County organized their first political club, the Kern County Political Committee. A few of the leaders in this movement were E. W. Winters, the first president, Henry Houston, Henry Simpson, the Pinckneys and Henry Spencer. Through the efforts of this club in 1916, Kern County received its first two Negro public servants: Joe Pinckney, of the city street department, and Clarence Boswell, a deputy sheriff. Although Boswell had no power to enforce the law, he still received pay as such. His son was a property owner and farmer in the Delano area.

During World War I, about five Negroes left Kern County to serve their country. Henry Spencer was one of these. Soon after World War I cotton growing was reintroduced in Kern County. This attracted all types of Negroes—good, bad, and indifferent. Soon there were about a thousand families living in the county. During the war the political club became defunct but it was reorganized in 1923. A few prominent members were Johnny Ward, Mr. Storry, Sherrill and Boyce Geary, Virgil Meeks and Mr. Drisdon. Action by this group increased the number of Negroes employed by the City of Bakersfield and the County of Kern. To the city's list was added the names of Virgil Meeks, Green Willis and, for the county, R. D. Grimes.

Since 1936 the Negroes have had a hand in electing city and county officials. In 1952 the first Negro city councilman in California was elected in Bakersfield. He was the Reverend Henry H. Collins.

There have been several active Negro political clubs in Kern County: the Kern County Voters League, the Women's Political Study Club, and a strong N.A.A.C.P., which was led by men like Robert Mosley.

The Negroes in Kern County have come a long way since 1884 when they first stepped off the train in Bakersfield. While the first arrivals were farm hands, some of their descendants are now city officials, doctors, attorneys and educators. With education and understanding, the sky is the limit.

(*Historic Kern*, September, 1976)

Interview with William Henry Pinckney
by Richard C. Bailey

I was born near Seneca City, South Carolina on December 24, 1872. My father's name was David Pinckney and my mother's maiden name was Elydia Reece.

My mother and father were among the first colored people to arrive in the Bakersfield area. When I was twelve years old we and some other families left South Carolina in March of 1884 and rode in boxcars to Chattanooga, Tennessee where we met more families intended to come to California to better themselves.

From Chattanooga we rode in day coaches the rest of the way to Sacramento, California. My family and some others went to Los Angeles, Fresno, Tulare, Stockton and various other points in the San Joaquin Valley. As I recall, there were four carloads of colored people that came to California in 1884.

Many people don't know that cotton raising began around Bakersfield in 1884. Carr and Haggin, who brought in the colored people including my family through agents in the east, planted three sections between Wible Road and Kern Island Road. It was a wonderful arrangement for us since meat was furnished, as well as our housing and use of animals. They even brought around sacks of flour and dropped them off on the door steps. It cost us nothing. Carr and Haggin even paid the transportation of a lot of these colored people to California. However, so many ran away and would not work that the cotton was abandoned after about a year, and beets planted in their place. Many of the good colored people were really sad when the cotton experiment failed since they never had it as good as this in South Carolina. The families came out here on a one year contract, but most of them broke it and went off to work elsewhere. Most of the colored people who were brought to California at this time were city folks who were probably no good in the first place and didn't want to work. They spoiled it for everybody else.

When I arrived in Bakersfield I believe the city limits on the south was at Fourteenth Street, and I well remember when it was extended first to Fourth Street and then to the present line of Brundage Lane. In the block where the present Elks Club building and Catholic Church now stand, there was nothing but a jungle of willows where hoboes hung out and camped. It was a good place to stay away from. At the west of the present City Hall between "I" and "H" streets, there was a large blackberry patch owned by Dee Weber.

E. W. Winters, left, and Henry Simpson in Winters' second hand store on Nineteenth Street in Bakersfield in the early 1900s.

The Massena Hotel later stood on a part of this ground at the southwest corner of "I" and Truxtun streets.

I bought my present place at 812 "H" Street in 1900 and have held it since that time. I remember when the Town Ditch ran right down "H" Street in front of my house. I think some of the later pipes are still buried near the curb. In the next block north where Lowell School stands there used to be a camp ground where families used to stay during their visits to Bakersfield until as late as 1902. The Lowell addition was named for Wilmer Lowell.

In 1885 I worked as a butler for Dr. L. S. Rogers at his home located at Eighteenth and "H" streets where Judd's now stands. Dr. Rogers was head of the hospital which then stood on the later site of the Bakersfield High School Elm Grove. The hospital faced "G" Street and was a wooden board building.

In 1887–88 I worked up at Tehachapi handling cattle and then came down to work for two years as a stockman for Brown's Dairy. I think it was in 1890 or 1891 that R. E. Houghton brought the first Holstein cattle into the Bakersfield area. He had them where the Kern Valley Packing Plant is on Kern Island Road south of Bakersfield.

A man named Barnhard planted many of the umbrella and palm trees that still grow around the city. I well remember when the Valley Road came into Bakersfield in 1898, and I played tenor trombone in the colored band which was present on this occasion. It was known as the Kern Valley Band. Professor White was its leader. Henry Simpson, the gardener, also played with us later. This group was disbanded around 1905.

I remember the big Bakersfield fire of 1889. I was in church when I heard the fire bells. The fire even burned the volunteer fire cart and hose on Nineteenth between "L" and "K." They had to abandon the equipment and run for their lives. After the fire I became a hod carrier.

I also remember the flood of 1893 and the asphalt wagons coming into town from Maricopa. The Weedpatch Hay Market used to be where Hughes Drugstore now stands. It extended from Eighteenth Street to the corner where Hoenshell's Service Station is today.

I worked for James Curran for a while. At that time his brickyard, a couple blocks east of Union Avenue, extended from Eighteenth Street to Truxtun Avenue.

I remember James Ogden when he had charge of Henry Miller's affairs. These interests amounted to around eleven million dollars at that time, so I have been told. He later became city manager for Bakersfield.

I believe the first show in Bakersfield was the Nickelodeon located by the Beale Clock Tower where the Bakersfield Chamber of Commerce now stands. The admission price was five cents. The pictures did not move, but were slides that were pushed in and out of the projector. A skating rink was next erected on this property and, after it, the Ingleside Hotel.

I remember when the three-story Grand Hotel stood on the northeast corner of Twentieth and Chester, and when Sheriff John Kelley closed up stud poker gambling in the Arlington Hotel and other places. The Arlington stood on the southeast corner of Nineteenth Street and Chester Avenue and burned down in the big fire of 1889. The gambling element threatened to kill Kelly for this and did their best. He used to live near me on "H" Street, and I often walked home with him from town until he told me that "they" were out to kill him. After that, I saw to it that Sheriff Kelly walked home alone. Kelly later became wealthy after the discovery of the Kelly-Rand Mine in the Randsburg area.

August Kratzmer made the iron chains that surround the front of the present City Hall in his foundry, and I made the mortar for the fence that still stands at the same location. In fact, I did a lot of cement work on many of the buildings around Bakersfield.

I remember when a lot of hobo "stiffs" used to come into Bakersfield and hit all the ranches in this end of the valley for handouts. If I remember correctly they used to start at the old Murfitt ranch near Buena Vista Lake, then in turn go on to the Yellow Hamby, Deep Wells, Elk Grove, Buttonwillow and Hog ranches; then on to the Goose Lake, Fowler and Los Banos ranches. It was a regular circuit and everyone knew about it in those days. As I remember, the hoboes usually started this circuit around September. At that time Henry Miller was said to have around 100,000 hogs in Kern County. He would rather feed these men than have them steal or do damage to his property. The hoboes were allowed to come to the mess hall tables after the regular help had finished eating, and they really cleaned everything off the table. Miller had the hoboes stay in buildings near the various ranch headquarters to keep them from setting fire to the haystacks, which happened oftentimes on other people's property. He never let anyone go hungry. In those days men got seventy-five cents to a dollar per day for driving teams of two to four horses or mules. They received a dollar and a quarter to a dollar and a half per day when they drove a team of eight to ten animals with a jerkline.

I remember when Railroad Street, later Truxtun Avenue, was the main cattle, horse and sheep trail through Bakersfield. When animals were driven in from the west to be loaded at the railroad over where East Bakersfield now stands, the dust was something terrific. To keep it down somewhat, they used to throw straw on the road, but it was bad anyway.

I remember when the cowboys from Tejon Ranch, Miller and Lux, and George Coffee outfits used to come into town and take over on pay days. They would ride in in groups of fifteen or twenty. The red light district ran twenty-four hours a day at that time, and no matter what time these men reached town, they were always sure of a good time, whether it was two or six o'clock in the morning. They would often race up and down the streets lassoing chairs off the sidewalks. The city marshal would stay out of sight pretty well unless the shooting got serious. Sometimes they would ride the horses right into the saloons.

I remember later on when the English remittance men came into the Rosedale area. The Southern Hotel used to make them leave a deposit before having a party in order to be sure of getting payment for damaged furniture and other equipment. Those were really wild times.

September 28, 1899 I married a widow, Mrs. Amanda Randolph. From 1916 to 1945 when I retired I worked for the City of Bakersfield Street Department as a grader man. I have had a small ranch in the mountains above Lorraine for a number of years. Until recently, I always had a few head of horses and cattle up there. I spend my time mostly between there and my home here in Bakersfield. When in town, I live with my step-daughter, Hynda Randolph. I used to know almost everyone in Bakersfield but not any more.

Marcus Hall, the well-known colored singer, is my nephew.

(*Historic Kern*, October, 1951)

Russians in Kern County
by Dr. P. N. Root

It is a known fact that the Russians in California are as old as California itself. We do know, when we read Bancroft's history of California, that the Russians, who were mostly engaged in the seal industry in Alaska, were very unwelcome guests of unwilling but powerless Spain, and also that the Russians had a settlement in the region of Russian River, where there is the present site of Sebastopol and Fort Ross. There is also a supposition that Pismo Beach was named by the Russians, since the word Pismo in Russian means a letter. It is also known that, when they liquidated their assets in California, those assets were bought by Sutter.

We are discussing, however, the present Russian Colony of Shafter; and, as in the case of the Mexicans of California, the Russians of the present time have no connection whatever with the Russians of the early era. The Russians of our time may be very favorably compared with the Pilgrim fathers, and, it seems, they are the last group who came to the United States for the sole purpose of religious freedom.

While in my time Russia was allowing religious freedom to everyone (with certain exceptions), there was a strong "gradation" of the value of religions. The highest was considered the Greek Orthodox Church, while the Jewish religion was probably considered the lowest. It was arranged so that everyone could get from a lower religion into a higher, but no one had the right to get away from the dominant religion into any other. So all the Russians proper had to belong to the Russian Orthodox Church and had no right to get away into any other religious group, whether of an established order or of one of their own choosing. But, while the government tried to enforce this rule, many dared to disobey and to believe the way they saw fit.

Their history, up to the time of the beginning of the nineteenth century, is not definitely recorded. Only at that time they began to get some recognition. They were granted some religious freedom. But, with the ascent to the throne of Nicholas the First, when all other religious groups were stopped very severely, the Molokane were also deprived of their freedom. But the Molokane refused to bow before the authorities in their religious beliefs and were able to show only a great number of martyrs for their faith. The struggle was going on intermittently for about a century, and finally, about 1905, they decided to emigrate to the "Promised Land," as America was named by one of their prophets. How much of a promised land it turned out to be is not a decided question, since in the First World War they also suffered a great deal for their unwillingness to bear arms.

The Russian Colony of Shafter consists of two religious groups: the Doukhobory, or Strugglers of the Spirit, and the Molokane, or milk drinkers, a name which they acquired because during the Lent season they were allowed to use milk ("moloke" in Russian), while the Orthodox Russians were not allowed to use it. Of these two groups, the Molokane are the more numerous in the Shafter District, while the Doukhobory are more numerous in Canada, where they have a colony based on religious communism.

The oldest representative of the Russian Colony in Shafter is Nicholas J. Rilcoff, although the oldest was probably Vasili Poznoff, now dead. As it was said earlier, the Russians finally decided to leave Russia about 1905. He was born in Tiflis. He served in the army in the Caucasian region. Finally, when the edict of their religious leaders came out to refuse to bear arms, he took the step. The Russian government sent him to Siberia in exile. It took quite a time to get there, and the trip was anything but pleasant. Finally he left Russia and arrived in Canada in the Doukhobor Colony in 1905. He stayed there for a while, but apparently the communistic economy of life did not agree with him, and in 1907 he arrived in Los Angeles. His son, N. N. Rilcoff, former superintendent of Kern General Hospital, was born in Canada, and was brought here when he was a small baby.

In 1909 Rilcoff arrived in Shafter, which at that time was a flagging station on the railroad. Most of the land belonged at that time to the Kern County Land Company. They built fences around the farms to keep the jack rabbits in. For irrigation they had ditch water. There was at that time an attempt to settle a colony around Shafter, sponsored by a person named Henry Martin. It was mostly a promotional scheme, probably on the same basis as the colony around Rosedale. Mostly he brought out Russian Germans of the Mennonite and Seventh Day Adventist denominations. They founded a city, named Martindale, which is now Lerdo, but the project failed. The crops were mostly wheat and barley. It was planted in October and was dependent on the rain.

In 1914 the Shafter Colony was formed. By that time there were about twelve Russian families around here. They then secured homesteads somewhere near the present Jerry Slough and Goose Lake. Rilcoff finally sold his land and came to Shafter, where he bought twenty acres at seventy-five dollars per acre from the Land Company. There they began to dig deep wells. The water was reached at a depth of about thirty-five feet. Now it is about one hundred feet to the water, and they dig wells as deep as three, four, or even as deep as six hundred feet. They began to plant potatoes and sugar beets. Potatoes at that time produced one hundred to one hundred and twenty sacks to the acre. Later they began to plant grapes.

Of the old Russian familes there is the Poznoff family and one Mr. Dvortzoff in Rosedale. Mr. Rilcoff has lived on the present place since about 1920. He has forty acres and a beautiful home. The Chenobaeffs were the next settlers. His neighbor and brother-in-law is Carp Molofy. He left Russia in 1910. He lived for a while in Kharbin. He came via the Pacific and landed in San Francisco. He has lived in Shafter since 1915. He had, together with his father-in-law, Mr. Kousmin, twenty-two acres. In 1921 he bought forty acres at the present location. At the beginning the work was done by horses.

(*Historic Kern*, September, 1957)

V

Mining and Petroleum Industries

Among Kern County's exploitable resources, those related to the mining and petroleum industries have been most important. Starting with gold in the 1850s, followed by silver in the 1890s, the mining of precious metals was a mainstay of the economy. More recently emphasis has been placed on the production of borates, salts, gypsum, mercury, and other minerals for agricultural and industrial uses, including the production of cement. Assuring Kern County prominence in recent years has been its production of petroleum products, together with natural gas. Over the years the success of the mining and petroleum industries has greatly influenced the economic history of Kern County.

Monolith Vital to History
by Karl M. Backes

Monolith Portland Cement Company had its roots in the turn-of-the-century need of the City of Los Angeles to supplement its water supply from a source outside the Los Angeles Basin. By 1906 that city had determined the extent of its need, secured an entitlement to water in the Owens Valley, and begun development of a transmission facility to bring the water to Los Angeles. One of the first projects undertaken was the construction of a cement plant at Monolith, California, at the site of good limestone and clay deposits located near the geographical center of the proposed transmission facility. Initially a 120-acre tract located southwest of the mill site and nearly due south of Tehachapi was the source of limestone for the manufacture of cement until 1912. Beginning in that year a site located directly west of the mill supplied limestone through the term of the city's water project.

The cement plant was constructed during the years 1906 to 1908, and it had a milling capacity of about 250,000 barrels of cement per year. Except for an idle period sometime between 1910 and 1912, the plant operated continuously until the water project was completed in 1914. After an unsuccessful attempt by Los Angeles to operate the cement plant as a source of cement for public use, the mill operation was terminated and the facility was closed down. In 1920 Fred A. Ballin, president and principal owner of the Supple Ballin Shipyard and Pacific Marine Iron Works, Aman Moore, one of the first cement engineers in the United States, and Coy Burnett, a successful young attorney, formed an association which obtained a five-year lease of the cement mill with the intention of producing potash. The association was known as the U.S. Potash Company. Ballin served as president, Moore as vice president, and Burnett as secretary-treasurer. In 1920 the U.S. Potash Company obtained exclusive rights to the manufacture of waterproof cement, a new product in the field of cement uses, and by the end of the year the company had produced 43,767 barrels of cement.

In 1921 Moore sold his interest in the U.S. Potash Company to Ballin and Burnett, and the name was changed to Monolith Portland Cement Company. After improvements were made in the production facilities, the new company manufactured 320,000 barrels of cement in 1921. In that year a long-term lease agreement with J. W. Jameson, the owner of nearby ranch lands on which were cement deposits, allowed the company to extract limestone and clay. Geologists determined that these deposits to the north and west of the plant would supply enough raw materials to sustain more than one hundred years of operations.

With the assurance of ample raw materials and the growing market for Monolith Portland Cement Company's fine quality product, major improvements in the milling facilities were made in 1921 and 1922, which increased the rated capacity to 450,000 barrels per year. The new "Jameson" quarry was opened, and new raw grinding, burning, and finish grinding facilities were installed. George A. Fisher, an experienced cement manufacturer, was plant superintendent at that time. In 1923 Fred Ballin sold his interest in the firm to Coy Burnett, at which time the latter was elected president. Under him the Jameson quarry was further developed and the processing facilities were expanded. Older kilns were augmented by new ones until the productive capacity reached 650,000 barrels during 1923.

Improvement of the cement processing facilities continued until by 1925 the rated capacity had been increased to 1.4 million barrels of cement per year. In 1926 an improved quarrying method was developed with the addition of a "glory hole" operation. A cone-shaped hole was dug from the upper level of the quarry to a tunnel running into the mountain at the crusher level. Rock quarried at the upper level was dumped into the "glory hole" and moved through chutes to rail cars in the tunnel. From there it was hauled to a crusher. The construction of a natural gas pipeline from the Taft oil fields made possible a change in the kiln-burning operation from fuel oil to natural gas. Electric power, which had been generated at the job site since the mill's inception, was provided by a public utility in 1926.

In the 1920s Richard Requa of San Diego, a friend of Coy Burnett, was instrumental in putting Monolith's waterproof cement to use in Spanish-type architecture in Los Angeles. Many structures in Hollywood and Beverly Hills afford evidence of the widespread use of waterproof stucco at that time. The Los Angeles County Hospital was constructed from Monolith cements. Between 1927 and 1930 there was little activity in plant construction, and a downward trend in production which began in 1928 continued through 1932, from 1,450,000 barrels in 1927 to 815,000 in 1932. By the latter year a new Hi-Early strength cement had been developed, and in 1933 a method of hauling bulk cement was available. The easing of market conditions after 1932 brought renewed activity in plant construction. The production had increased to 1,800,000 barrels of cement per year by 1936. Between 1937 and 1940 the cement-making process was improved by redesigning the electrical system and improving the grinding and burning facilities in order to produce a higher quality cement. During the late 1930s production remained fairly constant at just below 2,000,000 barrels per year.

In 1940 the Monolith Portland Cement Company purchased the Jameson ranch properties which surrounded the plant site, and for nearly a decade the company operated this cattle ranch. With the subsequent termination of the cattle business, the land was leased for grazing operations.

With the outbreak of World War II in 1941, the United States government laid a prior claim to all production at the Monolith Portland Cement Company. Its cement was used in the construction of the vast Naval Ammunition Dump at Hawthorne, Nevada. For the first time Monolith-developed bulk delivery bags were used in order to speed up the handling of the cement. After nearly all of the plant's production was used in construction at Hawthorne during the years 1940 to 1942, virtually all of the subsequent wartime production was used in construction of the naval base on Guam.

During the decade following World War II Monolith's cement-making facilities were further upgraded, and dust-collecting equipment was installed on all kilns, making a considerable contribution to the reduction of dust-fall in the surrounding countryside. In 1955 the Monolith donated to the City of Tehachapi sixty acres of land for the development of religious, charitable, and community projects. Other land was donated for the development of Little League and Babe Ruth baseball facilities. In 1958 the Tehachapi High School football stadium, a project of the local school district and Monolith, was dedicated to the president of Monolith and named Coy Burnett Field.

By the mid-1960s the Monolith Portland Cement Company had installed additional production facilities which enabled the plant to produce a record 4,000,000 barrels of cement annually. This production helped meet the need for materials for the construction of buildings, water projects, and highways in southern California. In the late 1960s Monolith made plans to modernize its facilities, increase the output, and eliminate the stack emissions. Completion of this program in the 1970s promised to increase the productive capacity to 5,000,000 barrels per year, move Kern County closer to a fuller utlitization of its resources, and contribute to a cleaner air environment in which to use them.

(*Historic Kern*, December, 1970 and March, 1971)

Red Rock Canyon
by Richard C. Bailey

Red Rock Canyon, located one hundred and twenty-five miles north of Los Angeles and twenty-five miles north of Mojave, is a spectacular gash at the western extremity of the El Paso Range where it joins the higher Sierra Nevada. It is now well-known by reason of the magnificent sweep of freeway that serpentines between the red cliffs from which its name is derived. Travelers along U.S. 6 have often described the area as a sort of California Bryce. Others are reminded of portions of the Grand Canyon. Comparisons like these are warranted, although in extent Red Rock is considerably smaller than these more famous natural attractions.

Although its genesis is in the distant past, Red Rock became known to history little more than a century ago. The accidental discovery of gold at Sutter's Mill in 1848 set off a tide of emigration from the East that was soon to alter completely the course of California history.

In their eagerness to reach this land of promise a number of emigrant divisions chose to follow the questionable routes in traversing the unknown mountains and desert expanses that barred their way west. Among these were several groups popularly known as the Death Valley parties. After blundering into the great basin with the macabre name, these units made their painful escapes south and west over wastelands considered among the most awesome in North America.

In January, 1850, a number of these footsore survivors camped in Red Rock on their way south to safety. They were the Bennett and Arcane families plus a division of the Illinois Jayhawkers. The former had recently been rescued from Death Valley by Lewis Manly and John Rogers who had returned from southern California with food barely in time to save their lives. Neither they nor the Jayhawkers were apparently impressed by the wonders of the canyon through whose depths they passed. In later years, if they thought of it at all, it was most likely to recall how hungry, cold, and weary they had been at this time. Four decades later Lewis Manly in his famous book, *Death Valley in '49*, was content to state simply that the pass was now known as Red Canyon. His descriptions of other points on their route are often vivid and detailed, and his failure to enlarge on what he undoubtedly saw here is inexplicable.

The formations of Red Rock date back to late Tertiary times. Judged to be at least 2,500 feet thick, they are composed mainly of bedded volcanic tuffs, sandy and shaly beds, and two lava flows. Their strikingly tilted facades have been eroded and weathered into fantastic and weird forms.

During the 1890s hundreds of miners sifted the sands for gold among the conglomerates and tuffs that lined the beds of the various gulches. That their efforts were richly rewarded is evidenced by the report that around sixteen million dollars in gold was taken from the canyons within a few years. The largest nugget known to have been found here was unearthed by Dave Bowman in Santa Monica Canyon. Having no scale large enough to determine its weight, Bowman, with the help of Clinton Todhunter, another miner, estimated its worth by balancing the nugget against a four-pound single jack and four cans of condensed milk. They were not far off its actual value, which approximated $2,000.

MINING AND PETROLEUM INDUSTRIES 141

Another fortunate prospector was Rudolf Hagen, who has been credited as the rediscoverer of Red Rock Canyon gold in the 1890s. Coming here in the spring of 1893, he and his associates are said to have washed more than two and a half million dollars worth from surface workings. They are then reported to have spent a considerable amount of this in litigation to protect their claims. One of his partners was Charles Canfield, a well known pioneer producer in Kern County's Midway oilfield. Hagen subsequently acquired quite a few thousand acres in the Red Rock area, and a considerable part of this property is now held by his heirs.

The early trail through Red Rock was always difficult due to the sandy soil. It was subject to frequent washouts by torrential cloudbursts which even now rage through the gulches during winter months. Freighters and stageline drivers, however, for many years cursed their way through the gorge over this unimproved road on the passage between Los Angeles and Owens Valley. Their alternative was the detour around the east end of the El Pasos which was difficult and too long to be practicable.

Ricardo, a canyon stopover, was established during the 1890s by the early miner Rudolf Hagen, and named by him in memory of his son Richard. The original building fell victim to a flood some years ago and was rebuilt a short distance to the west. This later structure is now abandoned and near obliteration.

During the 1920s the road through the canyon was first black-topped with oilsand. Then in 1931 a modern paved highway section was dedicated, which in 1958 was succeeded by today's four-lane expressway. A short distance within the southern entrance, where the concrete bridge spans the main streambed, the present roadway passes almost over the original site of Ricardo. Early accounts mention the nearby location of Sullivan's Spring where miners and travelers secured drinking water. This spring still exists a few hundred yards northeast of the road, protected by weathered timbers placed here long ago. Two miners, named Sullivan and Black, ran a placer claim in the vicinity in 1899; the spring is presumably named for the former.

In 1908 the City of Los Angeles contracted with the Southern Pacific Company to construct a nine mile branch rail line from

Cantil Siding up Red Rock Canyon to the site of the Owens Valley aqueduct, which then was under construction. This standard-gauge line was completed in January, 1909, and operated almost continuously for twenty-two months. It was then dismantled and its material sold to the railroad and the U.S. Reclamation Service.

Once a cloudburst ripped out a section below the canyon's south entrance, and a number of the twisted rails lie rusting in the wash, not far off the present highway. Nearby stand the remains of a stone and earthen dam built by Hagen; most of this was also carried off by a canyon flood.

The entire aqueduct was completed in October, 1913; and since that date has transported water over 225 miles of desert and mountains to the expanding metropolis in the Los Angeles basin. The section along the Sierra Nevada, west of Red Rock, required the drilling of a two mile tunnel through a soft sandstone formation, an operation that was completed in seven months. The tunnel was then completely lined with concrete during the next eight months. During the month of August, 1909, this job saw the establishment of a new world's mark for rock drilling when crews of the Jawbone Division cut a record 1,000 feet, eclipsing all former standards.

Red Rock has been a popular mecca for "rockhounds" since the hobby's birth several decades ago. Although the area has yielded considerable material, diligent searchers can still find a variety of excellent specimens. Among these are agate, quartz crystals, and small opals. Chalcedony in various mixtures and colors is also present, as well as brown, green, and red moss jasper. Petrified wood is still available, but the once noted "petrified forest" in Last Chance Canyon no longer exists. The fossil remains, formerly so plentiful on the surface, have been entirely carried off by voracious collectors.

After numerous abortive attempts Red Rock Canyon was acquired by the State Department of Parks and Recreation from its owners during 1968 and is tentatively scheduled to be opened as a public facility sometime next summer. Its boundary will encompass an area of more than five thousand acres, although the exact total has not yet been determined. This is good news to all persons concerned with the preservation of this California geologic and scenic wonderland.

(*Historic Kern*, December, 1968)

Borax Mining in the Frazier Area
by Thomas A. Larkins

In 1899 Colemanite was discovered in the northern part of the Lockwood Valley in eastern Ventura County at an elevation of 5,200 feet by a prospector named McMillan who opened up a small deposit near the top of the ridge facing the valley. F. M. Smith of the Pacific Coast Borax Company heard of the find and came out to look at it; but McMillan was drunk at the time and took no interest in showing him the claim. Smith stated that he could find no commercial ore in sight. About this time Gail Borden (Borden Milk Company) became interested in the claim and bought out McMillan.

John Stauffer and Thomas Thorkildsen took over the mine from Borden, Stauffer owning 49 percent and Thorkildsen 51 percent. Stauffer operated the mine where work had begun as early as July 1901. This was the first Colemanite that was opened up in that district. Two other mines followed (Columbus and Russell).

A letterhead used in 1908 lists the following officers of the Frazier Borate Company: C. DeGuine, president; John Stauffer, secretary; and Thomas Larkins, superintendent.

The post office address was Griffin, and as this was one and a half miles distant from the mine which received nine-tenths of the mail, a petition was circulated and a new post office was established in the mine store and called Stauffer. I was superintendent from 1904 until the mine closed down in 1908. When I arrived at the mine, a long tunnel was being run at the bottom of the hill to intercept the ore body and drain the water which was being pumped from an inclined shaft.

At 1,000 feet there seemed to be no indication of ore, so it was decided to drop down 100 feet from the shaft entrance near the top of the hill and start another tunnel in order to tap the water and get rid of the pumps, hoist, boilers, etc. When this middle tunnel reached the ore bearing shales, the water from above was encountered together with a deposit of high grade Colemenite, some of which was in the nature of brownish crystals that was sacked in the mine, without being sorted.

The lime formation surounding the ore body had a tendency to swell when moist so that the timbers used in the tunnels and stopes had to be renewed often. These timbers were cut from pinon pines on the mine property and were never properly seasoned, so that eventually a small saw mill was installed in the Seymore Valley north of the mine to cut up some of the larger trees. This mill proved inadequate and a larger one was built at 7,000 feet elevation on Mt. Pinos where agreement was made with the U.S. Forest Service to furnish stumpage. This mill could only be operated from May to October each year on account of logging and road conditions, so that a storage yard had to be established on the ridge just above the mine to stack the output of the mill to use during the winter months.

As labor was hard to get in this region, men who applied for work were never turned away. If there was no opening in or around the mine, they would be put to work temporarily in the saw mill or in building and maintenance of roads. All timbers and lumber were hauled from the mill to the mine, a distance of seven and one-half miles by four-horse teams which were based at the mine camp. The saw mill reduced the cost of timbers and logging from twenty-three dollars per M, Bakersfield, plus haulage charges of six dollars per ton, to eleven dollars per M for the material produced from the mill F.O.B. the mine yard.

Prior to 1905 a shortage of seasoned timber for the mine kept development back; but when the saw mill began to operate we not only produced all the materials we required but sold all kinds of lumber to the ranchers for miles around. A general store building housing the post office and office was built on the left side of the camp and a number of cabins and houses for the married men on the right side. A large barn was erected at the south end of the camp to take care of at least fifty head of stock and store 100 tons of hay. This proved invaluable when heavy snow storms obstructed the roads.

The only transportation for ore and supplies was by wagon road

MINING AND PETROLEUM INDUSTRIES

to Bakersfield, in Kern County, or Lancaster, in Los Angeles County, as no roads had been built through the mountains to Ventura. The original road to Bakersfield was crude, crooked and steep in places, and this had to be corrected by degrees at our own expense.

The most practical team for ore hauling was made up of eight mules and two big wheel horses with a large lead wagon and small trailer. To the end of the trailer was attached a light two-wheel cart having a box body with tie-rings to be used at road camps to tie the stock at night and when feeding at noon stops. The round trip from the mine to Bakersfield was made in seven days. The first hauling was done by Johnny Morris, a rancher living five miles south of Bakersfield on Union Avenue, who operated a string of three ten-mule teams. He generally accompanied the teams although he did not drive.

As production at the mine increased other teamsters became interested until at one time there were some 150 head of stock used to haul the output of the mine. The average tonnage was one ton to the mule hauling ore. The back freight was rarely over six tons to the team on account of the uphill grade.

An effort was made to substitute a tractor for the mules. The three-wheel Holt steam drive farm tractor with a 16-ton iron wheel wagon made two trips, one to Bakersfield and one to Lancaster. Each trip took one month. The tractor was forbidden to use the county roads and had to break a way for itself as it went. On steep grades the front end of the tractor rose in the air and turned the machines around and down hill. At the mine, the approach to the ore bin was so steep that a wooden crate had to be built and filled with stones to hold the tractor down on the road. After the Lancaster trip the contractor abandoned the idea of hauling by tractor.

At various times the teamsters would stop hauling and demand more money. This made it necessary for Stauffer to go into the hauling business. Three ten-mule teams were purchased and put on the road and not only proved a success but broke the uncertainty of hauling costs and shipments and assured us of regular in-bound freight and supplies for the mine.

A description of the mule team as developed might be interesting at this point. The twenty-mule team, the trademark of the Pacific Coast Borax Company, was used in a comparatively straight flat country with few turns, where only a few animals could pull at the same time, hence the ten-mule team was about the most practical stretch to have in front of the wagons, although at times the contractors put on twelve and even sixteen mules to haul more tonnage. This additional tonnage made it so hard on the "pointers" going around the turns that the stock had to be renewed after a few trips.

I have known "skinners" to go into a corral of young stock and without much hesitation pick out a leader. As the leader represented the life, brains and future success of the team, I often marveled at the intuition or knack these desert teamsters possessed. Having picked the leader, the rest of the team was broken and placed in the team according to their speed or freeness in walking. In some cases where the mules were too free, they were held back by a "buck" strap extending from the singletree through the hame rings to the bit.

The best job of breaking pointers was done by the "swamper" riding the tongue of the lead wagon. He generally used a long bamboo fish pole. As soon as the mule had learned his name and been hitched up on the end of the tongue, the swamper called his name, tapped him on the side of the head in the direction desired and when the mule had turned out, a tap on the rump made him jump the chain and pull. If he attempted to jump back before completing the turn he was met with the extended pole. He soon learned to jump and pull until called back. When the mules were taught to "point" at the tongue, they were moved up in the team to the sixes and eights.

At the camp along the road, upon rising in the mornings, the teamsters rolled their beds, fed and harnessed the stock, and ate breakfast. After breakfast the leaders were led out first and hooked up to the end of the long chain. Each pair knew its place and would stand there. The wheelers were hitched up last. The driver had a jerk line (window cord) to the leaders, a jockey stick between their heads so that a pull on the line would guide the lead mule to the left. A jerk on the bit would turn him to the right. The wheelers by the way were generally held in reserve along the straight stretches so that they

MINING AND PETROLEUM INDUSTRIES 147

could do extra duty on swinging the tongue around the turns. In addition to the regular harness, on the last wheel horse was a plain saddle where the "skinner" rode in the mountains and could direct his wheel horses and apply the brakes by using a heavy strap to the lead brakes and a longer rope to the trailer brakes. These brakes by the way were made to apply pressure to the back as well as the front of the wheels and were shod with buckeye blocks cut from trees along the road.

A word about the ore wagons. In general they were specially built, having heavy high wheels with double iron tires on the rear of the trucks to off-set the friction generated by the double brakes on the down grade stretches. Tubes fitted to the inner side of the hubs extended to the boxes so that the teamster could by means of a spout can apply heavy castor oil to the axles. When the wagon was under headway, the "clucking" of the wheels against the axles could be heard long distances. The wagon bodies were hand built, with tongue and groove materials on the sides held together with iron bands. Some were lined with sheet iron. Angle iron was bolted along the bed plates so that the floor boards extending from side to side could be slid backwards when the tailgate was removed. This allowed the ore to drop to the platform at the destination. There also was a "jockey box" in front of the lead wagon, together with various other containers and hooks along the sides to carry accessories. For holding the wagons on the grades, hardwood chock blocks with chains attached to the ore beds were so arranged that they could be dragged along behind the rear wheels.

Our shipping point was just north of the old freight depot at Kern (East Bakersfield), where a raised platform was constructed about the height of the railroad car floors. We had a contractor to load the ore by the ton into the box cars by using a wheelbarrow, and it was forwarded to the points as directed by the main office of the Stauffer Company.

About one-half mile east of the Frazier Borate Mine a discovery of Colemanite was made on the east side of Seymore Creek and was developed by a former resident of Ventura County, W. H. Russell. A vertical shaft was sunk to a depth of 200 feet and tunnels run north and south to intercept the ore body. Some low grade ore was encountered in the northern drifts and was shipped to Stauffer Chemical Company. But the water problem and continued low quality of the ore proved too costly. An oil burning calciner was purchased to reduce the waste material and was hauled to the mine and partly assembled but not completed at the time the property was taken over by Stauffer Chemical Company.

The Columbus Borax Mine was just east of the Russell claims and was developed by Calm Brothers of Chicago. It was also a shaft mine with cross-cut tunnels. The ore was low grade and like the Russell ore contained so much waste that only a small amount was ever shipped directly from the mine. This was hauled by horse teams to Lancaster in Los Angeles County, and forwarded to Chicago where Calm Brothers at that time produced a preserving powder that was used in meats, etc. but it was eventually banned by the U.S. Government pure food laws.

(*Historic Kern*, December, 1957)

Story of the Yellow Aster
published in the *Brooklyn Eagle*, 1899

In the town of Los Angeles, California, there stands a splendid modern mansion, surrounded by magnificent grounds, a monument to the saying, "A rolling stone gathers no moss." The house is the home of F. M. Mooers... While the culmination of this story reads like a romance, the strike was not a sudden one, though the means that enabled Mooers and his partners to develop the mine [at Randsburg] were remarkable results of good fortune. The rest of the story of this rise from poverty to affluence, from wild and reckless living to ease and fortune, from the desk of a bookkeeper through the hardships and desperate life of the West to the luxury of a splendid home and a fortune which cannot be estimated, can best be told by himself.

"The life of a prospector," he says, "is always fascinating, whatever may be the hardships, providing he has enough to eat. Indeed, to the experienced prospector, the man used to the ways of life, the hardships are generally more fancied than real where want of food does not figure. To follow your faithful burro through deserts and over mountains, to lie down at night when night overtakes you, with only a saddle for a pillow would probably seem unique to a society man of Brooklyn Heights and perhaps not comfortable. Indeed my friends tried to dissuade me from such a life, saying the hardships would kill me, but I have yet to find the man who would tire me, when I have been compelled for 'a grub stake' to hammer a drill or run an ore car in some of the big mines of Colorado, or drive a six mule team from daylight to dark, to procure the wherewithal to pursue what too often turned out to be a will of the wisp in my eighteen years' search for an El Dorado. But that life had been pictured too much to be interesting to the readers of the Eagle now. Suffice it to say that I drifted with indifferent success, passed through more or less perils, until I wandered into California.

"I went from Nevada to the desert between the Arizona border and the Sierra Nevadas. Here are the great Calico-tinted mountain peaks, some of them rising to an altitude of 10,000 feet, but between them and around them a great undulating sea of sand, a prehistoric ocean which once lapped the foothills of the Rocky Mountains, fifteen miles to the east.

"Here is desolation supreme, but soul inspiring in its awful stillness. Here was a geological problem that I often longed to solve. It was a grand study in itself, this great desert. But somehow I longed again for civilization and after a time I found myself in the City of Los Angeles. Laying aside my sombrero and duck clothing, I once more devoted myself to newspaper work with more or less energy in the Southern metropolis of California.

"It was not for long, however, as the news of the gold placers on the desert broke out and excitement ran high at a place called Goler, about 150 miles northeast of Los Angeles. Once a miner, always a miner you know, and once the news reached town, my nomadic life gained the better of me and I donned the sombrero again and was soon on the march for the new gold fields. I do not know why it is that distance lends enchantment to the prospector. But it is true that it does. If one-thousandth part of the money spent in the frozen Klondike, where privation, untold hardship and death itself stares the inexperienced prospector in the face at every other step could have been spent in prospecting that great geological ocean bottom, the great Mojave desert which lies at the very door of the garden spot of the world, California, it would have produced more gold in a single year than Alaska and Colorado combined.

"Thousands of square miles, as unexplored as darkest Africa, lie open to the prospector who can work in his shirt sleeves every day in the year and at night can roll himself up in his blanket and sleep under the stars in comfort. Yet the average prospector is easily lured by fabulous tales of wealth in distant lands, and his nomadic disposition leads him away to regions where more excitement and adventure is met with in the search for treasure.

"There were more than 2,000 people camped at Goler at one time, satisfied to make from two to five dollars a day in the dry placer mining. The present town of Randsburg was only ten miles from the spot and yet there was not the slightest indication of the footprint of man or beast when I first visited that region which is now producing $200,000 in gold bullion per month. I first was there in April, 1895. It is currently reported that tenderfeet usually stumble into the best mineral finds. You can rest assured, however, that actual geological study found Randsburg and made it what it is. Many were the sleepless nights my partner and myself spent in the study of where all the gold came from that was found in the placer mines. Singleton and I knew the gravel was all original quartz, of course, but where were the ledges and what had brought this auriferous gravel to that spot?

"There was no evidence of water courses, except those caused by the cloudbursts in the desert mountains. All of a sudden it dawned upon us that we were in the center of a volcanic belt about ten miles wide; that formed ledges of quartz. The mother of gold had traversed the region. The north, the archean rocks were in place, the granite, horseblende, siorite and mica schist existed there. Why not that range of mountains to the south, never before explored, we wondered, be the other border to this volcano? There were evidences of tremendous disturbances and upheavals in the past. Extinct craters everywhere gave evidence of tremendous heat, which probably disintegrated and burned out the ledges and left the gold in a molten state, in small nuggets and coarse grains.

"This thought was an inspiration to us. The winter rains had been unusually severe and the gravel was in bed rock. Our dry washing machine had been standing idle for a month or more. The hungry coyote began to sniff in the tent door, too uncomfortably like the proverbial wolf. Our provision man wore a sour look when he brought our monthly supply from Mojave.

"'I'm sorry, boys,' he said rather despairingly. 'You'll have to dig up. Yet I don't see what you will dig for the ground won't dry for your machines until June. Now, the fact is, I did not come here for my health and it takes money to buy groceries.'

"Something had to be done immediately. I remembered the case of the Gallagher brothers at Leadville, who had reached the same stage in the grub question and who were told that another week's supply was their limit. It seemed all up with them but at that very moment they discovered that every bucket full of the heavy stuff they had been lifting out was carbonates and worth a thousand dollars a bucket. I remember passing a joke about its being a good omen, for you've got to strike bedrock before you reach gold and we had struck bed rock in grub.

"Now was the time to put our theories into practice. The want of a team to haul water had prevented us up to this time from exploring the unknown range to the south. I had the year before made a hurried trip to the region and had built a monument right in what proved to be the very heart of the bonanza.

"I had only a canteen of water with me at the time and was glad to get back to camp, with my tongue parched and hanging out. Water is a very serious problem on this arid waste and one does not dare to wander far from the source of supply.

"Now C. A. Burcham, one of the prospectors in camp, had the only team that was there and we tried to persuade him to make the trip, although he had no confidence in our geological theories. However, he finally said: 'If you'll pay for the horse feed and three barrels of water, I'll go with you.' We agreed at once and loaded up our picks, shovels, drills, powder and mortar and pestle and horn spoon to sample our rock and with our scanty supply of rations started off. We three were very soon under way. I taking the lead to pilot the trail for the load was heavy. The tourists by rail who have seen this hot and parched region in the summer, as they have been whirled at the rate of fifty miles an hour from Needles to Los Angeles, have possibly seen no beauty in this desert.

"The red sandstone and barren mountains skirt plains of endless alkali with no shrubbery but the greasewood bushes, the sage brush and the yucca tree, with its bayonet type leaves. The gray coyote is about the only thing seen sneaking over the sandy plains. As the traveler plods wearily on he will see some distance off a beautiful lake, relecting the shrubbery that surrounds it and countless waterfowl appear to float on its placid bosom. How many pilgrims have been beguiled to leave the trail and with parched tongues and crippled feet pressed on to the spot, only to find it merely a mirage. To many that has meant the straw that breaks the camel's back, and skeletons tell the sad tale to those who follow them. Not a drop of water, nor a tree nor a shrub, but a vast expanse of hardened sand and clay, baked and polished by the hot winds from the Death Valley until its surface is like a mirror, is where the lake appeared.

"But this is April, 1895, that I tell about. The winter rains have been ample and behold the transformation. Standing on Mount Olympus, or Randsburg, a perfect carpet of wildflowers is spread at one's feet, making impossible to step without crushing them, their beauty only enjoyed by rabbits, hundreds of which jump on every side.

"Two hundred miles to the northward, a succession of mountain peaks of the snow capped Sierra Nevadas pierce the sapphire sky. To the northeast, southwest, all around you, are the desert peaks (the range of vision in this rarefied air comprising a radius of two hundred miles) chiseled in every conceivable architectural design and painted by their mineral constituents in every hue of the rainbow.

"The blue and purple shadows rest on carmine or hematite of iron hills, the pea green denoting copper, the gray granite constantly changing, never alike, but all barrenness and desolation except for the wildflower and the gold. This is April. In July, all will be parched and brown again from the furnace blasts from Death Valley, seventy miles away and yet while the thermometer will rise to 135 degrees in the shade, there is absolutely no humidity and I have suffered worse in New York with the temperature at 90 degrees. At night the trade winds of the Pacific fan a man while he lies under his blanket.

"We reached the present site of Randsburg April 22, 1895; not a footprint or hoofprint had impressed the telltale clayey soil since I was there over a year before, with only a canteen of water and no tools to sample the rock. I walked ahead of my companions up what is now Rand canyon and came to a large quartz cropping, seven feet above the grass roots. I knew there was gold in the gravel, for I had found gold in it, and here was a mass of the mother lode which had escaped the erosion of countless ages, with sparkling particles as big as wheat grains shining all through it. Here was a mine, indeed, a vein of it in sight on top, six feet wide. Enough to make many men rich. Carload after carload was afterward milled that gave $165 to $175 to the ton, from this one ledge, before the mill was ever thought of.

"But this proved to be a very small affair when the mountain whose summit was 4,800 foot altitude was geologically investigated.

"The whole mountain was ore. The country rock was a diorite, a metamorphosed granite. Through some gigantic convulsion, this diorite had been rent asunder in the remote ages, making an enormous crevice in the earth's center 500 feet wide and this had molten quartz and gold. In some successive age, eruptive dikes of porphyry ore were shot up, to break through. This was the mineralized quartz.

"Many times I have been asked how it feels in a moment of poverty to be suddenly confronted with millions. My answer has always been one of gratitude to the Divinity which shapes our ends, and mine has been rough hewn enough that we might have great wealth to trust to benefit our fellowmen. It was thus I felt when this seemingly inexhaustible store of treasure lay before me. Still the millions had yet to be gotten out of the earth's treasure vault and the conditions at this time seemed unfavorable to us. Here was a mountain of ore but no water for many miles on this arid waste. The old dry washing machine was brought into use again and here a kind Providence intervened and helped us.

"The great ledge had decomposed through the ages so that only on the very summit of the mountains $50 per day was 'dry washed' from the gravel. This enabled us to have the claims surveyed, some 400 acres in all, and to put a few men to work to develop the property. From two carloads of ore, we three men realized $10,500 and with this money began developments on a large scale.

"But now came the dangers that are greater than any encountered on the desert. As soon as the strike got abroad, it was the signal for the most outrageous blackmailing schemes ever conceived by man or devil. It is the wonder of the mining world that this mining property which experts have conceded to rival the great Comstock, should still be in the hands of its original discoverers. It would take columns to describe the many schemes to rob us of our property. We three men, who were virtually down to our last pot of beans in April, 1895, have fought, unaided by any outside capital, the greatest scheming legal brains of the Pacific Coast and found ourselves the producers last year of $650,000 in gold bullion, which with our new mill, will be doubled this year. With this money we have bought a water plant that is the equal of any municipality. We have built and paid for the most complete thirty stamp mill on the coast and paid $210,000 in dividends the past year.

"We have 3,000,000 tons of ore by actual measurement from the 600 foot level, up, that will mill ten dollars per ton, taking it as it comes, without sorting it, at a cost of not over four dollars a ton, to mill and mine. There are veins on the hanging wall that will yield ten dollars per pound and there are great masses of ore in the so called 'bridal chamber' . . . that will yield one hundred dollars a ton, over a million dollars being exposed to view in the wonderful chamber 600 feet beneath the surface of the summit."

(Historic Kern, June, 1958)

The Early Days in the Oil Fields
by George E. von Breyman

The following is a little about the early life, living conditions, and a good many things that happened in those early days in the oil fields here, and in some of the other oil fields of the San Joaquin Valley. Where I worked the fall of 1902 and the spring of 1903 on the Canfield Lease the living conditions were not too bad, for that day and age. We had a bunk house with a second roof above the regular house roof, so that air could circulate between these two; and there was a covered porch on both sides of the house which sheltered the main building a little. As there were no refrigerators in those days, the only way that I ever saw in use at the cook house to try to keep the food from spoiling was a water drip system. A skeleton frame was built, and burlap sacking was covered over this (it had a solid flat top), and a water pipe was brought to the top and was allowed to drip; as the water saturated the sides of this makeshift cooler, it did very well.

Very often superintendents and drilling crews alike were, you might say, green cut of the field. So, you can imagine that things were sometimes rather hectic. There were quite a few drillers who came out here from Pennsylvania, Indiana, and Ohio who were competent enough to drill the shallow wells of that date. But when the mad rush started here in the Kern River Oil Field, it seemed as though every merchant, farmer and such thought that they should become an oil magnate overnight. So, the rush to do so. (You might think that I am exaggerating, but nevertheless, it is so.)

As it was in this mad rush for a while at least, there was a dearth of drillers. So here is what was done about it by some of the oil operators. In the evening they gathered out in front of the Southern Hotel, and would call out, are there any oil well drillers in the crowd? A number of men who did not know the first thing about drilling a well, thought why not take a chance? I might just as well get six dollars a day, that is better than skinning mules for a dollar or so. I knew of one of these mule skinners who made the try. He had to spud in. The stem, which was as a usual thing twenty-four feet or so long, was lying out on the walk. To pick it up he screwed the rope socket onto the top of it and started the steam engine that actuated the bull wheels on which the drilling cable was wound. So far, so good, but when the stem was brought in as far as it could possibly go to the back of the derrick, it came up against the top of the derrick entrance. Well, Mack was stuck. So when the boss came along, he said, "Mack, let's go to the office. I think that you would do better skinning mules." The way we did this was to hoist the rope socket up into the derrick a ways and take it out through an opening between the braces and let it down to the walk.

A little later when I was over on the coast I took over the drilling

Lakeview gusher near Maricopa, 1910.

of a well for an oil operator who had hired a couple of drillers who had spudded in and had made only eighty-five feet in two weeks. I had been fortunate enough to work with some of the drillers who came out here from the eastern oil fields who were capable men, and got the wells down. I had been drilling for one of these men and he recommended me. In those early days everything in the oil field was in the horse and buggy days as compared with today. Often when we did not have a tool that was required for a certain job we went to the shop that was doing oil well tool work, and helped the shop devise what was required to fit the occasion.

When the oil boom started here a good many men commenced to take up U.S. federal government land. They used the old placer mining rule, if I express myself correctly. Under the placer mining law a man was entitled to file claim on each alternate twenty acres. Some of the big interests, as I will call them, hired men for a few dollars to go out. (I believe it had to be the first of the year. I knew one man who did this on the paid basis. He said that he had to go out at midnight so that someone else would not file ahead of him.) Then as there was considerable gypsum on the West Side, some of those who filed on this land held it by doing assessment duty on these gypsum deposits.

Many times these claims were bitterly disputed; sometimes open warfare. The way the story went of one of these battles was that two men held a claim that someone else disputed. The two men referred to had a tent on the claim, and one night after they had crawled into their blankets, suddenly shots came from every direction. They were wounded but they crawled into a gully, and as they had anticipated what might happen they had rifles and shot back. Well, the report was that they made it so hot that they left a buckboard and team that they had hired from Benettina who had a saloon and stable in McKittrick. There were very strong feelings about some such things as this. Here was a hired man; who hired him, and who hired the men who hired the team? Sometimes it was wild and woolly in Kern County in those early days. One night, so the story went, a couple of men got into a fight in Benettina's saloon and one of them went out and got a shotgun and came back and killed the other man. As far as I know he was never caught.

I knew a rig builder over on the coast who, so I heard, had been a deputy constable at McKittrick about the time of the above happenings. He always carried a Manlicher carbine rifle out on the job with him. I often wondered why he did this—whether he was looking for someone, or whether he was looking over his shoulder?

When I worked in the Kern River oil field my living conditions were of about the usual run for that day in the oil field. But here are a couple of instances that I ran into. The summer of 1903 I went to work for the San Francisco & McKittrick Oil Company. I had to build my own bunk out of one-by-twelve rough boards, and no mattress furnished. (In all the rest of the camps they at least furnished a cot and mattress.) Of course we worked twelve hours those days, and the company boarded us. When my driller and I came in at midnight there was supposed to be something to eat for us on the dining room table, but most generally the crew that went to work on the A.M. shift had the table about cleaned. This oil property was five miles north of McKittrick. I don't know, but it might be near where the Standard Oil Company and the Shell Oil Company brought in the big wells a short time ago. The wells that we drilled at the time that I was there were shallow, and produced heavy oil.

Referring back to the federal land grabs, when William Howard Taft was president, he decided that he had better take a hand in this, and withdrew it from entry. And some of those who disregarded his dictum had their holdings taken away from them at least temporarily. One such case was the Obispo Oil Company. Howard Payne was appointed receiver, or possibly that term should be referee. He took about $3 million and deposited it in a bank in Sacramento, where it was held until the courts decided the case. I believe it was eventually returned to the Obispo Oil Company.

This is a brief summary of those early days here in the oil fields, some of it was good, some not so good. There is another thing I might mention about the time that I was here in the Kern River field. There was a beer wagon that made the rounds daily through the field. A good many of those early drillers were heavy drinkers. I left it alone. And I might add that Bakersfield had the name of being quite a wild town.

(*Historic Kern*, March, 1966)

VI

Mountain and Desert Communities

Mining activity along the Kern River in the mid-1850s stimulated the founding of several small trading centers. For nearly a decade, the economic and social life of the miners centered at Keyesville, near the confluence of the North and South forks of the Kern River. By the 1860s, that town had declined while other towns developed, such as Kernville, Havilah, Claraville and Sageland. When Kern County was created in 1866, Havilah was chosen as the county seat, only to lose that political plum to Bakersfield in 1874. Mining activity along the Kern River had declined by the 1890s when extensive mining activity began east of the Sierra Nevada in the Mojave Desert. There rich gold and silver discoveries brought into existence towns like Garlock and Randsburg. Later open pit borax mining led to the founding of Boron. In the meantime completion of the Southern Pacific Railroad between San Francisco and Los Angeles in 1876 afforded Mojave importance as a shipping point for a vast hinterland extending as far as Death Valley and the Owens Valley.

Havilah, Kern County, California
by Richard C. Bailey

"And a river went out of Eden to water the garden; and from thence it was parted, and became into four heads. The name of the first is Pison: that is it which compasseth the whole land of Havilah, where there is gold." (Genesis 2: 10–11)

The mining town of Havilah came into being after the discovery of gold at Keyesville, Quartzburg and Whiskey Flat in the Greenhorn Mountain Kern River area. According to the generally accepted story, a camping party consisting of Ben T. Mitchell, Alexander Reid, George McKay, Dr. C. de la Borde and Asbury Harpending accidentally happened on a rich quartz deposit a few miles to the south of the then known developments. Harpending is said to have given the new camp its name of Havilah, plucking it from the Book of Genesis in the Bible. This biblical Havilah was described as having been a land of much gold, and the name was quickly accepted as appropriate by the wishful thinkers. July, 1864, is usually the date recognized as signaling the birthday of the town.

The Harpending mentioned above was a Kentuckian who had been involved in an abortive plot to seize California for the Confederacy during the Civil War, which was still raging. The plot failed, and Harpending, hearing that southerners were welcomed in the Kern River mines, decided to seek sanctuary there. He arrived just in time to cash in on the Havilah boom and left there eventually with around $800,000, according to his own account. Later in San Francisco he became prominent in real estate and gained a degree of notoriety through his involvement in the Great Diamond Hoax which was exploded by Clarence King, the famous mining engineer.

Havilah became the center of the rich Clear Creek Mining District, and soon outstripped the earlier camps in development and population.

At its peak in 1866, Havilah had nearly a score of flourishing mines in its vicinity, with nine stamp mills of from five to twenty stamps each in operation. A stage ran daily between Whiskey Flat (later Kernville) and Caliente, through Havilah. There were thirteen saloons and quite a few gambling and dance halls as well. Horse

Kernville street scene, c. 1890.

racing along the principal street was a popular sport. Holding up the stage was another method of killing time. In fact, holdups became so frequent that the express company nearly went out of business, and finally refused to carry any more bullion.

In 1874, after having been the county seat of Kern since the organization of the county in 1866, Havilah was forced to take a back seat to the rising town of Bakersfield out in the San Joaquin Valley. In a hot and closely-contested election Havilah lost her pre-eminence, and it was not many years before her mile-long business street began to take on the semblance of so many other ghost towns in California history.

Today only one of the original structures remains—only a few crumbling walls and foundations still exist as evidence that here once thrived a sizeable community.

(*Historic Kern*, February, 1936)

Recall Ballot Battle of 1873: Havilah Loses County Seat
by Charles P. Martin

Kern's historical battle of the ballots—when Bakersfield wrested the county seat from Havilah in a bitter contest—was recalled when the thirty-three ballots cast at Havilah in the special election of February 5, 1873, were discovered under a pile of debris in the attic of the Bakersfield City Hall, the former Kern Courthouse, where they had lain unmolested for decades.

There, too, were uncovered other historical documents. There was the great register for Kern County of April, 1879; ballots used at the general election held at Hot Springs on September 3, 1879, a poll list of the election held at Havilah on January 24, 1883, at which nine men voted; a book of certificates which proved certain individuals had the necessary qualifications to teach in the secondary schools of Kern County, and several scattered ballots showing a list of office seekers of more than half a century ago. Most of these records are the oldest of their kind in Kern County.

The Havilah ballots were in a long envelope which had been sealed and signed by A. A. Bermudez and E. Cohn, the election clerk and his deputy; Inspector F. W. Goodale and Judges E. P. S.

Andrews and John P. Miller. Sacrilegiously, the envelope was torn open, and within were found the ballots, penned by husky miners who voted to a man to retain Havilah as the county seat. But Bakersfield won the ballot contest and Havilah's glory began to dim, until today it is but a specter of its former self, a ghost city with but a rock-rimmed graveyard to remind passers-by that once it was Kern's greatest community.

In the great register of 1879 there were 1,330 voters registered. Therein was found the name of Abia Taylor Lightner, who had resided in Kern County longer than any other person up to that time.

The ballots cast at Tejon and Hot Springs several years later showed Hugh J. Glenn, W. F. White and George C. Perkins fighting for the governorship of California. In Kern County, Ben Brundage and Theron Reed were battling for Judgeship of the Superior Court. Charles E. Jewett and F. W. Craig sought the county clerkship. W. R. Bower and A. O. Collins asked favor of the voters for the sheriff's job, and Mrs. D. B. Rogers and F. S. Wallace were running for the superintendent of schools post. Alex Williams was in the race for supervisor of the third district. And at the bottom of the ballot voters were given an opportunity to express their views on Chinese immigration. In most instances the voters opposed immigration of the Orientals. Practically all voters were Democrats.

Interesting was the school certificate book. It showed that on June 8, 1873, Superintendent of Common Schools J. N. Cornwall gave J. W. Berry of Glennville a certificate to teach. Berry's was the ninth to be issued, and in six years following, under the regime of Superintendent L. A. Beardsley, only nine more teachers were given certificates. They were Forrest E. Grover of Linns Valley, William B. Booth of Kern Island, J. T. Gray of South Fork, James Binnie of Kernville, Mrs. Hattie Gould of Glennville, Miss Cora McGrann of "Mohave," Mrs. E. P. Venack of Bear Valley, John Hickey of Linns Valley, Miss N. E. Mauldine of Bakersfield, and Miss Rachel Morrison.

The poll list of Havilah for 1883 showed that there were only nine voters left in the district. They were Pat Murphy, W. E. Chapman, Patrick O'Brien, John W. Farning, Martin Walsh, all election judges, and Henry E. _____, Edwin J. Reynolds, William F. Main, and Michael Graham.

The documents were found by City Building Inspector R. H. Hubbard and the writer, who were going through the attic on another errand. Kicking over a pile of debris, they found the old Kern County records.

(Historic Kern, January, 1953)

A Havilah School Teacher
by Caroline Payne Harris

In June, 1911 I graduated from Los Angeles State Normal School. The most important thing in my mind at that time was to get a job. I was living with my aunt and uncle then. They had previously lived in a little mining town called Havilah in Kern County, where my uncle had worked in the Big Blue Mine. So one day my aunt said to me, "I think that I will write to Mrs. Billy Wood in Havilah and see if they need a teacher there for the next year. Mrs. Wood is a very good friend of mine and I am sure that if there is a vacancy in the school there, she will do everything possible to get the position for you."

My aunt immediately wrote to Mrs. Wood and explained the situation to her. Very soon a reply came saying that a teacher was needed for the following year.

I corresponded with Mrs. Wood several times and soon I got a letter from Mrs. Waters, who was the clerk of the school board. She asked me the customary questions and after an exchange of several letters I received a contract to teach in the school at Havilah the following year 1911-1912.

At this time I was very young and inexperienced and had never been away from home. I was very thrilled at the prospects of getting my first teaching position and starting out on my own. During the summer I corresponded with Mrs. Wood many times. She invited me to room and board at her home.

On September 1, 1911 I got on the train in Los Angeles and started for my new home and teaching job. After an all night ride through the Tehachapi mountains I finally arrived at Caliente about

Havilah, a mining ghost town by the 1880s.

7:00 a.m. I was met there by the stage driver, Mr. Payton Moore, who took me over to the Caliente Hotel for breakfast. There were other passengers waiting there to go on the same stage as I was taking. This stage was a traditional stage, very high off the ground with perhaps four rows of seats extending across the bed of the stage coach with the driver sitting up in front. I believe it had a top to protect the passengers from the weather. I guess Mr. Moore had discovered by this time that I was a very scared green young person, so he let me ride beside him on the front seat.

The stage coach was drawn by six horses. This alone was a big adventure for me because I had never seen a stage coach before, let alone ride in one.

At about 8:00 a.m. we started on our way up through the mountains. Some of the passengers were going to Walkers Basin, some to Havilah, others to Bodfish, Kernville, or Walkers Pass.

The road was a fairly good mountain road as roads went in those days, but it was very steep in places and I remember the driver stopped several times to let the horses rest a bit. The passengers then got out and stretched their legs and looked around at the beautiful scenery which to me was something very wonderful as I had never been in the mountains before. After about four or five hours we came to Walkers Basin. Here we stopped at the Rankin Ranch for lunch. This was the first time I had met Mr. and Mrs. Walker Rankin, Sr. I later had the privilege of visiting with these wonderful people many times.

After lunch and a rest we again started on our journey. At about 6:00 o'clock in the evening we approached the town of Havilah. As we came up the one and only street we noticed a lady standing in the middle of the road waving a cloth vigorously. The driver stopped when we approached her. She asked if the teacher was on the stage. So I got off with my new trunk and other belongings and was escorted by Mrs. Elizabeth Wood into her home. This was to be my home for the first year I stayed in Havilah. Mr. and Mrs. Wood were very wonderful to me and did everything possible to make me happy and comfortable while I lived with them. At this time they had two little boys Leslie, six years old, and Elmer, about five years old.

The first evening they told me so many interesting things about

Havilah, and later I found out some very fantastic stories which these mountain people enjoyed telling to greenhorns like myself. I was a very good subject for these fictional yarns as I was very gullible at that time.

In the morning, Mrs. Wood introduced me to Mrs. Waters, the clerk of the school board. After a short visit we walked down the road to look at the schoolhouse. It was a one-room unpainted building made of mountain lumber, with a front porch and a belfry in which was installed a large bell with a rope hanging down in the anteroom so that the bell ringer could easily get hold of it and ring the bell at the necessary times. In the anteroom at the entrance of the building was a bench up against the side wall on which was a five-gallon galvanized bucket which held the drinking water for the children and the teacher. A tin dipper with a long handle stood in the bucket. At one end of the building there was a five- or six-foot space partitioned off for the storage of wood. An iron potbellied stove stood at the other end.

The playground was not fenced so it was not unusual to find cattle near the building or lying down at the entrance of the schoolhouse.

The first year I received $75.00 a month salary and the second year I got $70.00. The reason for the decrease the second year was that the first year I carried a bucket of water from the creek every day for our drinking water. I also did the janitor work which amounted to sweeping the schoolroom once a week and building the fire every morning. After I was there a short time I found a boy friend who built the fire and carried the water for me.

Havilah, which once was a thriving mining town and the first county seat of Kern County, was now almost deserted. On each side of the street were old deserted store buildings which were rapidly disintegrating. The foundation of the old courthouse and other public buildings were still there. There were many abandoned mines. The King Solomon Mine was the only one working. At this time only ten families were living in this deserted village. These were Mr. and Mrs. Gus Miller, who operated a small store; Mr. and Mrs. Waters, who operated the post office; Mr. and Mrs. W. B. Wood; Mr. and Mrs. Wilson, who ran the hotel; Peter McGuirk, an old miner; Mr. and Mrs. Zook; Mr. Andy Polkinghorn; Mrs. Gunderson; Mr. and Mrs. Ross Wilson; Mr. and Mrs. Nielsen; and Billy Menzel.

For recreation I would often go home with one of my students, Walter Hayes, who lived at the King Solomon Mine, four miles up in the mountains. He would let me ride his burro, Togo, and he would walk beside me with his little black dog following behind us.

At regular intervals he would tickle the flanks of the burro and make him kick up his heels. This amused Walter very much and brought screams and threats from me to tell his mother if he didn't stop. Just before we reached the mine he would always make me promise that I wouldn't tell his mother.

After an enjoyable week-end at the mine I would ride down the hill Monday morning in time to start the school.

Other times I would go to dances either at Caliente, Bodfish, Kernville or Borel.

In the evenings I would visit the various families and play cards, which seemed to be a very important leisure activity then. I spent much time riding my horse in the hills during the week-ends.

I remember one time that there was a very important dance in Caliente and the stage did not get back to Havilah until 10:30 on Monday morning so I thought that I could not go on account of my teaching. A day or two before this Mrs. Waters, a board member, visited my school. While there she asked me if I was going to the dance. I explained that I would not be able to get back in time for school on Monday morning. She said, "You go right along and I will come down and open the school and take care of the children until you get back." So I went to the dance. The stage let me off at the school Monday morning. There was Mrs. Waters taking very good care of my class until I returned.

All transportation was done by horses and mules during my first year there. The first automobile came up through these mountains the second year I was in Havilah. It was a Stanley Steamer. This created a great deal of excitement. Before the end of the year the horse stages were replaced by automobile stages and many people through the hills bought cars for themselves. The hauling of freight was still done by mules and horses for several years after this.

At the end of the second year, which was June, 1913, the enrollment of the school dwindled until there were not enough children to maintain a school, so the old school building was torn down.

(*Historic Kern*, June, 1956)

Kern County One Hundred Years Ago
by Eugene Burmeister

Activity in the fledgling County of Kern centered 100 years ago around Havilah, with smaller settlements at Keyesville, Claraville, Glennville, Kernville, Scodie, Lavers' Crossing, Petersburg, Quartzburg, Kern Island, Old Town and Willow Springs. The booming mining town where gold was discovered along Clear Creek in 1864 had been chosen in April as the county seat. The town's voting population in September, 1866, was 900.

The first county election in July had seen the Democrats electing a full slate of officers by a substantial majority. Serving on the three-man board of supervisors were Henry Hammel, chairman, James J. Rhymes and Samuel A. Bishop. Other county officials included William B. Ross, sheriff; Henry D. Bequette, clerk, recorder and auditor; Ezekiel E. Calhoun, district attorney; David A. Sinclair, treasurer; Redmond B. Sagely, assessor; Colonel Thomas Baker, surveyor; Dr. Joseph Lively, coroner and public administrator; Dr. Joseph B. Riley, superintendent of schools; and Theron Reed, circuit judge. Serving the county in the state legislature were James W. Freeman in the Senate and Joseph C. Brown as a member of the Assembly, both Democrats.

All county business was carried on in buildings leased from Bella Union Hotel owners Henry Hammel and Andrew H. Denker, and from Luther F. Humiston until the $2,200 courthouse could be finished in 1867 by South Fork Valley millwright Thomas H. Binnix on an $800 lot purchased from H. C. Harding in Havilah's public square. The sixteen by twenty foot two-story $1,600 jail, approved by the board of supervisors at its August 1 meeting and being built by Thomas B. Stuart, was nearing completion. The county and state tax rate was $2.61 on each $100 valuation.

Farming and ranching had been well established in the county in Walker Basin, South Fork Valley, Linn's Valley, around Fort

Tejon, Kern River Valley, Tehachapi Valley, and along the Kern delta. Cattle and sheep were raised by large ranch holders, and wheat, potatoes and hay were important crops. Butter was selling at Havilah for fifty cents a pound, flour at twelve dollars a barrel, potatoes three and a half cents a pound, eggs at sixty-two cents a dozen, sugar at thirty cents a pound, and kerosene at two dollars and twenty-five cents a gallon. Hay was bringing forty to fifty dollars a ton.

There was no railroad here 100 years ago. Roads were few and most of these were mere trails. The old Butterfield Overland Mail route crossed the county from north to south, although the stage had abandoned the southern route with the coming of the Civil War in 1861. There was no bridge across the Kern in the vicinity of Bakersfield and several ferries took stages, wagons and passengers across the treacherous river. The McFarlane Toll Road had been completed over Greenhorn Mountain in 1864. The Los Angeles-Havilah wagon road had been opened in mid-1865 by way of Elizabeth Lake, Willow Springs, Tehachapi Valley and Walker Basin, and later that year a road had been completed between Visalia and Havilah through Glennville and Kernville.

There were no public schools at this time. Private tuition schools operated at Havilah, Kernville, Old Town and Kern Island (Bakersfield). The board of supervisors would establish in November, 1866, the Havilah, Linn's Valley, Kelso and Tejon school districts.

Indian troubles in the county had subsided, brought about through the efforts of General Edward F. Beale in getting most of the Indians to move to the Sebastian Reservation, and by the army troops stationed at Fort Tejon from 1854 to 1861 and by California volunteers until the fort was closed in 1864.

After relying on Los Angeles, San Francisco and Visalia newspapers until August 18, the county now had its own newspaper, the *Havilah Weekly Courier*, published every Saturday by George A. Tiffany, with Havilah physician-surgeon Dr. Charles W. Bush as editor. Editor Bush asserted that the purpose of the paper was to advance the interest of mining, agriculture and business, and that the paper would espouse the Democratic cause.

Father Daniel Francis Dade, a Catholic priest from Visalia,

presided over St. Joseph's Church and a parochial school at Havilah. Episcopal services were held in the booming mountain mining town by circuit-riding divines who also visited Glennville, Kernville and South Fork Valley, and by several local businessmen who preached in the courtroom on the Sabbath.

Along the Kern delta, Colonel Thomas Baker, who had settled there September 10, 1863, was busy selling land and laying out streets. Baker's field of alfalfa east of the present civic center was a popular grazing spot for travelers through the San Joaquin Valley. Heat, occasional floods and mosquitoes plagued the area, and malaria and typhoid created serious health problems. The town's population was small but within three years would grow to 600.

This was Kern County 100 years ago.

(*Historic Kern*, September, 1966)

Claraville and Sageland
by Steve Ginsburg

In the southern Sierra Nevada twenty miles to the southeast of Kernville are located the remains of two relatively unknown ghost towns, Claraville and Sageland. The two towns are ten miles apart in distance and another 2,500 feet in elevation. Claraville is located in the forested area on Piute Mountain at an elevation of 6,300 feet. Sageland, at 3,800 feet, is in Kelso Creek Canyon, a semi-desert region.

Claraville was the first of the two towns to come into being. The year was 1862. Two prospectors, Robert Palmer and Hamp Williams, discovered gold on the northeastern slope of Piute Mountain. They staked out their claims and organized a mining district called the Mt. Sinai Mining District. Within a few months other miners trekked to the site from Kernville and other towns. A principal mine of the district, the Bright Star, was located seven miles northwest of where the miners made their camp in a flat meadows area, now known as French Meadows.

Supplies and machinery were hauled to the mine over the steep and tortuous Geringer Grade located southeast of the mine and camp. The road began in Kelso Valley and rose to an elevation of

7,000 feet at the summit before dropping down into the meadows. The equipment was hauled over the incline by oxen trains, each having a double wagon and pulled by fifteen to twenty oxen. With such a long train, the road had to be made as straight as possible so that the trains could negotiate the grade. When the trains reached the summit, the wheels were tied together, thus acting as a brake so that the wagons would not run away on the downgrade.

The small camp soon blossomed into a town which was given the name Kelso. However, this name was changed in 1864 to Claraville, after Clara Munckton, the daughter of a miner. The town grew to have all the buildings of a typical mining town, stores, saloons, homes, and a hotel. In 1865 Claraville was the metropolis of Piute Mountain and was the third town in size in Kern County, with only Kernville and Havilah having larger populations. Roads had been built by this time to Havilah, Kernville, and the Mojave Desert. A "courthouse" was erected and the town had its own justice court that year. By the end of 1865 the population had reached more than 500—in only three years' time.

Besides the mining at the Bright Star, there was lumbering and milling in the forested regions of the meadows. Numerous lumber companies cut their timber and many of the companies made Claraville their headquarters.

In early 1866, Palmer and Williams sold their mine to the Pettus Gold and Silver Mining Company of Providence, Rhode Island. The new company built a four-ball quartz crusher and a ten stamp mill to step up production. The ore was quite rich, selling for more than $200 a ton.

Later that year another gold strike was made on Kelso Creek below Claraville. The founders organized the El Dorado Mining District, which included three mines that sparked the boom at what became Sageland. They called the mines the St. John, the Burning Moscow, and the Hortense. A small town with a few stores, saloons and cabins was built in the valley midway between the three mines. By the end of the year, the Sageland population had increased to 200 and there were stages running between Sageland, Claraville, and Havilah.

Promoters of the El Dorado Mining Company built a twelve

stamp mill at one mine, and the Gold Hill Company built a mill of ten stamps at another. The ore was not as rich as that of Claraville, selling for only twenty-five dollars a ton.

Back at the Bright Star, work continued. The Pettus Company sold its holdings to three brothers who continued operations. The three shipped the ore to San Francisco. In mid-1867, more machinery was needed to deepen the shafts, and it happened that their company was bankrupt. The three had drunk up all their profits. The mine closed down. The town started to wither and die. By the end of 1868, Claraville was deserted. Yet its six years of existence had been profitable, for more than $1,000,000 in gold had been taken from the Bright Star Mine.

Sageland was just beginning to enjoy its life. Mining operations went reasonably well at the three mines and life went on rather peacefully. In 1868 the town claimed an opera company, the Sageland Opera Troupe, which performed in the early part of that year for the inhabitants. The town's peaceful existence continued until 1873 when the mines closed and Sageland began to die as had Claraville a few years earlier. By 1874 Sageland was completely dead, too.

Today it is almost impossible to locate the sites of the towns. All that is left of Sageland is the cemetery, situated on a hill above the road. Claraville has a little more to preserve its historic site, including modern cabins and one old building. This last is about a quarter of a mile from the road. The two sites are best reached by a paved road from the small community of Weldon on California Highway 178, twelve and one-half miles east of Isabella. From Weldon it is sixteen miles to the site of Sageland and another nine miles up the steep Harris Grade to the site of Claraville. The general area of summer cabins and homes is known as Pine Cove.

(*Historic Kern*, June, 1962)

Sageland: Its Rise and Fall, 1866-1876
by William Harland Boyd

From a watershed in the Piute Mountains Kelso Creek flows eastward to the base of the range and then northward to the South

Fork Valley. The creek was named for John W. Kelso, who in the mid-1850s hauled freight between Los Angeles and Keyesville. The latter was a Sierra Nevada mining camp which sprang into existence during the Kern River gold excitement of 1854-55. Kelso approached the Sierra Nevada by way of Jawbone Canyon, and then he made his way over a crude road through Kelso Valley and along Kelso Creek to the South Fork Valley.

In 1861 prospectors worked their way into the Piute Mountains and opened the Mount Sinai District near the top of the range. With the rise of mining in this mountain district, Claraville, a trading center, had come into existence by 1866. From Kelso Canyon the steep St. John grade was used by teamsters in hauling supplies to the miners of the Mount Sinai Districts.

Tragedy struck on Kelso Creek in 1863 when Martin Hart, Oliver Burke, Moses Hart, William Dawson, and James Hazlum, who were hauling freight between Los Angeles and the Kern River mines, were attacked by Indians waiting in ambush. Two of the teamsters were killed, while the others barely escaped with their lives.

Some restless Claraville miners in 1866 went on a prospecting trip, and in their ramblings they discovered promising quartz veins near the eastern base of the Piute Mountains. Once their find became known, other miners joined them. The story of El Dorado, the gilded man, had helped lure the Spanish gold-seekers onward in their search for gold. The miners in Kelso Canyon in 1866 formed the New El Dorado Mining District.

The mining settlement which sprang up in the new district at first was called El Dorado Camp, but by 1867 the name had been changed to Sageland. Besides the arrivals who came from Claraville, there soon were at Sageland several who migrated from Havilah, a mining town at the western base of the Piute Mountains. Some of the newcomers engaged in mining, while others opened businesses at the new settlement.

Among the miners who acquired holdings in the New El Dorado District were Felix Serre de St. Jean, Isaac M. Taylor, Thomas Bridger, Charles W. Keeney, Jasper Harrell, Ralph H. Rogers, Henry Hammel, and Andrew H. Denker. Well-known mines of the district included the St. John, Hortense, Burning Moscow, and Italian Lead. Although the first rock was crushed in horse-powered arrastres, by 1867 several stamp mills were in operation in the New El Dorado District.

As Sageland became "alive with visitors and workmen," several business houses were opened. Among the Sageland businessmen were several proprietors of businesses at Havilah who founded branches of their firms in the new settlement, including William G. Sanderson, Jacob Asher, and George H. Bodfish. They were joined by other businessmen who included William F. Weir, George Snow, and Joseph Hoffman. The Telegraph Stage Company, which was already in service between Visalia and such mining towns as Havilah, placed a stage on the route between Havilah and Sageland in 1868.

During the heyday of Sageland it was a boisterous mining camp, and not unlike the typical mining community, much of the social life of the miners was centered in the saloons and gambling halls. Yet the Sageland Opera Troupe was organized in 1868 and gave several performances before well-filled houses of appreciative audiences.

By 1869 the activity in the new El Dorado mines was beginning to decline, and with this came a lessening of the business and social activity at Sageland. In 1872 many of the buildings were moved to the St. John mine, where a small town sprang up. While during its heyday some eight hundred to one thousand miners gathered on Sundays at Sageland, by the mid-1870s, as a newspaperman reported, "scarcely a vestige of the old town remains to mark the spot where it once stood..."

(*Historic Kern*, March, 1969)

On the South Fork
from the *Californian,* May 25, 1895

W. W. Sanders has just planted a small orange grove on the South Fork. He has a sheltered location and has every reason to think they will do well there.

A settler from Owens river, returning from a trip to Hanford, was impressed with the sad results of the alleged depression in the fruit market. He was going back from that rich country better satisfied than ever with the conditions of his frontier home.

Charles Whitlock has a homestead with about 100 acres of good land commanding the outlet to Little Lake, where there is a steady flow of 150 to 200 inches of water. It is on the road from Mojave to Keeler, sixteen miles distant from Salt Wells and seventeen miles from Mt. Spring Canyon. It is 1,000 feet higher than Salt Wells and he thinks 700 or 800 feet fall could be had within eight miles or less. As power is much needed and very expensive at Mt. Spring Canyon, it might be a good enterprise for someone to develop and transmit this power. It would prove a sure enough bonanza on the bonanza lead of Mills and Stiles.

Frank McCutcheson, who is assessing property on South Fork, estimates that there are not less than twenty thousand acres of mesa land there that might be reclaimed by a reservoir system in the mountains and a canal taken out above where the water sinks in the quicksand late in the season. This does not include land in Weldon canyon or on the mesa opposite the home of J. V. Roberts, which is too high to be reached by a canal of moderate cost.

Mr. Thomas Smith has been on South Fork since 1862. By improving available reservoir sites he thinks the irrigating capacity of the river could be increased at least three-fold. There is plenty of mesa land that could be reclaimed. Walker's Pass is on a direct line to Barstow and he expects some road will soon run through that section and doesn't see why they should not run between the river and the point of rocks across the road from his house. He regards the pending and threatened litigation regarding water rights as likely to result in general loss, not to say calamity.

A. C. Wirth has lived twenty-one years in this section and thinks Mr. McCutcheson's estimate of reclaimable mesa land on South Fork none too high. As demonstrated by the half section that A. Brown has watered just west from the Paterson place, it is about the best land in the valley for fruit or alfalfa. These lands are enough above the level of the valley to be in a thermal belt of their own, and comparatively free from frost. Honors gained at Chicago have advertised this as one of the favored apple sections of the United States. Mr. Wirth will plant 400 more trees next spring of selected winter varieties. The Kennedy meadows are a good reservoir site that could be made available at slight cost. The engineer of the Sweetwater dam reported that the Monache meadows would make the second largest reservoir anywhere. Below either of these sites the fall is so rapid that it would be possible to generate a vast power. The main problem is to find a market for this power.

Joseph V. Roberts settled at the head of South Fork in 1860 and has seen the river dry at this place ten or twelve times.

Kennedy meadows are one and one-half to two miles long and one-half mile wide, which would make a good reservoir at moderate costs. The West Fork carries from 1,000 to 2,000 inches of water and is well adapted as a site for water power. The flow is constant and the place very easy of access.

By crossing the river at Kernville and taking the trail leading up the canyon near Frank Thurston's house one saves a great deal of hard climbing in seeing the grand monarch of all our mountains. Stories of trout fishing at the Big Meadows sounds apocryphal. The idea of throwing away hook and line and landing seventeen golden trout at one cast of a barley sack is too much for common credulity.

The road over Greenhorn mountain is being well repaired and will soon be in good condition for travel. After leaving the foothills one will find attractive scenery and many a brook of sparkling mountain water. It is sixty-five miles by way of Glennville to Kernville.

At Glennville Mr. Kromer, recently from Maryland, has a very neat store and a postoffice, accessible from the platform in front. Although this is a mountain town and these are hard times, he is doing a cash business, to the plain advantage of all concerned.

(*Historic Kern*, March, 1958)

Walker Basin
by Eugene Burmeister

Little is known about the early history of Walker Basin. No records are found to tell who first looked down into the rich valley from the surrounding ridges, and few Indians remained there when the first white settlers arrived in 1857. The Kawaiisu of Shoshonean origin and also known as the Plateaus, Paiutes, and Tehachapis had a village in the valley. There they found an early paradise, for the basin had plentiful game, good groves of trees for camping, small lakes and a fine stream for water and fish, and rugged mountains offering protection from enemies. The earliest known pathfinder to the area was Joseph Reddeford Walker, who discovered Walker pass in 1834 on his route east out of the San Joaquin Valley and for whom the pass a few miles northeast of there is named. The basin also got its name from this early explorer as did the famous Joe Walker Mine.

The earliest settlers in Walker Basin were stockmen and farmers, enticed to the valley by its good grass, rich soil, adequate water, and ideal climate. The first to settle there was Charles H. Weick in 1857. A native of Germany, Weick raised a few cattle and farmed at the west end of the basin. After his death January 8, 1873, at the age of fifty, he was buried at his request on a little mound on his ranch.

Weick was followed the next year by the John Becks, the Bob Wilsons, the Blackburns, and three bachelors, William Weldon, Joseph V. Roberts, and Gabriel Lockhart. The March 16, 1859 edition of the *San Francisco Alta California* gives an account of a fisticuffs between Roberts and Lockhart following a disagreement over a dog. Roberts' dog had gone with Lockhart into the woods and stayed there all day. When they returned home in the evening, Roberts thrashed the dog and tied him up. Lockhart then fed the dog and angry words arose, ending in blows between the two bachelors. Roberts and Weldon moved a few years later to South Fork Valley where they went into the butcher business in connection with their stock ranch, supplying meat to the miners along the upper Kern, and where Weldon founded the town named for him.

Abia T. Lightner, Sr., who was born in Pennsylvania in 1801, moved to Keyesville in 1855 from Santa Clara County where he had conducted a Baptist seminary for five years. When he found his mining and milling operations unprofitable, he sold the Mammoth Mine and in 1858 bought land, a three-room adobe house, farming implements, and about one hundred head of Spanish cattle, "little and lean and wild," at the southwest end of the basin from Bob Wilson, who moved to the Fort Tejon area. Lightner raised pota-

Walker Basin in the 1890s.

toes, wheat, and large quantities of alfalfa which he sold at the booming mining town of Keyesville for forty to fifty dollars a ton, and later delivered to the soldiers at Fort Tejon for sixty dollars a ton. He built a grist mill on Basin Creek in 1860 and ground the wheat raised locally on shares. The census of 1860 shows that he had 160 acres of improved land and 80 acres of unimproved, valued at $1,500. His farm implements were valued at $200. He owned three horses, three mules, twelve milk cows, twenty-five beef cattle, and four pigs, with a total value of $1,000. It was while hauling produce to Havilah one frosty morning in 1867 that he lost his life. On a downgrade, his foot slipped from the brake and he was thrown forward under the wagon wheels.

Daniel W. Walser, a native of Missouri, moved from Tulare County to the basin in 1864 where he bought Myron Harmon's hay field from Hamp Williams, who had bought the land from George Walker, and engaged in farming. Harmon, who operated the Summit Sawmill and an ice house on Greenhorn Mountain, had a blacksmith shop in Keyesville. He came to the basin each year and cut the rank hay that grew on the subirrigated meadow in the east end of the valley.

Walser cleared willows from a meadow along Walser Creek, grubbed and broke the soil, erected ranch buildings, and in 1869 set out a fine orchard. He added to his holdings until he owned 2,700 acres. In 1866, he was appointed as one of four commissioners to organize Kern County. His son, John "Cas" Walser, served as sheriff of the county from 1923 to 1935.

A few long-horned Spanish cattle were brought in and turned loose in the hills, but it wasn't until 1867 that the first purebred cattle were introduced to the basin. That year Walker Rankin, Sr., a native of Pennsylvania, arrived, acquired a large amount of land around Caliente and in Walker Basin, brought in the first Herefords, and soon built up a sizeable White Face herd. The following year Rankin married Lavenia E. Lightner, daughter of Abia T. Lightner, Sr., born in Missouri in 1847. Their son, Walker Rankin, Jr., who married Mary Alice Williams, still lives on part of the old Lightner ranch and has followed in his father's footsteps as a rancher and farmer.

Other early basin ranchers included Jim Miller, Pete McGuirk, William H. Johns, and Tom Williams. Williams' son, Nicholas, who was born at Havilah May 25, 1866, just fifty-three days after Kern County was organized from parts of Tulare and Los Angeles counties, was the first white child born in the newly-organized county. When Williams lost his ten stamp mill down the Kern River in the flood of 1867, he moved his family into a small cabin on the Walser ranch where he worked as a ranch hand. The family located a few years later on Thompson Creek and bought a few cows from Walser for ten dollars a head. Nick Williams also followed the ranch business, acquiring 5,500 acres through purchase and homesteading in Walker Basin and on Piute Peak.

The first settlers came to the basin before roads came to the area. Prior to the opening of roads, neighbors got teams and wagons together twice a year for trips to Los Angeles or Visalia for provisions. In either direction the trip was a precipitous one. To the south, they came to one very steep point coming off the Old Lions Trail into what is now Oyler Canyon. There the wagons were lowered by ropes or cables. When they returned from the shopping trip, the wagons were unloaded at the foot of the hill and pulled up to the top, while the contents were packed up on horses. The load was then picked up and hauled home. On August 6, 1863, upon returning to Fort Tejon through Walker Basin from Camp Independence where his troops had been sent to quell the Indians in Owens Valley, Captain Moses A. McLaughlin, Company G, Second Cavalry, California Volunteers, wrote: "From Walker Basin to Aqua Caliente, distance about twelve miles, the road is almost impassable, being obliged to lower the wagons by means of ropes attached to the hind axle tree." David Smith carried the mail on horseback between Visalia and Tejon, passing through the basin, until his death in 1857 when the route was taken over by James Dunlap of Linn's Valley.

By the fall of 1854, a road had been beaten over the divide from Hot Springs Valley to the newly-established gold camp at Havilah and on to the basin. It was mid-1865 before funds solicited from Los Angeles merchants and residents of Elizabeth Lake, Willow Springs, Tehachapi Valley, and Walker Basin opened a road to the south.

Later that year, funds solicited to the north opened a road between Havilah and Visalia. Two years later, in 1867, Colonel Thomas Baker, the founder of Bakersfield, completed Baker Grade, or Baker Toll Road, connecting Bakersfield with Havilah via Walker Basin.

It wasn't until 1875, with the arrival of the Southern Pacific to the railroad terminus at Allen's Camp, which was renamed Caliente by the Southern Pacific, that a road was built between Caliente and the basin. The Oyler Canyon Road, named for John Franklin Oyler, a Keyesville businessman who became Sycamore District road overseer, was owned by Judge Theron Reed, Edwin R. Burke, and John D. Cochran, and was built by Cochran. The group later bought the Baker Toll Road for $1,200 to eliminate competition, but the toll road between Caliente and the basin proved a failure and it was soon sold to the county. The road was improved in 1878.

Several stage lines operated through Walker Basin. The John J. Tomlinson Stage Company established service between Los Angeles and Havilah in 1865. When Tomlinson withdrew service in 1871, interests represented by Samuel Harper took over the line, and in 1871, George Andrews acquired the line. Wells Fargo and Company began express service through Kern County in 1867 with an agency in the basin. The Inyo Stage Line ran from Caliente through the basin to Owens Valley during the 1870s. All of the stage lines were confronted at times with highwaymen, and history records a number of holdups in the Walker Basin area.

Teamsters from Los Angeles hauled supplies through Walker Basin to the new county seat at Havilah. Because of the winter isolation, freight wagons came through in the fall, pulled by as many as ten animals. The suppliers returned in the spring to replenish stocks. With the closing of the mines and the coming of the railroad at Caliente, most of the stage lines ceased operations. Smaller, privately-owned lines continued to haul passengers and freight for some years, however. One of these was the line owned by Nick Williams, who ran a four-horse, two-seated Concord between Walker Basin, Caliente, and Piute from 1906 to 1912. Williams sold out in 1912 to Sam Maxson who put into service one of the first motorized stage lines in the county between Caliente and Kernville via the basin.

With the gold boom at Havilah, along Caliente Creek, and in Walker Basin in the 1860s, the Joe Walker Mine in the Quito Mining District soon became one of the most profitable in the area. It was located in the northeast part of the basin March 20, 1866, by Hamp Williams, father of W. Hamp Williams, discoverer of the "Big Silver" at Randsburg. Finding a rich ledge on the surface, Williams staked a claim, selling it a few days later to Burdett and McKeadney for $2,000. After a 14-foot shaft had been sunk, a third interest was sold to Edwin R. Burke for $12,500. A 350-foot shaft was sunk on a seventy degree angle, the shaft consisting of three compartments. A 100-horsepower steam engine was used to operate the twenty stamp mill, compressors, and hoist. Wood for the boiler was hauled from nearby oak groves. All machinery for the mine was hauled in with oxen through Visalia from San Francisco.

A sizeable settlement sprang up around the mine, known as Joe Walker Town. More than a dozen families comprised the burg, plus at least one hundred single men from the mine. Quite a social event took place in October, 1866, for the inauguration and christening of the new twenty-stamp mill. The *Havilah Courier* of October 29 reported that "Everything navigable was brought into use, stagecoaches, buggies, saddlehorses, and burros were mounted and the cavalcade started . . . 100 persons, including ladies."

A wide, rich vein soon brought profitable returns to the investors with a six-day cleanup netting $12,000. As the shaft was sunk, however, underground water began to create problems. Pumps were installed but were unable to keep ahead of the flow. A Cornish pump, weighing more than eleven tons, was brought in from England via San Francisco and Visalia, but it also failed to keep ahead of the water. The mine was acquired a few years later by Judge P. T. Colby, who hired G. P. Kellogg, long connected with the management of the famous Crown Point Mine in Nevada, as superintendent in November, 1873. It was transferred to Senator J. P. Jones of Nevada in 1876, but he soon abandoned operations. During its operation the Joe Walker produced about $600,000. Idle for some sixty years under the ownership of the Phoebe Hearst estate which had acquired it for a debt, the mine was bought by Dan Cronin in 1939, and assisted by Tom Duffy, operations were begun in 1941. Water again forced its abandonment. More recently, water from the underground river which flows through the mine has been put to profitable use irrigating sugar beets, sorghum, hay, alfalfa, and grazing land in the basin.

Roundups were annual events for the ranchers. The basin and surrounding ranges were unfenced in the early days and cattle roamed at will for miles. Cattle from the basin strayed as far as Rose Station on the plains of the Tejon Ranch and each spring a general drive was made to brand the calves and to push the animals back toward higher country. In late summer the beef cattle were gathered. Then, a four- to five-day drive was made to Bakersfield where beef sold for fifteen to eighteen dollars per head. Later cattle were driven to Caliente and shipped by rail.

The increase in grain acreage prompted Daniel and William Lightner, sons of Abia T. Lightner, to construct a grist mill on Basin Creek near the Weick home in 1869. Grain also was hauled for grinding from South Fork Valley, Kern Island (Bakersfield), and the Tule River area. The two-stone mill was completed in December at a cost of $10,000. Walker Rankin, Sr. was listed as owner. In January, 1870, the first wagon load of flour from the mill arrived in Bakersfield. The mill also supplied the Kernville flour market. By 1871 it had proved so profitable that the Lightner brothers had paid off the debt. The two also ran sheep near Allen's Camp.

About 450 acres of wheat were planted in the basin in 1876, but expectations for a bumper crop were dampened by a killing frost, high winds and hordes of grasshoppers. The wheat yielded only twenty-five bushels per acre. The barley crop was limited, also, to only 200,000 pounds, and potatoes, gardens, and fruit were badly damaged. The year saw the abandonment of efforts to raise fruit there. The basin also had 400 acres of meadow in 1876 of which half was in hay.

A school was established in the basin by the Kern County Board of Supervisors May 10, 1877. It was a one-room school with Miss Cora McGrann as the first teacher. First located on the Lightner ranch, the school was built on skids so it could be pulled by horses or mules to the basin's population center. The Walker Basin School District became part of the Vaughn School District August 8, 1932, later became part of the Twin Oaks School District, and in 1949 joined the Caliente School District.

Walker Basin still holds an air of real western living. Dominated by Piute and Breckenridge mountains, with other alluring peaks and ridges in the distance, it is a land of hay, deer and cool nights. It remains a cattle paradise and many of the ranch holdings are still in the hands of families of the original settlers. In recent years, more and more farming land has taken over what was once grazing land. Barley, oats, alfalfa, and potatoes are among crops now under cultivation, dial telephones have come to the area, a dude ranch is under construction, and there is talk of getting a new road to connect the Southland with the Lake Isabella recreational area, but as yet, the face of the basin has changed little since the first settlers came here more than 100 years ago.

(*Historic Kern*, December, 1964)

S.P. Changes Names of Two Stations
from the *Daily Californian*, December 29, 1905

The Southern Pacific Company has changed the names of two of the stations on the mountain and the change took place Tuesday, a bulletin being posted in the dispatcher's office to that effect. The stations are Girard, which will now be known as Marcel, and Pampa, which will be called Bena. The change was made on account of the names conflicting with those of other stations on the line of the Southern Pacific. In Texas there is quite a large town called Girard and there is also another small place called Pampa. The signs on the stations on the grade will be altered and when the next new time card is issued the new names will appear.

(*Historic Kern*, December, 1976)

Woody Newest Kern County Town
from the *Bakersfield Californian*, July 12, 1909

Joseph Weringer today filed a map with the Board of Supervisors embracing eighty acres of his famous mountain ranch, dedicating streets and roads to the county, and with the well-defined plan of establishing a town to be known as "Woody," and selling in addition to town lots, acreage property for the raising of oranges, lemons, figs, apples and other fruits, all of which mature to perfection in the equable climate of that section.

Mr. Weringer has an ideal mountain ranch, one that is abundantly watered by numerous springs, and for the land that he disposes of he purposes to furnish water for irrigation. The raising of citrus fruits on the Weringer land is no experiment. Around his home place there is a grove of orange and lemon trees, and the fig also thrives wonderfully well there.

The climate of Woody is unsurpassed both in the summer and in the winter seasons, and Mr. Weringer believes that many valley people will be attracted by his offer and that a flourishing little town, surrounded by numerous small orange groves will result from his enterprise. Though in the foothills, the land he offers is level and may be readily irrigated.

The Greenback copper mine, which is located on Mr. Weringer's property, is shortly to be opened up and there is much interest in other copper claims in that locality.

(*Historic Kern*, September, 1975)

Saltdale

This company community began in 1914 when the consolidated Salt Company started operations at Koehn Lake in Fremont Valley. In 1911 and 1912 it was superseded by the Diamond Salt Company.

About 1928 this firm was sold to the Long Beach Salt Company. Since 1950, the Long Beach Salt Company has been a wholly owned subsidiary of the Western Salt Company. In 1916 a post office was established there but moved to Cantil in 1950.

Saltdale is located near the Red Rock-Randsburg Road about thirteen miles west of Randsburg.

(*Historic Kern*, March, 1971)

VII

Bakersfield and Sumner

The location of Bakersfield was determined by the geographical characteristics of the southern end of the San Joaquin Valley and the meandering course of the lower Kern River. Settlers were attracted to the broad, fan-shaped, alluvial plain formed by the Kern River as it emptied into the valley. That plain became known as Kern Island, defined by the several channels of the Kern River. Here was rich, level land where the water of the river could be diverted for irrigation. As the gold boom of the upper Kern lost its luster, both miners and tradesmen saw in Bakersfield a more profitable and permanent site. Settlers from outside the county were attracted by the relatively inexpensive and available land. By 1870, Bakersfield had its own post office and the county's only newspaper. And by 1874, the voters of the county favored Bakersfield over Havilah as the county seat. With the arrival of the Southern Pacific Railroad in 1874, the future of Bakersfield as a growing community was assured.

The Birth of Kern County
by W. Harland Boyd

The creation of a proposed Kern County, redesignated Buena Vista, had been authorized by an act of the state legislature as early as 1855. The new county was not organized, however, in spite of the fact that by a second enactment in 1858 its organization had been extended for a year. The growing importance of the mines in the 1860s, especially after the rise of the Clear Creek district, encouraged those who sought the creation of a new county. At Havilah, early in 1866, a public meeting was held for the purpose of urging the Tulare County members of the state legislature to seek the creation of Kern County. Serving as chairman was William B. Lilly, and as secretary, William L. Kennedy. After he had explained the objective of the meeting, the chairman was authorized to appoint a committee to draft appropriate resolutions and petitions. Among the committeemen were Henry Hammel, Henry D. Bequette, Joseph Caldwell, William Marsh, and Alexander Reid. Soon after, James W. Freeman of Tulare County introduced a bill in the state legislature providing for the creation of Kern County, which, after passage, was signed by Governor Frederick F. Low. Kern County comprised territory formerly included in Tulare and Los Angeles counties, and the county seat was established at Havilah.

The creation of Kern County once assured, politics was in the ascendancy, and the Democrats and Republicans organized their respective county organizations. Candidates were "as numerous as frogs after a thunder shower," wrote a correspondent as the summertime election drew near. When the election of county officials occurred, the Democrats, by substantial majorities, were able to elect a full set of office holders. Henry Hammel, Samuel A. Bishop, and James J. Rhymes were the first county supervisors, although within a few months Bishop resigned and was succeeded by John M. Brite. "Well and nobly done," wrote a Los Angeles journalist, following the election and launching of the county, who welcomed the county into the "sisterhood of counties, and predict(ed) for her at no distant day the proud position of one of the leading counties of the state."

(*Historic Kern*, March, 1956)

The arrival of the San Joaquin Valley Railroad at Bakersfield in 1898 was celebrated with a parade, shown here at the corner of Nineteenth and Chester. The parade was led by the Chinese contingent.

Reminiscences of a Growing City
by George W. Wear

I don't know that I have been here long enough to be able to tell anything regarding the early days of Kern County that would be of interest. I have only been here sixty-three years, and some people—perhaps I among the number—learn but little in that length of time.

However, a few things that come under my observation I retained in memory, and I will try to write them down. In the month of May, 1875, while I was in Los Angeles, I received a telegram telling me to come to Bakersfield as there was a position for me on the *Californian*. I told a chance acquaintance of it and he raised his hands in horror, saying, "Why, you surely don't intend to go to that death hole, do you? No one can live there. It is the sickliest place on earth. Even a fly can't live there." I asked if everybody died there how they disposed of the bodies. He said that newcomers would cast them out and bury them and that in a little time other newcomers would bury those whom they found there and that the wheel of death continued to rotate.

The statement that there were no flies here appealed to me and I decided to come to Bakersfield. But I found the statement about there being no flies here was slightly exaggerated. I found that the population consisted of several hundred families and each family had a large family and that each member of the family also had a large family.

At that time the Southern Pacific railroad was not completed from the north to Los Angeles, there being a gap extending from Caliente—then known as Allen's Camp—to San Fernando, but work was being pushed on both ends.

I boarded the train at Los Angeles, transferred to a stage at San Fernando, crossed the desert and mountains to Caliente and took the train for Bakersfield. My trip on the stage was one to be remembered. An old style concord coach, at some points drawn by four horses, at others by six animals, and others by eight. There were eighteen passengers on the stage, a number of them riding on the top of the vehicle. I happened to get a place on the driver's seat. When we entered the desert we ran into the worst sandstorm that I have ever experienced. At times the horses could not face it and would stop until the blast had passed. Mojave consisted of a large crude barn, where relay horses were kept, and nothing more.

We came down the mountains in the dark, the horses on a run. Being tired out from the long ride, I went to sleep holding to the guard rail of the seat, and nearly fell off the stage, but the driver caught my arm and pulled me back on the seat with the admonition, "Look out, young man, if you fall off you will perhaps land a thousand or more feet below." I kept awake the remainder of the trip to Caliente.

Arriving at Bakersfield, I took a room at the James Hotel, conducted by H. P. Olds, a very nice little place as frontier accommodations went, but scarcely up to the Waldorf-Astoria. After removing the grime and sand which I had accumulated on my trip over the desert and mountains as best I could, using the pint of water which the pitcher contained, I went to bed and slept the sleep of the innocent.

When I came down in the morning there was an argument or controversy going on between Mr. Olds and a 240-pound man. "I don't understand," said the 240-pounder, "why you charge me nine dollars a week for board when you charge the others seven dollars." "Why," said Olds, "you are so large that if I charged you less I would lose on you." "Oh," said Mr. Obese, "you charge according to size, do you? Now, there is that little shrimp over there that would not weigh more than ninety pounds. I suppose you charge him less than seven dollars." "No," said Olds, "the food is before him and if he doesn't eat it, it is up to him."

After breakfast I struck out in search of the *Californian* office, which I found at the point where Lowell Store now is (1516 Nineteenth Street). The paper was owned and edited in a fiery manner by Julius Chester, a man who by reason of vitriolic editorials had aroused the enmity of numbers of people, but whom, to this day, I regard as one of the best friends that I ever had.

There were two papers, the *Californian* and the *Courier*, both owned by Julius Chester, he editing the first named, but he had given control of the *Courier* to J. S. Brittain, the latter to pay the expenses and receive the profits of the paper. But from some cause

Brittain failed to pay the expenses and every Saturday night Chester would pay the wages of the employees of both papers. The only property that I ever knew of Brittain owning was a horse, and in confidence he one day told me that he was going to sell the animal as he needed money. I asked him how much he expected to get for it, and he said ten dollars.

I found the *Californian* a typical cross-road plant. A Washington hand press worth perhaps $250, about $40 worth of type, a couple of high stools, and the essential office towel, so black and stiff with dried ink that it stood in the corner of the room. The press that we used in the early days had a capacity of about 300 copies an hour. The old *Californian* was a four-page affair with a circulation of about 300 copies.

When I first came here I was told that editing a paper in California was a dangerous occupation, as someone was liable to shoot one of the editor's eyes out at any time, but I never found it so. After working for Chester for several years, I took charge of the paper and afterwards I published the *Gazette* for twenty years or more. The nearest I ever came to getting obliterated was when an irate candidate for office whom I was opposing breezed into the office and in no uncertain manner announced that if I ever said another word in the paper against him he and I could not both live in the same state. A tramp printer showed up and I put him to work and the next issue of the paper had little else than articles denouncing Mr. Candidate. I found him a man of truth, as I am still living in this state and he is not.

But what about Bakersfield in the early days of its existence? When I arrived the town had a population of four or five hundred people. The business center from Nineteenth Street and Chester Avenue extended about two blocks to the north, south, east, and west, with more vacant than occupied lots intervening. P. Galtes and George B. Chester had mercantile establishments where overalls and other coarse goods as well as barbed wire, nails, and some other articles might be obtained. The post office was behind the counter of a corner of Chester's store. Dr. Bratton had a drug store which was superintended by J. C. Drury, and if you called for some remedy Mr. Drury would tell you that he didn't have it, but that he had something just as good. The town had a school, the building thirty feet square being located at Eye Street at about Fifteenth Street. There was one teacher and about fifteen pupils. Quite often the pupils, on going to the school building, would fail to meet the teacher, as he was off holding a conference with John Barleycorn. On other occasions the teacher would find no pupils in attendance as they had taken a few days off for fishing or other amusements. The town had a livery stable, blacksmith shop, barber shop, brewery, perhaps a dozen saloons, several professional men, and several unsavory dancehalls, as well as two or three other places called hotels.

There were no street lights and no sidewalks. A sprinkling cart threw a light shower of water on the main streets daily. But the reputation Bakersfield had attained as an unhealthy place was not undeserved as fever was prevalent during the summer months and no one escaped. It was not a fatal disease, though it was severe.

The population of Bakersfield and Kern County increased very slowly, and there was hardly a perceptible change until oil was discovered, and then people came by the thousands, and now the once insignificant village shows up as a wonderful and still growing city.

I had been in California but a short time when I came to Bakersfield, and many things were new to me. When I went to the hotel for dinner the day after my arrival the menu announced a number of desserts, among them being "Captain Jack Pudding." I was familiar with a number of puddings but the "Captain Jack" was an unknown variety to me, but I was young and anxious to learn and ordered it, and was served with a chunk of decidedly coarse corn-bread covered with molasses. Then I knew what Captain Jack Pudding was.

Chinatown was located close to the hotel, and when I retired that night I heard what to me was a confused jumble of sounds coming from Chinatown. I went to the open window and listened. I decided that it was some kind of a musical instrument, but was uncertain if it was someone wrestling with his first lesson in music or a skilled professor giving the Chinese national anthem. I learned afterwards that the instrument was a Chinese fiddle.

While we did not have the many means of entertainment those days that have developed since, we nevertheless enjoyed ourselves. We had picnics, shows, dances, buggy rides and some other forms of entertainment, and on one occasion five horse thieves were taken from the jail and hanged. Some historian has said there were six. I say five, and I should know as I saw them hanging, and I have the name of each and every one of them.

Editor's Note: This article was written for the Kern County Historical Society October 25, 1937 by the late George Wallace Wear, who was born February 28, 1852, in Mississippi. Mr. Wear arrived in Bakersfield in May, 1875 to take a position on the *Southern Californian.* The *Californian* and the *Courier* were combined in May, 1876, and on October 1, 1878, Mr. Wear became head of the mechanical and business department of the *Courier-Californian.* Later Mr. Wear became the publisher for the *Gazette*, which had been established October 30, 1875, by John F. Linthicum.

(*Historic Kern*, March, 1964)

Bishop's Narrative—November, 1881
Old Mexico and Her Lost Provinces
by William H. Bishop (1889)

Bakersfield, capital of Kern County, seventy-five miles farther south, somewhat smaller than Visalia, boasted at one time the distinction of a malady peculiar to itself. The Bakersfield form of malarial fever, whatever the fine difference that distinguished it from others, had a position apart in the medical works. The sanitary condition of the place, however, has been greatly improved by the extension of drainage and irrigation works, and can, no doubt, be made all that could be desired.

Bakersfield takes its tone essentially from livestock. It has special resorts for drovers and sheepherders. Its streets are generally full of horses, caparisoned in the Spanish style, tied to hitching posts and awaiting their owners before the stores and taverns. The sheepherders, a lonely race, become morose and melancholy in their long wanderings with their flocks apart from the habitations of men and human speech. They are far removed from the shepherds of Boucher and Watteau. Some are said to go insane through the monotony of their lives; and it is an occupation taken up only as a last resort, and unfitting him who pursues it for any other. Strangely enough, there is a rather English tone among them. Young prodigals of good family are found who, after trying their fortunes in Australia, India, and elsewhere, are eating the husks of repentance here in true Scriptural fashion.

The shops in Bakersfield, as throughout our travels, are kept principally by the Jews, who are great pioneers. No people are growing up more ardently with the new West; and where they are found business is pretty sure to be good.

The Chinatown is a district of compact little streets, of an extent that indicates a population almost equal to that of the rest of the place. An irrigating ditch surrounds it like a moat. The cabins along this, picturesquely reflected in it, are gray and weather-beaten, varied with patches of bright Orientalism, and shaded by a line of tall poplar-trees. The Spanishtown, close by, is a cluster of dance-houses and corrals, between which swarthy Joses and Juanitas are seen passing.

As if this were not foreignness enough already, we stumble upon a camp of strolling gypsies, their tents pitched on the borders of Spanishtown. They are English, and have come from Australia, dropping their "h's" all along the way, no doubt, as liberally as here. They are like types of Cruikshank and Dickens. An apple-faced Mrs. Jarley appears in a large velvet bonnet with plumes. A very tightly-dressed, slender individual, with a weed on his hat, might pass for Sam Weller. He is a horse-tamer and jockey. At his heels follows a belligerent bulldog. Behind one of the tents a child of nine, Cassie by name, with fine, dark eyes, is making a toilet before a bit of cracked mirror. She pastes down her wet hair into a semblance of the "water-waves" of fashionable society. When interrupted with a compliment on the arrangement she affects displeasure, and tosses it all abroad again with a native coquetry.

(*Historic Kern*, September, 1977)

Bakersfield
by A.J.H. (probably A. J. Hanson, Methodist minister)
from the *Bakersfield Courier*, October 24, 1874

At the extreme southern limit of the great San Joaquin Basin lies the subject of this sketch, a town of growing importance for the section of California in which it is located. Nearly three hundred and fifty miles by rail from San Francisco, and far removed from other centers of traffic, it seems almost out of the world to him who has never paid it a visit. Los Angeles is 150 miles southward, Santa Barbara, 90 westward, and Visalia, 75 northward. Yet we are here in civilization and constantly behold faces that but a few days since were seen in San Jose or San Francisco, and but just a moment ago there came to the ear the familiar whistle of a passing locomotive, drawing its freighted train across the magnificent railroad bridge which spans the Kern River.

Step on the train which leaves San Francisco at four p.m. and by ten a.m. of the next day you will be delivered safe and sound at our Bakersfield depot... After a wearisome ride over one broad expanse of dry, sun-browned plain, it is quite refreshing to enter a place green and luxuriant with the vegetation of a semi-tropical climate... Low and moist, it becomes hot and somewhat malarious in summer months, yet as cultivation is bestowed and a thick growth of willow underbrush cleared away, less trouble is experienced and in time the place can be made quite as healthy as any other in a similar situation.

Some 700 inhabitants compose the town, and of these quite a large number are Spanish and Chinese. Our American citizens have gathered here from various parts of California, as the history of the place extends back but four or five years, and but few from older states have found their way directly to this spot. Active, enterprising and respectable people are these, who occupied the best social position in other places and are here endeavoring to make pleasant society for themselves and children.

The county seat has been recently transferred to this place from Havilah, a mining town some forty miles distant, and we are favored with the presence of the various officials of the body politic. A court house costing $30,000 is to be erected soon, and that will add to the significance of the town.

Our M. E. Church has been erected within the last year, costing about $1,800, but still unfinished on the inside. When complete, it will be a very neat structure, accommodating between 200 and 300 worshippers. Ours is the only church publicly represented at present, though we learn our Presbyterian friends expect to organize ere long, and that Catholics design to erect a place of worship shortly. We need religious teachers, so let them come and do what good they can.

Here are published two weekly papers of good character, the *Kern County Courier* and the *Southern Californian*, so that our appetite for news is entirely appeased.

There is a bank in town with moderate capital, which serves the purpose of trade quite well.

In the way of entertainment there is a brass band, which furnishes music of a very respectable character, while a circulating library furnishes considerable reading matter at moderate cost.

Seven or more saloons are in full blast, and sending out constant streams of moral (?) influence. There is a brewery in town; so unfailing fountains of lager beer gush out in our midst. No want of the necessaries of life, you will perceive.

Prices are high, board still higher, and money scarce, though business is becoming better as the cool weather approaches. When winter is upon us, rain falls in the valley and snow covers the mountain heights nearby; no spot in California can be more attractive.

(*Historic Kern*, September, 1958)

China Grade

China Grade is a mystery to most folks of the Bakersfield area. They surmise that it has something to do with Chinese, but beyond that, fancy runs wild. The truth is somewhat prosaic.

Back in the 1870s, not long after the first Chinese came to Bakersfield, watercress was discovered growing in wild profusion on the slope of a hill near the Kern River. This hill, which we now call the Bluffs, topped by Panorama Drive, was steep and no paths led to where the watercress grew. So the Chinese made a path, which they gradually widened. Years later, when a highway was built here, it closely followed the original track made by the Chinese. As a result, this section of the road came to be called "China Grade."

An automobile race was run over this course in July, 1911, in which a number of noted drivers participated. Sections of oil well casing were driven into the ground to keep the drivers from going over the edge. Portions of them still remained on the uphill grade for many years.

(Historic Kern, December, 1980)

Sumner, a Place Almost Mythical
by Henry Raub

Mesa Station, the short-lived Southern Pacific train stop on the north bank of the Kern River, welcomed its first steam passenger train from Lathrop on August 1, 1874. This was the end of the line until the river was bridged, so it was "All out for Bakersfield, Fort Independence, Panamint and Los Angeles." From here on passengers rode stage, wagon or horse.

While two steam pile drivers drove aromatic Oregon fir timbers into the muddy bottom of the sluggish Kern River, bridge mechanics sawed and hammered into place the supports and cross pieces that lengthened the new railroad bridge. Two miles to the east men cleared and prepared the site for the railroad depot to serve the Bakersfield area. The depot marks the intersection of Sumner and Baker streets today.

The *Courier* editor, in spite of his personal feelings regarding the railroad company's selection of a spot not in the town of Bakersfield of that day, tried to objectively describe the site. He wrote that it was an "entirely uninhabited plain of treeless, waterless and barren soil. This location, although not so close to town as many might desire, yet is as near as the company would have placed it consistent with the possession of vast elbow room it professes to require..." Southern Pacific wishes today it had twice as much "elbow room."

At this time, according to the *Courier*, Chinese laborers again began appearing in Southern Pacific track construction gangs in Kern County. Apparently the memory of the cholera terror at Delano had faded sufficiently for Charley Crocker to send down more than a hundred Cantonese to help grade the desolate stretch eastward from the heretofore secret station site.

Ten days after the last construction worker stepped off the completed railroad bridge, the first passenger train rumbled resoundingly over the solid wooden structure. With bell clanging it wheezed and creaked to a stop at a spot north of town, probably where Chester Avenue crosses the rails today. The travelers alit to find buckboard transportation into Bakersfield, a mile south. County road equipment hastily opened a road from town to the new railroad.

Among the new arrivals from the East, many "had the means and leisure to flee the icy winter of the Eastern states to bask . . . in the equable, temperate and spring-like temperature of this country."

One train traveler, a writer for *Christian Advocate* magazine, described Bakersfield as "so far removed from other centers of traffic that it almost seems out of the world to him who has never paid it a visit."

Mesa depot building may hold the world's record for serving as a railroad station for the shortest period of time in railroad history. Carpenters started dismantling it for removal to the new Bakersfield area depot site as soon as trains began unloading freight and passengers on the eastern end of track already mentioned. Meanwhile, men skilled in moving buildings hauled the Tipton station building down from Tipton to the new station site where they combined it with the Mesa station house.

Tracklayers completed the rail line to the strange new depot and prepared sidings by October 26 when the first combination passenger and freight train chugged up alongside the loading platform. The company announced regular scheduled passenger service November 10, 1874, with trains arriving at 7 a..m. and departing at 9 p.m. for the return trip.

Around the depot flimsy shanties popped up on lots purchased by persons attending Southern Pacific land sales. Most lots measured 24 feet by 150 feet.

It was about time that the natives in Bakersfield should be shook by a bombshell, and Southern Pacific had the bomb.

One morning some bystanders looked up and saw the name SUMNER boldly lettered on the depot building. One historian claims the railroad company named the station in honor of one of its vice-presidents. Regardless, the fat was in the fire.

The *Courier*'s editor stated that the railroad had attempted to extinguish the name of Bakersfield by calling "our station, Sumner... a place almost mythical." He shoveled scorn on the "sorely disappointed Sumner citizens" who had been led to believe the "business of Bakersfield would soon center around them." With monstrous sarcasm he drew attention to the main attraction in "the Sumner lava beds" that consisted "in the arrival of a load of water from the Kern Island Irrigating Canal which is an occasion of no little excitement and constitutes quite a break in the general monotony of things."

"Sumner, as a town, is an abortion," editorially shouted the infuriated journalist after taking three deep breaths to ward off immediate apoplexy. The hated name of Sumner, however, stuck for many moons until it became Kern City, East Bakersfield, and lastly Bakersfield.

(*Historic Kern*, September, 1969)

East Bakersfield Vignette
by Richard C. Bailey

East Bakersfield came into existence in 1874 when the Southern Pacific Railroad laid out a town plat which they named Sumner. The S.P. had originally intended to run its line through Bakersfield, but an argument over property bordering the right of way ended in a bitter impasse. Rail officials determined to "fix" Bakersfield. They would build their own town and leave the Kern Island politicians out on a limb.

The company town of Sumner was soon laid out and christened. Bakersfield merchants nervously gnawed their mustaches at the loss of the railroad; there was little else they could do. But the relationship between the older town and the up-start community was not entirely broken. In 1887 a horse car rail line service was inaugurated between the county courthouse in Bakersfield and the Southern Pacific depot in Sumner.

The little town, aided by its position as a rail point, continued to grow and was soon incorporated in 1893 under the new name of Kern, or Kern City as it was also called. The Southern Pacific agent, W. V. Matlock, became the first mayor, with A. W. Marion, city clerk; George M. Whitaker, marshal; John F. Dugan, treasurer; and Thomas J. O'Boyle, recorder. Ben Ardizzi became the first postmaster.

The next year, 1894, saw the establishment of the first fire department, a volunteer organization with headquarters in a small wooden building near the northwest corner of Sumner and Baker streets. M. J. Benson was its first chief.

The early business section encompassed four blocks. Stores and other establishments extended a block east and west of Baker on Sumner facing the railroad track, and continued one block south of Sumner on Baker, taking in both sides of the street.

Perhaps the oldest store in Kern was that owned by Amy and Ardizzi, later Ardizzi and Olcese. Among the earliest hotels were the Central, Lindsay, Noriega and Verdier. The general stores owned by J. J. Murphy and the partners, Dugan and Ryan, were other pioneer firms. For those interested in recreation and refreshments there was Conrad Richmond's saloon, bar and dance hall on Baker Street.

But all was not sweetness and light. The year 1893 saw Kern City holding an anti-Chinese meeting for the purpose of removing the threat of Chinese labor from the community, but the movement seems to have fizzled out after a brief period of shouting and arm waving. Next year the "Great Railroad Strike" occurred which was broken by General Wm. R. Shafter of later Spanish-American War fame. Local trainmen had struck in sympathy with railmen in Illinois, and since ice was brought in from Truckee by rail at this time, local saloons were forced to sell warm beer to their customers until traffic was resumed.

(*Historic Kern*, December, 1976)

Virginia Colony

In September, 1888, Henry W. Klipstein concluded a visit to Kern County, and returned to his home in Virginia, where he enthusiastically reported on the bright economic prospects for Kern County. Not only did he determine to move to Kern County, but he also encouraged his Virginia neighbors to join him in the move. In January, 1889, Klipstein settled on land near East Bakersfield, and soon several of his Virginia neighbors had followed him to Kern County. In the fall of 1889 the newcomers established "The Virginia Colony." It was reported in January, 1890, that three hundred acres of land had been sold in the colony to twenty different purchasers, who acquired an average of fifteen acres each. By then the settlers were busy clearing the land of sagebrush in preparation for the planting of trees, vines, and alfalfa.

(Historic Kern, December, 1975)

Bakersfield's Public Utilities
by W. Harland Boyd

Late in 1860 San Francisco and Los Angeles were linked by the Pacific and Atlantic Telegraph Company whose line passed through the foothills east of the future Bakersfield. Early in 1869 J. Newton Ewing, who was in charge of the local facilities, established a telegraph office at Bakersfield. In the 1870s, after several consolidations and changes in name, the firm became a part of the Western Union Telegraph Company.

Bakersfield was afforded telephone service late in 1888 by the Sunset Telephone and Telegraph Company, with Charles E. Tyler in charge of a small exchange. The company's original twenty telephones had increased to nearly sixteen hundred by 1904. Late in 1906 the Bakersfield firm was absorbed into the newly-formed Pacific Telephone and Telegraph Company.

In mid-1875 the Bakersfield trustees, during a short-lived period of incorporation, enfranchised the Kern Island Irrigating Company to supply water for "agriculture, manufacture, and domestic uses." The firm was authorized to dig ditches along the streets and alleys

Bakersfield street scene before the Fire of 1889.

and regulate the use of the water. The water was used mostly to irrigate trees, lawns, and gardens, while domestic water was drawn from private wells.

By the early 1880s some of the wells were becoming polluted with surface water, which resulted in a bad-tasting water and a presumed source of disease. A group of businessmen, among whom was William H. Scribner, formed the Bakersfield Water Company. Their water system, consisting of a steam pump, water tower, and distribution facilities, was completed late in 1883. Double the number of expected customers asked for water service as the system was being placed in operation.

In mid-1897 the Electric Water Company, a subsidiary of the Kern County Land Company, began to furnish water to customers living in the western quarters of Bakersfield. In the following year this firm absorbed the Bakersfield Water Company, and the Electric Water Company, in turn, was sold to the California Water Service Company early in 1927.

The Bakersfield Gas and Electric Light Company was organized late in 1888, and, under the management of Leonard P. St. Clair, began operating with fifty-two gaslight customers early in 1889. At first the company produced gas from naptha, but within a few months the gas was being extracted from coal. In mid-1890, after the installation of poles and wires, along with a steam-powered generator, the company lighted the downtown streets, and later in that year business firms were afforded electric service. The generating facilities were improved in mid-1892, at which time electric power was afforded the homeowners of Bakersfield.

Early in 1897 the Power Development Company completed work on a hydroelectric power plant located on the Kern River, at the mouth of Kern Canyon. The Power, Transit, and Light Company, formed late in 1902, acquired both the Power Development Company and the Bakersfield Gas and Electric Light Company. Early in 1911 the Power, Transit, and Light Company was merged with the San Joaquin Light and Power Company, which, in turn, early in 1939 was absorbed into the Pacific Gas and Electric Company.

(*Historic Kern*, December, 1968)

The Kern County Courthouse in Bakersfield after its reconstruction in 1896.

Southern Hotel
by W. Harland Boyd

"Our hotel accommodations have long been insufficient and unavoidably not of a nature to be attractive to the better class of guests," stated the *Kern County Californian* in September, 1887. By then the Southern Hotel Association had been formed with a capitalization of $100,000, by a group of Bakersfield businessmen, whose secretary was Celsus Brower. Architectural drawings for the new hotels were prepared by Benjamin G. McDougall and Son of San Francisco and San Diego. The site selected for the three-story building was on the northwestern corner of Nineteenth Street and Chester Avenue. The first story was designed for businesses, and the upper two stories, containing eighty-four rooms, all supplied with hot and cold water, were to be used for hotel purposes. As the building was being completed, it was stated that "from the foundation-stone to the tip of the golden dragon's spear" the structure was "substantial and durable, a mold of fashion and graceful form." The bay window at the corner was "the largest of its kind in the state," and it added "beauty to the structure." Contractor William J. Doherty had almost completed the hotel when it was described as "a lasting monument to the sturdy courage of certain . . . citizens" who had earned "the right to be called men of public spirit." The Southern Hotel Association formally accepted the building in March, 1889.

Bakersfield businessmen sensed that their town was about to enter an era of great material progress, but then a disastrous fire in July, 1889, destroyed the business section of the town. In spite of the staggering financial losses, the businessmen, including the proprietors of the Southern Hotel, set out to develop a bigger and better downtown Bakersfield. Many decades later, in 1947, the Southern Hotel was demolished to make way for a modern building.

(*Historic Kern*, September, 1975)

First Television Station West of Mississippi River
by Paul Biermann

KPMC is celebrating its twentieth year as a radio station here in Bakersfield. Before that, it was television. Not the same as the TV that is seen here by thousands today, but still it was television and some of the old-timers thought it was the best kind of entertainment in this part of the state. In those early experimental days of 1932, people came from a great distance to watch the television near the present studios of KPMC on East Twenty-first Street. It was a mecca for the curious—it was home to a handful of performers who knew they were in a strictly pioneering venture. The television efforts of the early founders of KPMC were well recognized as the first of their kind west of the Mississippi.

But television and radio as they are known now were farthest from the dreams of the Schamblin boys, Frank, Leo and Charlie. It all started out as a backyard hobby of Frank Schamblin who is now the general manager of the Pioneer Mercantile Company, a hardware-automotive firm that has stores in Fresno and Taft, as well as three in Bakersfield. Frank Schamblin had collected all the paraphernalia he could find and worked quietly yet effectively to make the parts fit together and produce something. It wasn't long before the local efforts came to the attention of Lee DeForest, who is now called "father of modern radio." DeForest was here on the west coast when he heard about the experimental television efforts of the Schamblin boys. He made a trip to Bakersfield from Los Angeles. Then as he saw what was happening he became more interested and the trips were more frequent. DeForest actually worked for a while as a consultant to the local television station. Chief engineer in those days was the late Ralph Lemert.

Despite the unbounded interest of individuals, it soon became apparent that much more development was needed by men much more highly skilled before television would be seen and enjoyed by everybody. Old-fashioned scanning discs would never become popular in living rooms of the nation. When the limitations were recognized here, the Schamblin yen for the entertainment field turned to radio. In 1933, the local application for a commercial radio station was filed with the proper authorities. It was not long before a broadcast license for the only high fidelity radio station of the region was granted. W6XAI was on the air commercially. About eighteen months later, there was a uniformity worked out for naming radio stations and the present call letters were adopted. KPMC has been known by that name ever since. K is the designation for stations west of the Mississippi. PMC stands for the initials of Pioneer Mercantile Company, which still controls the destiny of the station. Control is still in the hands of the Schamblin family, but Leo Schamblin has now taken over as general manager of radio. He moved up when Frank took over as guide of the destinies of the hardware and automotive outlets. All three brothers combine talents frequently for company decisions. A sister has stock in the company but lives in Southern California with no personal part in station management.

Somewhat unique in the radio industry where rapid personnel turnover is taken for granted, KPMC can boast a longer work record per employee than most stations in the nation. Curt Sturm has been on the staff as assistant manager for longer than this was a radio station. He joined the staff in the waning days of the first local television effort. There are others on the staff who have worked more than ten years for KPMC. Company loyalty has been fostered through good management and liberal wages.

KPMC went on the air commercially at first with a starting time of noon and a closing time of 10 p.m., but that soon changed to the present eighteen hours a day from 6 in the morning till midnight. At first, there was a staff of only seven employees including engineers, office help, announcers and entertainers. That has grown to the present staff of fourteen. On the staff have been some of the well-known people of the community—and some people who went on to greater fame in the radio industry. Ralph Kreiser of the *Californian* was the first news editor of KPMC, to be followed by Murray Arnold, now also with the *Californian*. Bill Whiting, now head of the Kern County radio communications system, was at one time an engineer for this station. Richard Bailey, now assistant Kern County museum director, once had a regular program giving historical background of the county and the valley. Beth Henley once gave regular book reviews on KPMC—she now works for the *Californian*. City Fire Chief Phil Pifer and Sam Pinnell of the city fire department, together with Cliff Baughman of the county health department, developed a program of "civic talks" designed to tell people what the various departments of city and county government were supposed to do. Dick Wynn worked as announcer for KPMC—then joined the networks as the announcer for the "Cisco Kid." Bill Woodson was an announcer on the local staff. Woodson is now heard in the part of the "Count" in the "Count of Monte Cristo." He is also the narrator on "This Is Your FBI."

Never on the staff but on the air on KPMC were such people as Spade Cooley, who made his first appearance on radio on this station, the late Ben Bernie and the late Walter Huston. Max Baer made a few guest appearances here. So did Joel McCrea. And there were many others who have been heard on KPMC as they flashed through the local spotlight through the years.

(*Historic Kern*, March, 1954)

Beale Clock Tower
by Chris Brewer

The Beale Clock Tower, long a familiar Bakersfield landmark, originally stood in the intersection of Seventeenth Street and Chester Avenue, in downtown Bakersfield. This picturesque brick structure, standing some sixty-four feet high, was modeled after a Moorish tower seen in Spain by Truxtun Beale. He was the son of General Edward F. Beale, the long-time owner of the large Tejon Ranch in the Tehachapi Mountains. Truxtun Beale donated the clock tower to the city in memory of his mother, Mary Edwards Beale, in 1904. The clock mechanism was built by Seth Thomas, and the time was indicated by hands on lighted five-foot dials, as well as by the ringing of a thousand pound bell. For forty-eight years the clock gave reliable service, but then disaster struck when a series of earth tremors hit the southern San Joaquin Valley in July and

August, 1952. Before a hastily organized Beale Clock Tower Restoration Committee could act, the Bakersfield City Council ordered that the tower should be dismantled.

Subsequently civic-minded citizens restored the Beale Clock Tower on the grounds of the Kern County Museum, using as much as possible of the salvageable material from the original structure. The ground breaking ceremony was held in May, 1961, and in December, 1964, the completed phoenix-like structure was dedicated. Once again the citizens could point with pride to one of the best-known symbols of Bakersfield.

(*Historic Kern*, June, 1978)

VIII

Valley Towns

The founding of Kern County towns in the southern part of the San Joaquin Valley followed agricultural development, railroad building, and oil activity. Bakersfield had its beginnings as a farming community, located where the abundant waters of the Kern River met the rich, alluvial soil of the valley. In several cases, towns were started and promoted by large land companies. Thus, Miramonte and Smyrna were promoted by Haggin, Tevis, and Carr in the 1880s; Rosedale Colony and Shafter by the Kern County Land Company; and Buttonwillow by Miller and Lux. Among other efforts to sell land after the turn of the century was that of the Home Extension Society, the promoters of Wasco Colony, and the Edison Land and Water Company, which developed a "citrus belt" on the mesa east of Bakersfield. After the railroad arrived in the 1870s, the Southern Pacific founded Delano, Sumner, and Caliente. Following the 1899 discovery of oil in the Kern River field near Bakersfield, oil activity spread westward. Within a decade the oil economy had given birth to booming towns like Maricopa, Taft, McKittrick, and Lost Hills.

San Emigdio Indian Village
by Barbara B. Gray

The village of San Emigdio where the Spaniards battled in 1824 was about three miles north of present ranch headquarters. Probably this village existed for a great length of time as the site provided water, trees and a natural gateway into the San Joaquin Valley. In 1889 Dr. C. A. Rogers of Bakersfield attended a sick woman at the rancho. Not far from the mouth of the San Emigdio Canyon, he said, there was a village of twenty-five or thirty neat adobe houses, some stained blue; and a church, not distinctly mission type but evidencing considerable age. Leopold Vignave had a store at the south end of the settlement, and there were two graveyards nearby. Godey told of the vaqueros who came from far and near to attend the fiestas in the village, dressed in their best. Old vaqueros had tales of how they happened to come to the San Joaquin Valley.

"Many came *de huida* (in flight), others to make their homes, and some by mistake. J. J. Lopez missed the San Fernando Mission where he was to meet its majordomo and came to San Emigdio where Alex Godey sent him to Tejon."

Rows of poplar, cottonwoods, and figs shaded the homes of the Mexicans and Indians who lived here, while abundant water irrigated small vegetable gardens. Thirteen families lived on the sides of the creek and in the '90s Kern County Land Company acquired the interest of the people and to hurry natural disintegration of the buildings took off the roofs. Some buildings still stood in 1930 but now only a scar marks the village of San Emigdio.

Today Kern County Land Company's San Emigdio Ranch is several times as large as the Spanish grant, although retaining its name.

(*Historic Kern*, September, 1957)

Delano: Random Notes
by Cecil Dyar

Delano is ninety-one years old in 1964 and will have been incorporated fifty years in 1965.

When the surveyors of the Central Pacific Company reached the area of which Delano is now a part, they saw miles and miles of nothing but prairie covered with sagebrush and wild feed. Now and then there were probably a few deer. Waterfowl from the great Tulare Lake were still numerous. The Indian had long since gone to the reservation and his fading trails were now used by the sheep and cattle men. If the surveyors' vision ranged far enough they might have seen an occasional willow or cottonwood tree along the dry beds of White River, Poso Creek or Rag Gulch.

After much political maneuvering and by an act of Congress on June 28, 1870, Section 11, Range 25, Township 25 Mount Diablo Base Meridian (Delano Townsite) was deeded to the Contract and Finance Company, a holding company for the Southern Pacific Railroad. This transaction was handled through Columbus Delano, the secretary of the interior at the time. It was signed by President U. S. Grant. The railroad did not patent the land, however, until March 4, 1881.

It is generally accepted that the first construction crews reached the Delano townsite from the north early in June, 1873. The rails followed close behind because the construction crews could not go far ahead because of the lack of water. It has been said by historians that at the time there was not a house or well within thirty miles of the place. Water was taken from Kings River and transported by rail in water cars.

This same lack of water caused the only settlers in the area to live along the edge of the foothills where water was easier to obtain from springs and mountain creeks. Among the pre-railroad settlers were Harry Quinn, Joel McMillen, Colonel Chin, Archibald Leitch, John T. Clark, and J. V. Caldwell.

The *Bakersfield Courier* on July 19, 1873 carried an ad by the Southern Pacific Railroad that service would be available from Delano after July 14, 1873, and that trains would leave regularly at 12:20 a.m. and 8:30 p.m. The depot had been built and the town officially named "Delano" in honor of Columbus Delano.

The rails stopped at this point, probably because the Depression of 1873 tied up the assets of the Southern Pacific's "Big Four." The construction had used about six hundred men, mostly Chinese, to get to Delano. It started south again a year and fifteen days later with one hundred men and thirty teams. Sixty Chinese died of cholera during the stopover and are buried in the local cemetery.

Delano thus became a railroad terminal, a sheep shearing center and a shipping point for wool, wheat and ore. As all boom towns, it literally was thrown up overnight, but remained for some time a Chinese camp, composed mainly of tents and box cars sitting on a siding. Several water cars were always on hand. The townsite was not surveyed until 1887 and before that time people just put up their shack or place of business any place that looked good to them. The first actual lease found recorded was not granted until 1883—ten years after the founding.

Bakersfield newspapers of the time did their best to pacify the citizens of their city by not publicizing the business boom going on in Delano. Many of the old history books have done the same thing by limiting the history of Delano to only one paragraph.

Emile Chauvin apparently had one of the early stores in the town and he was the first postmaster on October 21, 1874. Most of the early business houses faced the railway on what is now High Street but a great fire in 1890 wiped out the business district and the town was reborn in a more orderly fashion on today's Main Street. The Valencia House and the Tyler Warehouse (now H. P. Garin shed) are two of the buildings still standing in the heart of town that survived the fire.

By 1921 the Box Factory, Raisin Growers' Storage Yard, a concrete pipe company and implement houses were replacing the sheep shearing pens and grain warehouses. The depression in the late '20s and early '30s closed many businesses. Some that survived were the Delano Hardware, Stradley's Market, Mitchell Baker's, Ramsey Pharmacy, Talentine Department Store (later Morris's), Bill Smith's Meat Market, and several real estate agencies, two garages, Delano Theatre and a few smaller businesses.

At various times it was planned to bring water from the Kern River but to no avail. In 1890 the Spangler brothers built a dam on Rag Gulch above the Quinn Ranch and attempted to bring water to their places east of Delano. This also failed mainly because of the lack of water but in part was due to poor engineering. The dam was in poor repair for years and in April 1926 it broke, washed out railroad tracks near Richgrove, and flooded much of the area east of Delano.

In the early 1880s the windmill became established and replaced the mule power used to pump some wells. The general water level at this time was about forty feet in and around town. Many homes still used the hand pump. The development of the double plunger pump in the early 1900s and the discovery of plenty of water east of town at 90 to 140 feet below the surface offered a bright future for the area. Alfalfa, peaches, grapes and oranges were planted on a large scale. The first vineyard was planted about 1891. In 1908 the Morris Development Company began the development of the present Sierra Vista Ranch The big freeze in 1913, when the temperature dropped as low as fourteen degrees, almost put an end to the planting of orange and lemon trees in this area. The Morris Development Company is said to have lost 320 acres of lemons in one night. In 1915, A. B. Embler planted Thompson Seedless grapes between rows of trees in his olive grove. By 1919 these vines were producing three tons of raisins per acre. Some wet years, good prices and the invention of the turbine pump sent land prices soaring and the hey-day of the wheat and sheep men was over.

Cotton and row crops began to take the place of vines and trees as they were removed beginning in the early twenties. However, larger holdings such as the Earl Fruit Company which had acquired the Sierra Vista Ranch holdings, the California Grape Products Company under the supervision of A. Perelli-Minetti, W. J. Wallace and the Delano Fruit Company supervised by Charles Ladow, planted large acreages of grapes.

With the repeal of national Prohibition in 1933, construction of wineries began. The grape juice plant started by Perelli-Minetti in the mid-twenties was converted into what is now Cresta Blanca. Next Wallace built what is now called the Grower's Co-op. Minetti and sons built their own winery south of town and then came California Grape Products.

These large holdings required many transient workers. The "other side of the tracks" was born. Many minority groups established homes on the west side of town with a predominance of single men. Gambling houses and "red light districts" reached their peak in the area in the early thirties and for the most part shut down as the army moved into Minter Field in 1938.

The first elementary school was established May 7, 1883, almost ten years after the founding of the town. Delano High School was started in 1911. The first graduation class was in 1914 with six members receiving diplomas.

The town was first incorporated in 1910 with a population of 501. However, it was discovered that money which had been budgeted by the county supervisors for the grading of streets could not be used in an incorporated area. The incorporation lapsed and the town was again incorporated April 13, 1915 with a population of 575. By 1940 the population was about 4,573. Immediately after the attack on Pearl Harbor by the Japanese, the Delano Airport was enlarged and a patrol bomber base was established. The barracks for the base were at the corner of Lexington and Garces. Later the airport was a training center for night fighters. Before the end of World War II the barracks were used for German prisoners of war. In 1949 the Bureau of Reclamation established a base here and work was begun on the Friant-Kern Canal which was completed in 1952. With this assurance of another good supply of water the town has shown rapid growth.

In 1964, the community facilities include one general hospital with a bed capacity of forty. Other medical facilities include eight physicians and surgeons, five dentists, three optometrists, and two chiropractors. Educational facilities include four elementary schools, one high school, and one Catholic and one Seventh Day Adventist elementary school. There are twenty-eight churches, one library, one newspaper and three banks. Recreational facilities include three theatres, three parks, three playgrounds, and a new nine-hole golf course at Memorial Park. The 1964 business licenses total 603, including the following: amusements devices, four; barbers and beauty shops, twenty-one; bars and restaurants, fifty-three; contractors, sixty-three; delivery, sixty-seven; distributors, twenty-eight; garage and automotive, nineteen; hotels, motels, rooms, twenty-seven; packing sheds, nine; taxi, two; professional, forty-two; retail, one hundred forty-five; miscellaneous services, sixty; service stations, twenty-three; and solicitors, fifteen. The population has grown from 8,717 in 1950 and 11,913 in 1960 to about 13,250 in 1964.

Delano Historical Society has a Heritage House and a school building at the corner of Lexington and Garces in Delano which is being made into a museum.

(*Historic Kern*, September, 1964)

Caliente: Boom and Bust
by W. Harland Boyd

When the building of the Southern Pacific Railroad southward from Bakersfield station (Sumner) toward Los Angeles was begun in the fall of 1874, it became known that the next station would be some twenty-five miles distant. Early in 1875 Allen's Camp was selected as the site of the depot, a locale on a sand wash along Caliente Creek, in a narrow canyon in the foothills of the Sierra Nevada. Besides his name, only a crumbling cabin remained to mark the earlier presence there of Gabriel Allen, a rancher who had pastured his stock in this narrow defile. When the Southern Pacific sold town lots at the place in the summer of 1875, the name Caliente was bestowed upon the station, displacing the time-honored one of Allen's Camp.

Caliente's prosperity as a railhead appeared assured for at least a year, and perhaps longer, while the construction gangs threaded the rails through the mountains by way of Tehachapi Valley. A Bakersfield journalist early in 1875 stated that the "ravishing accounts" in circulation regarding Caliente were creating much excitement among businessmen who contemplated engaging in trade in the new community. By summer the Telegraph Stage Company, most recently operating between the end of the railroad at Bakersfield and the San Fernando Valley by way of Fort Tejon transferred its northern terminus to Caliente, as did also other stage companies operating between the railhead and the mining districts east of the Sierra Nevada. Business was good, and Los Angeles bound stages departing from Caliente were crowded to their utmost capacity and "extras" were dispatched almost daily. The travel to the eastern mines also increased greatly once the railroad had advanced this near. A highly prized business for Caliente came in the transfer of the operations of the Cerro Gordo Freighting Company to a railroad connection at this place, following the abandonment of the earlier connection with Los Angeles.

A Caliente resident, in the summer of 1875, wrote that the town, better known as Allen's Camp, was "the liveliest and most flourishing point of all the temporary halting places of the iron track, on the advance southward from Lathrop." The mushrooming town soon consisted of about sixty buildings, mostly designed to serve the purposes of eating, drinking, and sleeping. According to a contemporary description, the town comprised one wide street, with the depot buildings, tracks, and freight cars in the middle, not less than twenty-five saloons on the north side and all other establishments on the south side of the street. At the upper end of the flat was the headquarters of the Inyo freighting business, including stable, corral, blacksmith shop, granary, and warehouse. Arriving with incoming loads of bullion, the freighters acquired return loads of mining machinery, goods, and supplies. The Southern Pacific itself also brought in vast amounts of construction materials and supplies as the company drove its line through the Tehachapi Pass.

Receiving benefits that many older towns had been compelled to wait long for, Caliente was granted two justices of the peace, two constables, and a post office. There was even some talk of locating the Kern County seat at the new town.

With an estimated two hundred "permanent" residents in the town, Caliente also was the temporary base of operations for the two thousand or more railroad workers, most of whom were Chinese. There was no hazard that one might go hungry because of a shortage of food, but there was a chance that unless one spoke early for a bed he might have to sleep in a chair. While some of the businessmen and residents were from nearby towns like Havilah and Bakersfield, most were newcomers to the region. One visitor surmised that many were "old followers of the railroad, and possibly some of them... camped in every town on the road, from Omaha to Caliente."

As the town grew in prominence, Caliente was overrun by a host of professional gamblers, thieves, thugs, and other undesirables

Mack trucks hauling a bridge girder from Caliente to Kernville on the Lion's Trail, c. 1914. Note White Stagecoach.

who swarmed into the settlement. Crimes were common and scarcely was the community founded when the first of a series of shooting scrapes occurred. In lawlessness Caliente soon vied with the worst of the rowdy towns of the frontier West.

Meanwhile, work on the Southern Pacific through the Tehachapi Pass was "progressing with encouraging dispatch." Along a course that was "crooked and devious," from the point where the line plunged into the Caliente Creek Canyon, a contemporary observed, "it wiggles and twists and doubles up in a most perplexing and extraordinary manner." Near the end of 1875 the company began removing its headquarters from Caliente to a point not far from the town of Tehachapi. Work continued apace until by the summer of 1876 the line was completed to Mojave. The Telegraph Stage Company and the Cerro Gordo Freighting Company then transferred their operations from Caliente to the new terminus at Mojave.

As a consequence, Caliente was rapidly shorn of its glory, a development which doubtless came as no surprise to the farsighted businessmen of the community. The residents of the Chinese quarter left early in 1876, and scarcely a year after its birth many business buildings were being dismantled to be reassembled again at the "end of the tracks," or to be rebuilt at some older settlement like Bakersfield. Caliente had lived momentarily beyond the capacity of its normal economic setting to support it. Yet it was not destined to die, but only to rest quietly at the scene of its "better days."

(*Historic Kern*, September, 1953)

"Joyful"—A Dream Rooted in Optimism
by Frances Williams

In Kern County several organized attempts were made to turn from the questionable benefits of "civilization" to a life in harmony with nature. Broadly considered, this was the promotional outlook of the founders of such colonies as Rosedale, Edison, Greenfield, Shafter, and Wasco. Over the decades Kern County, with its promising and abundant resources, encouraged the concept of a "terrestrial paradise." Unique among these agricultural settlements was a utopian colony founded in the early 1880s by Isaac B. Rumford. Regarded by his followers as a man directly inspired by God, his principles were adopted by a sizeable group, which joined him in forming the "Association of Brotherly Co-operators."

Isaac B. Rumford was a native of Delaware, but as a young man of twenty-six, in 1860, he was farming near Oakland, California. There he experimented with Lawton blackberries. He apparently was subject to "dyspepsia and all sorts of ill," and in 1862 he had a bout with typhoid fever. By 1875 he had settled at Panama, in Kern County, and in the following year he opened the Kern Island Nursery a mile east of Panama, near the site of present-day Pumpkin Center. Rumford and his wife, Sara, were temperance and women's rights reformers, and they were concerned with the local laxity in morals. In a letter written to the editor of the *Kern County Californian* in December, 1881, he made an eloquent plea for adherence to the Christian way of life.

The Rumford farm was located just west of the Panama Slough and about one-fourth of a mile north of Panama Lane, near what is now Ashe Road. In a letter to the editor of the *Kern County Californian* written in January, 1882, Rumford praised the climate, soil, and water of the surrounding area. In subsequent letters he gave step by step advice for the guidance of those who might wish to join him in developing a law-abiding, moral, and healthful way of life paralleling his own at his fruit farm. By then he was thinking of himself as a modern Adam in a wilderness Eden. In October, 1881, the Rumford family turned to an Edenic diet of uncooked food. It was, as he explained, a means of preventing disease, as well as a means of freeing women from the drudgery of cooking. The diet consisted of "pure, live food, that had not been deprived of its magnetic, or best life-giving forces, by fire." Upon turning to the Edenic diet, Rumford stated that he became a "picture of health."

The formation of the "Association of Brotherly Co-operation" was an outgrowth of Rumford's dream-vision that the ills of humanity could be cured by the creation of simple community life based on the principles of Christianity. According to the principles of the association there was to be no gambling, use of tobacco, profane or vulgar language, or intoxicants of any kind in the colony. Dietary practices were foremost among the guiding tenents of the colonists. In January, 1884, the *Kern County Californian* reported that Rumford addressed a San Francisco meeting of "eccentrics and cranks" on the benefits of the Edenic diet of uncooked food.

The colony established at the Rumford farm was called "Joyful," and a little of its historical existence was preserved in contemporary newspapers and govenment records. A newspaper, *The Joyful News Co-operator*, was published during the year 1884, and in it are found some of the basic principles advocated by the colonists. A post office, with Rumford as postmaster, was established there in June, 1883, but is was discontinued in December, 1884. One can only speculate on the number of residents living at "Joyful" at its most flourishing point, but by November, 1884, no more than six were residing at the farm. Most Kern County residents doubtless continued to do "business as usual," being little affected by the "going on" at "Joyful." Outlasting the colonists at "the old Rumford place" were the plantings of peaches, apples, plums, pears, persimmons, figs, and nuts of the abandoned orchards, and these, recalled an old-timer, were the finest quality of fruits and nuts.

(*Historic Kern*, June, 1977)

Kimberlina Dates from 1889
(Sent to Richard C. Bailey
by Chester L. Roadhouse of Santa Rosa, California)

Your letter of February 9 is received in which you requested information about Kimberlina, a townsite in Kern County located on the Southern Pacific line about sixteen miles north of Bakersfield.

The townsite was named Kimberlina for my grandfather, James Monroe Kimberlin, who came to California in 1850 from Dickinson College in Pennsylvania to teach Greek and Latin at the College of the Pacific which at that time was located in Santa Cruz.

On account of his ill health Mr. Kimberlin resigned his teaching position and in 1868 became the pioneer wholesale garden seed grower of California. As a side interest in 1887 he purchased nine sections of land from homesteaders in Kern County and started growing wheat in the area between Lerdo Station and Delano.

He interested Mr. A. N. Towne, an official of the Southern Pacific Railroad Company, to authorize the construction of a switch at a point about sixteen miles north of Bakersfield. Mr. Kimberlin had a townsite staked out at that location. He built a hotel, a store building, and a blacksmith shop and planted ten acres of fruit trees. The railroad company named the townsite Kimberlina.

As a small boy I lived at Kimberlina with my parents for a year in 1889 while it was being developed. Rattlesnakes, centipedes, tarantulas and black spiders were numerous, but we were taught not to pick up loose boards or shocks of hay without first looking for such poisonous creatures.

The last time I drove through Kimberlina the area was covered with potato vines. The buildings that were constructed in 1889 had disappeared but I believe the railroad switch is still there and in use.

(*Historic Kern*, June, 1967)

Gosford
from the *Bakersfield Californian*, April 13, 1893

A corps of surveyors is now occupied laying out the site for the new station of Gosford, which is about ten miles from the Bakersfield depot on the Asphalto railroad.

A town site of 200 acres has been secured. The east and west streets will go by numbers and the north and south by letters. Lots will soon be ready for sale.

The railroad company purposes to build some warehouses and a depot as soon as the business will justify keeping a station agent.

The new town is a very fertile and productive part of Kern Valley and is destined to become a place of no small importance.

(*Historic Kern*, September, 1975)

Glenburn Becomes Jewetta
from the *Bakersfield Californian*, July 22, 1893

Glenburn is no more. This station—the first north of Bakersfield—is now known as Jewetta, and has been supplied with an agent and telegraph operator.

(*Historic Kern*, February, 1975)

Survey for the Town of Edison
from the *Bakersfield Californian*, June 24, 1903

Surveyors have been at work some time past, surveying and laying out a townsite at Edison. Edison was formerly known as Wade, a small obscure watering station on the line of the Southern Pacific railway about seven miles from Kern (East Bakersfield). Upon the advent, however, of the Edison Power Development Company in the canyon, about ten miles from Edison, the place suddenly came into prominence, as the company found it a convenient location for establishing a warehouse, which was used for storing machinery and supplies. At the time the supplies were shipped to Kern and from there hauled to Edison. At present all supplies are shipped direct to Edison, thereby saving considerable time and expense.

About forty acres of land belonging to the A. N. Towne estate and lying principally on the north side of the track is being subdivided and laid out into streets and soon will be placed upon the market. Wells will be sunk to provide water for the new site and with power which might be transmitted from the canyon Edison may in time become a prosperous manufacturing town.

(*Historic Kern*, February, 1975)

Will Call the Town McFarland
from *The Morning Echo*, January 1, 1908

When Hunt ceases to be only a siding and becomes a town with a postoffice and business houses, as is planned for the near future, its name will be changed to McFarland, in honor of one of its founders. For the present Messrs. McFarland and Laird have their business office at Anaheim, and Mr. Laird will maintain an office in the south until next fall. Mr. McFarland, however, is rushing work on his new house, and will move to the new town that is to bear his name as soon as the building is finished.

The town of McFarland is favorably located, having a large body of fertile land all around it. It is about midway between Delano and Famoso and not near enough to either to make one community an injury to the other.

(*Historic Kern*, February, 1975)

History of Arvin
by Betty Borden

Arvin lies in the extreme southeastern portion of the San Joaquin Valley. It is seven miles from Bear Mountain and about six from Comanche Point. Noted for its beautiful wild flowers and its delicious early fruit, Arvin has become famous throughout California.

There were, in Kern County, two tribes of Indians, the Yokuts of the valley and the Piutes of the mountains near Kernville. One of these tribes lived for a time near Arvin for one finds remains of an Indian cemetery in the foothills near Black Oak Mountain. The graves are so old that the bones have decayed, but the beads remain in the ground as a mute testimony of bygone existence.

From 1888 until 1893, this district was a productive dry farming region. Wheat was grown extensively. A few years later the present community of Arvin was started by a group of men in San Bernardino, California who wanted to colonize a place where land and water were cheap. They sold land to prospective settlers, and with the land, the owner received shares in the Foothill Citrus Farms Company. This company was organized by a committee of the stockholders on November 13, 1907 in San Bernardino. The purpose of this company was to drill wells and buy pumps to irrigate the 440 acres which comprised the colony. The original land owners were Ralph Haven, C. Meyers, David R. Glass, Maude M. Lochraine, A. A. Neff, J. R. Neff, A. A. Cox, F. L. Henry, H. A. Moyers, Lawrence Neff, A N. Habecker, and Sophronia Haven. In the fall of 1908, a year later, Arvin had a population of four families: A. N. Habecker, A. A. Neff, Arvin Richardson and Ralph Haven. At that time the only buildings were one house and one tent.

The next five years showed rapid growth in the population of Arvin and in 1913 there were enough children in the community to warrant the building of a school. When the directors of the Foothill Citrus Farm Company had planned the community, they had set aside the tract where Arvin is located for a town, and therefore, the school was built on this site. It was a two-room structure, which boasted two summerhouses, a stage and library, and a bell which could be heard throughout the community. Only one classroom was occupied during the first few years. The first teacher was Mrs. Adams, and the first pupils included: four Shoemakers, three Davises, two Tuckers, two Adamses, and one Heard. The first trustees were Ralph Haven, J. D. Tucker and George Richardson.

In 1908 the nearest store was at Greenfield, and the settlers were obliged to go about twelve miles as the crow flies for groceries. Before 1915, Skinney Williams opened a general store at Weedpatch, six miles away. The first store at Arvin was built on the site of the present Quality market by A. T. Staples in 1917.

In the early days, a mail carrier from Bakersfield distributed letters at Weedpatch corner, and anyone going to Bakersfield always got the mail for the entire settlement. Often a week or two elapsed with no news from the outside world. This was very unsatisfactory, but there wasn't much mail, and the Post Office Department didn't show a great deal of interest in the situation, so Ralph Haven, Ed Tanner, Mr. Nance, J. D. Tucker and Arvin Richardson got together and hired Warder Nance as mail carrier. At the end of three months the government paid Mr. Nance's salary. The first post office was on the property now owned by J. L. Krauter. Mrs. Birdie Heard was the first postmaster. Later George Richardson became mail carrier, and the post office was moved to an unused corner in Staples Store.

One of the most picturesque characters of the early days was Toby. When he was a very small pup, someone gave Toby to Ralph Haven, who cared for him until a new family moved into the community and then Toby promptly moved over to the new house. Each new resident was thus met by a welcoming committee of one, who resided with them gladly until another hardy soul ventured into the area, and then Toby deserted his former friends for the new ones. Everyone teased and petted him, and the community lost a whole-hearted supporter when Mr. Snowden took him to Los Angeles.

Every Sunday, the entire community would gather at the J. D. Tucker home for Sunday School. George Clark was the first minister. Whenever it was convenient for him to come, someone visited all the neighbors and told them that there would be preaching, and they would all come to hear him preach. Later, Philip

Ralph, who lived at Edison, preached at the schoolhouse every Sunday afternoon. From this developed the Congregational Church, which was formally established on June 17, 1914. The charter members were: Mr. and Mrs. J. D. Tucker, Mr. and Mrs. Ralph Haven, Pearly Gregory, Mrs. M. Adams, and Mr. Cameron.

The settlers were very neighborly in the old days. They were so far from anyone that they felt the need of one another, and did all they could to help one another. One day Della Tucker and Louise Smith decided they wanted some candy. After school was dismissed they put a saddle on old Dobbin, and without saying a word to anyone, started to Weedpatch, six miles away. They finally got to the store, purchased their candy and started home. A breeze was blowing and Louise's hat came off. Della stopped the horse and both girls got down. After recovering the hat, they were unable to remount Dobbin. After several unsuccessful attempts, they finally succeeded in getting on, but they had wasted a long time; it was growing dark. Meanwhile, the parents grew concerned—anxious, frantic. Finally Mr. Tucker told his closest neighbors, and Warder Nance rang the schoolhouse bell. Immediately all the settlers congregated at the school. A search party was organized. In buggies, on horseback, walking—all the loyal friends started out. Mr. Tucker drove his Ford, the only car in the community. Its headlights were rather temperamental and only turned on when the car was traveling full speed. Somehow he managed to track the horse to Weedpatch, and was half way back, when above the noise of the car, he heard the gun shot which meant the little girls were safely home.

The town was named after Arvin Richardson, son of George Richardson, and one of the prominent early residents. He came from a rather large family, and his mother could think of no suitable name for him, so she invented one of her own. When the post office was established the place had to have a name. Mrs. Heard sent several suggestions to the Post Office Department at Washington, including Heard, Arvin, Bear Mountain and others. The authorities at Washington chose Arvin.

The original pioneers of Arvin had intended to establish a colony of orange groves—designated by the name Foothill Citrus Farms Company—but the frosts were too severe for the delicate orange trees and they proved unsuccessful. People tried to raise apples, but there was no money in apples. During World War I, wheat was grown successfully, but when the European countries became normal again, there was no market for wheat. Fruit was tried, and Thompson Seedless grapes proved to be well adapted to the climate. The grapes from Arvin ripen earlier than those from other parts of Kern County, so the Arvin farmers get the best price in the Los Angeles market.

In 1919, the DiGiorgio Farms Company bought property north of Arvin, and now they own several sections of land, where they harvest plums, grapes, apricots, peaches and other early fruits. They employ several thousand men each season. In 1921, Lawrence Nourse and Tim Staples were influential in establishing the Bear Mountain Boosters' Club, composed of a group of influential citizens. The Booster Club sponsored the weekly newspaper, "Arvin Booster," which was edited by Jesse Stockton. For the two years that Mr. Stockton edited the paper, it was successful. When he left in 1923, the paper began to fail and soon ceased to exist.

By 1922, the school had three teachers and a small building had been built to accommodate the extra class. That year Arvin had a hotel operated by Mrs. L. W. Bornhauser. In 1923 the railroad was brought to Arvin. It was used only in the fruit season. The year 1924 saw the erection of the first church building, the present Congregational Church. A few years later the Nazarene Church was erected and still later, the Pentecostal Church was started.

In 1924, R. L. Thayer, in partnership with Mr. Weaver, opened the Brick Store, the first brick building in Arvin. Mr. Thayer had been delivering supplies to Arvin for several months and, believing that the community had a promising future, persuaded Mr. Weaver to go into business with him. Mr. Weaver soon sold his share of "Weaver and Thayer" to Earl Mitchell, who later sold his interest to Mr. Thayer. The building has been made larger and has become a small department store. This building now houses a jewelry store, beauty shop and restaurant.

In 1925, the Booster Club, now called the Arvin Booster Club, was reorganized, with Tim Staples serving as president. In 1926 he left Arvin and Merrill Barlow succeeded him as president of the club. At about this time several ladies of the P.T.A. thought that Arvin needed a troop of Boy Scouts. Victor LeMaster, with the help of Keith Mitchell, started the Boy Scout movement in Arvin. In 1928 Raymond Kendall, a teacher in the school (then enlarged to seven rooms), believed that connections with the headquarters of the Scouts was what the boys at Arvin needed, so he called a meeting of Mr. Thayer, Tom Downs, Warder Nance and Merrill Barlow. It seems that to belong to the scout group the troop needed $100, which they didn't have. The following year the Booster Club decided to sponsor the Boy Scouts and pay any necessary fees. They appointed Henry Bonesteel scoutmaster. There are now several Boy Scout troops in Arvin, as well as cub scouts.

On January 1, 1927, the Arvin Branch of the Kern County Free Library was opened. Prior to this, a branch library had been established in connection with the post office in Staples Store, but due to the loss of a great many books, this was unsatisfactory. County authorities were skeptical as to whether or not the new venture would succeed, but Mrs. Babcock, head of the county library, wanted to try it. Mrs. Cook was librarian for the first nine months, and then Mrs. Seat took over the work. Gradually it developed until now it is one of the larger branch libraries.

As the years have rolled by Arvin has continued to grow and prosper. Among the many interests here are the packing sheds where fruit and vegetables are packed and shipped to all parts of the United States; these sheds employ several hundred packers during the season. The school in Arvin has grown to an enrollment of nearly fifteen hundred pupils and has about fifty teachers. Construction on the Arvin High School began in 1948 and the school opened in September, 1949.

More and more churches have been established here, including a Catholic Church. There are several stores here now and a large post office, and 1949 saw the first house-to-house mail service in Arvin. Under construction is a new theatre and several homes.

Arvin still has a weekly newspaper called *The Arvin Tiller*, published and edited by Frank Reed. There are several clubs in Arvin and all of them are working for the good of the community.

(The first part of this history was taken from notes compiled by Virginia Krauter Swanson, loaned to me by her mother, Mrs. M. H. Krauter of Arvin.)

(*Historic Kern*, October, 1950)

The Beginnings of Taft
by Edith M. Dane

The known history of Taft and its vicinity carries back to the days of the Tulamni Yokuts Indians. Their village, Tulamnui, was on the western shore of Buena Vista Lake and about seven miles from the site of present Taft. During the winter of 1933 and the spring of 1934 the Smithsonian Institution and the American Bureau of Ethnology worked at excavating and screening the extensive shell heaps left on the site of the old village. Discoveries made there indicated the importance of petroleum and its various uses, even in that age.

The more modern history of the part of the west side of Kern County now known as Midway began in 1879. In that year United States Surveyor-General Benson conducted a survey of the area. In his party was a man named E. J. Boust. During the survey Boust observed some oil seepages and outcroppings of a tarry material, but at the time he attached no significance to his observations.

From the time of the completion of the survey until 1899 Boust was a deputy United States marshal for the district. He was acquainted with the Elwood brothers, the discoverers of the Kern River oil fields. While he was visiting them one day, Jud Elwood showed him oil indications in that neighborhood, advising him to file on some land there, but Boust became excited when he remembered seeing similar outcroppings on the west side during the survey of 1879. Elwood then advised him to make locations where he had seen these indications.

Being well acquainted in Fresno, Boust persuaded several residents of that city who had considerable money and a supply of adventurous spirits to go in with him. In May, 1899, they filed on ten sections in Township 32, Range 23, and four sections in Township

31, Range 23. Township 32, Range 23 was to be the location of the future and then unthought-of city of Taft. In November, 1900, they leased part of this land to the Oregon Midway Oil Company, with Gene Kay in charge.

A word here as to the origin of the word Midway for this area. It seems that in the old days of long-line mule team hauling, the distance between the fields at Old Sunset, east of Maricopa, and Asphalto, later McKittrick, was too long to negotiate without a rest. Hence a barn called "Midway" was erected, and here mules and skinners rested. Prior to the days of Boust, all drilling activity had been done either at Sunset or Asphalto.

In January, 1901, Boust formed the Producers' Guaranty Oil Company, located on the west half of Section 23 and the south half of 22, which would be about one or two miles in a southwesterly direction from the edge of Taft Heights. The first drilling in the field was done by the Oregon Midway, on Section 4, 32-23, which is between the present towns of Taft and Fellows. The drilling was done with a "patent" rig. Three wells were drilled, but 600 feet was the greatest depth to be reached with this rig, and the wells were dry. The company made preparations to secure a standard rig.

The drilling water for these first wells was hauled by mule team from the Miller and Lux hog ranch, about four miles southwest of Buttonwillow. The water cost $1.25 per barrel delivered at the well. After delivery the company had to permit the ten-mule teams used to haul it to drink from it, which used about half the water.

In 1901 the Producers' Guaranty Company, Boust's company, prepared to drill. In February drilling machinery was hauled across the bed of Buena Vista Lake, which at that time had been dry for three years. On the first well the drillers were paid five dollars per foot drilled, with the company furnishing all machinery, supplies, water and fuel. Fuel oil was secured from the Sunset field, and it is said it required four days for the teams to make the round trip. The oil cost two dollars per barrel, and hauling cost fifteen dollars per day for the team.

The first oil was struck on May 1, 1901, at a depth of 1,407 feet, with a 7⅝ casing. The first sale of oil occurred on May 15 and was to the Oregon Midway for fuel for drilling operations. The well had a production of twenty barrels a day, being pumped twelve hours a day.

In 1902 Buena Vista Lake filled with water, and the Producers' Guaranty, which then had four wells pumping, had water trouble. They thought that this trouble must in some way be connected with the water in the lake, as it disappeared two years later when the lake again went dry. In 1903 the oil industry in the infant Midway field "blew up," due to the extreme difficulties in shipping and to the fact that the vast quantities of oil produced in the Kern River field was selling for ten cents a barrel. The field lay quiet and shut in, given over once more to jack rabbits, horned toads and kangaroo rats.

In 1906 and 1907 increasing activity in the Sunset-Maricopa field and the drilling of large producers of better oil on the Maricopa Flats led to prospecting again in the Midway district. Boust and his associates formed the Knob Hill Oil Company and leased much of their land to other companies who began development work. In 1908 the Southern Pacific and the Santa Fe railroads, joint owners of the Sunset line from Bakersfield to Maricopa, extended the line to the Midway field and established a depot in a freight car, calling it simply "Siding Number Two."

Activity continued to increase in the field, and it became desirable to have a name for the business clustering around the freight car depot a little more distinctive than "Siding Number Two." For some reason it was called Moro, no one now seems to know why. However, that being easily confused with the town of Morro on the coast, they added an "n" and made it Moron. There was a town in Colorado by this name, and the post office department objected on the grounds that the abbreviations for California and Colorado were often confused. In July of 1909 it was decided to name the town for President Taft. This proved to be an appropriate name, as in September of that same year Congress, at the president's request, passed the Oil Land Withdrawal Order.

This meant that the many persons who had swarmed over the land locating oil claims must develop these claims if they were to hold them. These efforts led to a vast development in a short time, to

Downtown Taft, 1928.

unprecedented activity, and to the bringing in of some of the largest gushers the world has ever known.

Now, indeed, the little freight car depot became busy and was very soon replaced with a larger building to try to cope with the rush. It is said that for a year or more Taft was the second largest freight-receiving station in California. Freight cars came in so fast that at one time there were more than 300 cars waiting to be unloaded. The merchants who had been quick to establish businesses in the new town did their own unloading with wheelbarrows. Two passenger trains were run daily from Bakersfield and there was scarcely standing room on them. This little Sunset Railroad was for a time the most profitable bit of line in the world.

Most of the early businesses clustered along the railroad, but early in the morning of October 22, 1909, a fire started in the town bakery which almost wiped out the whole settlement. As the only water available was what was shipped in in tank cars and sold by the barrel, fire fighting presented difficulties.

The Southern Pacific engineers surveyed a townsite on the north side of the tracks and rebuilding started there. Town lots were placed on the market and sold at an astonishing rate. Business houses and homes sprang up overnight. The Blaisdell Opera House was built, a building which would have done credit to a much larger and older town, and many people from Bakersfield and elsewhere came to attend its opening. The descriptions carried by the early local newspaper of the gorgeous gowns worn by the ladies on this gala occasion show what a sophisticated affair this was.

The big gushers started coming in, startling the world. On March 6, 1910, the Mays gusher on Section 30, 32-24, broke loose and drenched the countryside. Its yield was never accurately determined, but it was conceded it ran into many thousands of barrels a day. Then at eight o'clock on the night of Monday, March 14, just eight days after the Mays gusher had furnished fierce excitement, the Lakeview, at the west end of Section 25, 12-24, threw its bailer into the crownclock and, with a mighty roar, shot forth more oil than had ever been seen before, carrying the derrick away like so much kindling. It is estimated that it flowed 18,000 barrels in the first twenty-four hours. Tuesday night the oil stopped flowing.

What happened at the bottom of the hole will never be known, but suddenly a great shower of rocks, sand and gas spewed forth and it literally rained oil over a huge expanse of the countryside. It was months before anyone got near it again. All efforts at controlling it were abandoned and all energies turned to throwing up dykes and making reservoirs in a frenzied attempt to keep the oil from reaching the waters of Buena Vista Lake, where Miller and Lux had threatened a million dollar suit for any contamination of the water with oil.

A great many other wells came in as gushers during this period, some of them catching fire and burning spectacularly. Excitement was intense! Excursion trains were run from San Francisco to the new town.

Enterprising businessmen began furnishing the town with utilities. In April, 1910, a small plant began furnishing electricity. In September gas was piped to the houses. In July a water system for the town was completed. Two tanks at the head of Sixth Street just south of the tracks were filled daily with water brought in tank cars and from there piped to the houses.

In 1909 the Conley School District was formed and the first school was in a one-room shack on the south side. In 1910 a two-room school building was erected, but by the time it was finished it was too small and a third room was started immediately. That year also saw the start of Catholic, Methodist and Presbyterian churches. On October 7, 1910, the citizens voted to incorporate.

E. J. Boust still owned about ninety acres of land he had filed on in 1899, and he formed a settlement there called Boust City. It consisted mostly of saloons and such places of business, flimsily constructed but with wide durable cement sidewalks. As was always the case, fires were frequent and at last it was burned out and was not rebuilt, but the cement sidewalks stretched away through the sagebrush for years, to the astonishment of a chance hiker who came upon them. Unfortunately, today Boust is mostly remembered for his notorious town and his pioneer oil work in the district is all but forgotten. He passed away in Taft on October 18, 1915, with lobar pneumonia.

In 1920 Sam Orloff acquired the Boust property and laid out Taft

Heights, a modern residential area. The original wide cement walks of Boust City may still be seen on B Street. While the excitement of the old pioneer days are gone, Taft's growth and the development of the Midway Oil Fields has continued, and she is proud not only of her wealth of oil, but of her homes, her fine schools, her many churches and her friendly people.

(*Historic Kern*, November, 1950)

IX

Flood, Fire, Flora and Fauna

This final chapter is a collection focusing on the wonders and vagaries of nature. On balance, Kern County has been relatively free of natural disasters. Floods, fire, and earthquakes have proved to be the principal forces of destruction in early Bakersfield. Prior to the completion of the Isabella Dam in 1954, the Kern River flooded with disastrous results on several occasions, most recently in 1950. In the days of volunteer fire departments, fire spread easily among the wooden buildings and entire towns were leveled. Historically, earthquakes have been more often talked about than experienced, but when they have occurred, as in Bakersfield in 1952, the destruction to property has been great indeed. Included here are articles which illustrate the variety of both plant and animal life in Kern County as well as the sometimes humorous human response.

The Kern River Flood of 1893
from *The Californian,* February 11, 1893

While a possible flood was not unexpected, owing to the heavy and continuous rains in the mountains for the last three days, the mighty rush of water through the city on Thursday night was a big surprise to everyone. Its volume and the suddenness with which it came left no time for preparations by householders in the northern part of town to remove themselves and household effects to places of safety. When the flood came nearly everyone was compelled to move in a big hurry.

About nine o'clock on Thursday evening a number of men standing on the Arlington corner heard the noise of the rushing water in the river and walked out to Chester Avenue to note the situation. When they reached the railroad they saw a vast sea of water spread out before them, and even while they looked they noticed it slowly rising. Even when it had reached the railroad embankment they felt no alarm, and supposing the flood would soon subside, returned to town. At two o'clock in the morning the flood had burst its barrier and rushed through the northern suburbs of town. Jeff Packard immediately jumped upon a horse, dashed into town, awoke Engineer Bernard of the fire department and the fire bell was rung at ten minutes past two o'clock. In five minutes a hundred men were shouting danger cries, and guns and pistols were shot off to warn the town of its danger.

The water came so swiftly that when the frightened people left their homes many were compelled to wade through water several feet deep. All the people managed to reach places of safety, and nothing but hysterics and nervous prostration among the women and children has resulted. Although no accidents happened, many had narrow escapes in the darkness from drowning. Among the many rescuers who did noble work were George Tibbett, Jeff Packard, Bob Withington, and several bus drivers and a score of others.

There were many generous and chivalric deeds enacted on Friday morning during the excitement attendant upon the inundation of the city and the adjacent country by our citizens, and mine host threw the doors of the Southern and Arlington hotels wide open to our people. Those who desired rooms were accommodated and others were made comfortable with warm fires, and at daybreak hot coffee was served the guests. Mr. Morrison exerted himself to make all comfortable and at home in his famous hostelry, and many were the compliments passed upon his courtesy and the clever attention of his corps of clerks.

There were over sixty ladies and children accommodated at the Southern and nearly a hundred at the Arlington. The lobbies of the hotels presented an animated scene of activity during the entire night commensurate upon so great an excitement. A number of patrons when they came to settle their accounts during the day were informed that it was open hospitality to them, and the edict was imperative in spite of all protests.

Harry S. Hall saved his dogs at the risk of his life. The new fire engine did effective work in pumping out cellars. Sam DeYoe moved his wardrobe of clothes twice to places of safety. The streets were deserted last night owing to the fatigue general after such an unusual episode. Lots in the Drury addition are in great demand, but J. S. Drury had concluded not to advance the prices. The headgates of the various canals are badly damaged and in a few instances have been washed out. A large number of cattle, calves and hogs were drowned and their bodies line the course of the mad waters. Houses were vacated at a moment's notice and abandoned to all practical purposes, but they were not molested. The dairy of H. W. Klipstein was swept clean of over one hundred gallons of milk and a number of cows and calves were drowned. Henry Miller's cup is running over with joy, over the Buena Vista lake reservoir's capacity to retain such a vast body of water that will reach it. The damage to the Southern Pacific track will be repaired by Monday, when trains will be run on schedule time again; trains are running regularly between Bakersfield and Los Angeles. There was an entire cessation of business yesterday and the excitement continued all day long. All communication with the surrounding country was cut off and it will be at least a week before a conservative estimate can be arrived at of the damage.

Ed Willow built two boats, one he named the Warrior and the

other Piedmont. He manned the Warrior and went in search of people in distress. On paddling over the Scribner's new fence he found a party of sixteen ladies and gentlemen full of Scribner's canned goods ready to depart, and loading the Piedmont with passengers, started off, but on reaching the fence the boat grounded on the pickets and it was found necessary to kick off the top of a number of pickets in the new fence to allow the boat to ride through.

Mr. Willow deposited his precious cargo in safety and was on another tour of rescue when he was espied by George Tibbett who was horseback wading through the water.

Mr. Tibbett, being wet and cold, on seeing Willow enjoying life so well, drew his lassoo and soon had it around Willow's neck; sticking spurs into his horse he drew the boat and Willow along at a rattling gait, but the speed was too fast for the Piedmont, and Willow was drawn through the water a considerable distance until he was properly soaked, when he was left to run the Piedmont, a wetter and not so enthusiastic man.

The flood played havoc with Klipstein's dairy and temporarily shut off the supply of milk used in this city. One hundred gallons of milk and the cans containing the same were washed away, and a considerable number of calves and pigs are missing, the exact number of which is not known at present. Seven cows were bogged to their necks in mud. In Hunt Bros. Kern Valley Nursery, 57,000 grafts were swept out besides a considerable number of young trees of different varieties. Two thousand palm trees received Wednesday evening are also gone. These palms were for the Kern County Land Company and were to have been planted on Nineteenth and Twenty-fourth streets.

The Ah Ming Company, which runs a vegetable garden two or three miles southwest of this city, on the Panama road, lost fifty hogs, 2,500 sacks of Irish potatoes and 1,500 sacks of sweet potatoes. The growing vegetables in the garden were also washed out, and a whole field of turnips, carrots, and miscellaneous truck is lodged up against a fence on the road to Panama ranch. The whole southwestern country around the Panama section is strewn with cabbages, and the men in the neighborhood who were not up in a tree yesterday were fishing cabbages off the plains. The Panama ranch itself was a vast sea of water yesterday, the flood being three miles wide and ten miles long.

One of the most remarkable railroad accidents that ever happened on the San Joaquin division of the Southern Pacific occurred last Thursday night a short distance up the road from the Chester Avenue crossing of the railroad. An "extra west" special freight train of thirty-nine cars leaving Sumner for the north at 1:15 a.m. was ditched by the engine jumping the track, and the circumstances surrounding the accident are such that in all probability traffic will be suspended for some days. The rapid rise in the river backed the water up against the track embankment, softening and rendering it unfit for travel. The train was running at a low rate of speed, and when the engineer reached the identical spot where the Gobel wreck happened last fall, the track sunk away on the lower side and the engine was overturned into the ditch. The two head cars were ditched, but the remaining thirty-seven did not leave the track. The engineer, W. N. Cole, and the fireman, B. E. Bryson, had a narrow escape, but fortunately received no injuries. Bryson and the head brakeman were thrown into the water, but dragged themselves out. Soon after the wreck the rising water washed the embankment from under the rails, and the water tore through in many places, cutting out great holes. The wreck is a bad one on account of the track which is sagged down in twenty places within a distance of 2,000 yards, and almost every car is inclined at angles up or down. It will probably be a week before the wreck can be cleaned away. A "shoofly" track cannot be built on account of the water on either side of the main track. A large gang of men was put to work yesterday morning on the Sumner end of the break. The train was an "extra west" with orders to meet 21 at Lerdo. The latter engine waited on that siding until 8 a.m. yesterday morning, then came down to Kern river bridge, and returned north. Superintendent Whitmer was aboard 21.

There was fortunately no injury nor loss of life sustained in the accident, which is due to the caution and judgment exercised by the engineer in proceeding at moderate speed over what is considered a very dangerous portion of the road. The damage will not exceed $5,000.

A camp of over thirty Chinamen, working near Hunt's nursery, were washed out of their tents Thursday night about two-thirty o'clock and lost almost their entire outfit of camp equipage, clothes and bedding. None were drowned as far as we can learn. This accident probably started the rumor that five Chinese had been drowned. No Chinaman in town will say anything about the accident.

(*Historic Kern*, June, 1980)

The Bakersfield Fire of 1889
by James Curran as told to Richard C. Bailey

At the time of the fire I was living where Beale Park is today. I had my horse hitched up in front of the house about nine o'clock in the morning, and my wife and I were getting ready to go somewhere. I happened to look toward town and saw a large black cloud. My wife said that she thought that it looked as if it were near the center of town.

I left my horse and started down the street on foot, since I knew that if it was a fire the horse would only be in the way. When I arrived near the intersection of Nineteenth and Chester, I saw that the smoke was coming from the Fish Building in which a furniture store was located at the corner of Twentieth and Chester, present site of the Bank of America. The Southern Hotel, one of the three brick buildings then standing in Bakersfield, was already on fire and I was quite concerned.

My brother, Will Curran, was the night clerk in the Southern Hotel, and I was worried whether or not he was awake and out of the building. Will Houghton and I ran into the hotel and got to my brother's room just in time to meet him coming out. He had his pants and shoes in his hand, and we all three got out as quickly as possible. Liquid solder from the roof was falling in big drops, and splashing about. That stuff was hot. The fire spread both north and south on Chester Avenue on each side of the street and burned every building from the slough that ran across Chester Avenue at present-day Twenty-third Street back to the location of the county courthouse (present Civic Center Building). The buildings on Nineteenth

Bakersfield after the Fire of 1889.

Street were also completely burned down. The fire spread over several adjoining streets and blocks, and the Bryant School was burned. It stood where today's Central Fire Station stands.

The only structure that was saved was Scribner's Water Tower. This was a wooden tower that stood at the corner of Seventeenth and Chester on the spot now occupied by the Standard Oil Station, next to the El Tejon Hotel. By the time the fire reached this spot the tower had been filled with water by the pump that they housed in a building alongside it. The pump house burned down, and the only reason the tower didn't burn was because Will Houghton climbed to the top of the tank where the upper windows were located and threw water on the spots that were afire as we yelled at him from the ground. The top of the tank was open beneath the roof and he dipped a lard bucket into this and threw the water out the windows between his legs.

The Kern Valley Bank at the southwest corner of Eighteenth and Chester where the Anglo-California Bank (now the Crocker-Anglo Bank) is today, was burning when Will Houghton and I went inside to see what we could do. There was a bathroom upstairs. We turned on the water in the tub and dipped water from there to throw on the fire until the water ran out. We soon saw there was nothing we could do so we left. We got out of there none too soon as the heat was something terrific. I wouldn't say for sure, but I would estimate there were around 10,000 persons in Bakersfield at that time.

There were only three brick buildings in town, as I said before. The Southern Hotel where Penney's now stands; Hirshfield's Store where Brock's is now located and the Galtes Building which stood on Nineteenth Street near the southeast intersection of Nineteenth and Chester. The insurance companies paid off insurance on the burned structures but this didn't amount to much.

After the fire three men from Bakersfield went to San Francisco to try to borrow money to rebuild the city. These men were Henry Jastro, Hugh A. Blodget, and Solomon Jewett, the banker. They went to all the banks in San Francisco, but were turned down by everyone.

Then, while walking down a street they saw a sign which read, "Daniel Meyer, Money Lender." Mr. Meyer and one other acquaintance of his lent Bakersfield enough money to start rebuilding. As I recall, the interest rate was nine percent, which was certainly extremely reasonable. I might mention that no insurance company would extend any credit for new buildings. A good many temporary wooden buildings were put up after the fire, later replaced by brick buildings. I had started a small brick yard in 1886 and I guess I furnished most of the bricks that went into the rebuilding of Bakersfield. Most of the downtown buildings today are constructed of the bricks from my yard. The present city hall bricks came from my place and those in the fence and gate bordering the Stockdale Country Club also were made in my plant. I merely mention this last because it might be of interest to some people.

A number of years after the fire, a group of San Francisco businessmen came to Bakersfield soliciting business for San Francisco. They addressed a group of Bakersfield businessmen and told what a wonderful city San Francisco was. Toward the close Alphonse Weill got up and reminded them of the experience of local businessmen after the fire of '89 when no bank or insurance company would lend money to help rebuild our city. The San Francisco spokesman replied that this was before his time and if his group had known of this incident it would never have come to Bakersfield.

Note: This account of the Big Fire in Bakersfield was related to Richard Bailey, director of the Kern County Museum, on May 1, 1950. Mr. James Curran, founder of the Bakersfield Sandstone Brick Company, came to this city as a young man in 1883 and was active in civic affairs until his death September, 1952, at the age of ninety.

(*Historic Kern*, April, 1962)

The Town of Kern Nearly Blotted out by (1898) Fire
from the *Kern Standard*, July 9, 1898

With the exception of a half block bounded by I, Baker and Kern streets and the alley between I and H, the business portion of Kern City is in ashes. An area of three and a half blocks covered with charred timbers, crumbling chimneys and the usual debris of a fire, constitutes the burnt district.

A few minutes after nine Wednesday evening fire broke out in the old California House on H Street, a district crammed with old wooden buildings, dry as tinder and only needing the application of a match to set them off. The alarm was given and the firefighting apparatus, such as we have, was quickly dragged to the scene, but the nature of the buildings doomed them to speedy destruction, and the heroic efforts of the local firemen counted for nothing. The flames leaped from building to building, licking them up almost as fast as if made of paper. The fire spread from the California House both ways on H Street and Verdier's corner, and the long row of little shacks eastward was soon demolished.

Ritzman's two-story building on the corner of Baker and H streets caught next, on the roof, and the flames leaped the street and fired the buildings on the east side, at the same time eating their way southward toward I Street. The town was compactly built and the back yards were full of sheds, barns and out-houses, so that the flames had food to feed them over almost every foot of the territory burned over. An attempt was made to blow up some of the intervening buildings to stay the steady onward march of the fire but they were not successful. The telephone wires were kept hot wiring for assistance from Bakersfield, but everybody was so excited that they probably failed to make themselves intelligible and finally a horseman was dispatched to Bakersfield to ask the department there to come over and help us. They arrived finally with the steamer which they planted on the Central Hotel corner, and to them must be given the credit of saving what little of the town is left. The men worked in a perfect hell of fire, but they stayed with it until the danger was past. Before they came, however, the switch engine, in charge of Engineer Frank Orr, did effective service in the block opposite the depot. On account of the inability of the hose to stand the pressure the engine pump could not work to its full capacity, but it did good work, nevertheless, and at one time had that part of the town saved. But when the firemen turned their attention to other threatened points the fire broke out afresh in the neighborhood of the Druid's hall and could not be again subdued. Persons who were in that vicinity at the time make no bones about declaring that the second outbreak was set purposely. In fact there is little doubt that the fire was incendiary in the first place. Several attempts were made after all danger was past to start fresh fires in the half block of buildings that was saved, but owing to the watchfulness of the marshal and his aides they were abortive. Traces of coal oil poured over fences and out-buildings were plentiful. If caught it is probable that short shrift would have been given the miscreants. The people were in a mood to deal with the dastards as they deserved.

The people on H Street, in the vicinity of the origin of the fire, lost most heavily in the way of personal effects. They had time only to save themselves. Those on the front street got out almost everything. The street was piled full of goods all night, but they were well-watched and no serious losses were reported.

Several residences on the north side of G Street were burned, including Mac Nunez's. Little or nothing was saved out of them. And many families living above or back of their places of business were rendered homeless and left, some of them, with nothing but the clothes on their backs.

At one time it looked as though the Southern Pacific depot and Wells Fargo's express office were doomed along with the balance of the town, and the officials there had all their effects ready to move at a moment's warning. But the work of the Bakersfield fire company prevented this added catastrophe. The wind, too, what little there was, was in their favor, blowing from the northwest. The fact that the wind was in that quarter had a great deal to do with saving the row of buildings west of Ardizzi Olcese's store. The fire in their rear threatened them seriously for a time and had the wind been from the south nothing could have saved them.

The total loss is variously estimated at from fifty to one hundred thousand dollars, and there are besides many small losses that cannot yet be ascertained. The individual losses with the amount of insurance on each is given below. The list is not complete but is as nearly so as it can be made at this writing. The insurance adjusters were here yesterday, and as soon as they are through the authorative figures can be obtained and will be published:

J. J. Murphy, $4,800, insurance $3,500 or thereabout; C. Ritzman, $10,000, insurance, $3,500; Jean Eyraud, $1,500, insurance, $400; Druid's lodge, $4,500, insurance $1,000; M. Cesmat, $10,000, insurance $4,000; Dussere & Philips, $800, insurance $400; Peter Ader, $2,000, insurance $1,000; Vivian Bros., $800, no insurance; J. L. Depauli, $6,000, insurance $4,000; Jacob Walters, $2,500, insurance $1,400; A. Cuneo, $250, no insurance; Simeon Phernio, $1,000, no insurance; Prince the Tailor, $1,000, no insurance; J. F. Dugan, $700 on store, insurance to be adjusted and store house on Front Street valued at $300; James O'Hare, $1,500, no insurance; E. Verdier, $12,000, insurance $3,500; Sartiat Bros., $5,000, insurance, $1,400; J. Neideraur, $2,100, insurance $1,100; Pabst Brewing Company, $1,500, no insurance; C. A. Morris, $2,500, insurance $1,500.

No terms of execration are too strong to apply to the class who, under the guise of helping a man move his goods out of a building threatened by fire, really engages in it for the purpose of theft. A person who would do that kind of petty thieving will do anything— nothing is too low or contemptible. Wednesday night's fire furnished plenty of instances of this dastardly work.

One life was lost in the fire Wednesday night. Joseph Gallien, a Frenchman employed about Verdier's stables, was burned to death. He was known familiarly as "Whistling Shorty" and had been around town several years. He retired early Wednesday night in a small building adjoining the stables, and it is supposed slept so soundly that he was not awakened until the flames began to lick his limbs. That he got out of bed and perhaps made an effort to save himself is known from the position when his charred remains were found. They were several feet distant from the place where his bed stood. The remains were a ghastly sight. Little was left but the trunk and the stumps of arms and legs. A small box contained it all.

(*Historic Kern*, June, 1957)

Nineteen fifty-two Earthquake Notes
by Richard C. Bailey

The quake of July 21, 1952 that shook the southern end of the San Joaquin Valley was the strongest experienced in California since the San Francisco earthquake and fire of 1906.

It was probably the largest seismic disturbance in the populated

Downtown Bakersfield under reconstruction after the Fire of 1889.

western portion of southern California since the Fort Tejon tremors of 1857.

The shock was felt over a very large area. It shook the densely settled Los Angeles region, and was felt at San Diego and points farther south in Mexico, more than 200 miles away. It was also felt at points north of San Francisco, and at Reno and in a large part of southwestern Nevada.

In Santa Barbara, the Carrillo and California hotels were damaged by the quake, and the Balboa Building was seriously damaged. A great deal of broken glass and cracked plaster was reported.

In Los Angeles there was considerable damage also. The elevator shafts in the Prudential Life Building were so twisted that elevators could not be used, and employees were dismissed on reporting to work. Among the structures damaged were the Roosevelt Building, the Van Nuys Building, the Rowan Building, Mays Department Store, the Mayfair Hotel, the Town House, the Gaylord Apartment House, and the Tishman Building far out on Wilshire Boulevard. The Statler Hotel estimated that 500 rooms were damaged, with a possible loss of $100,000.

Other towns affected by the quake were Lancaster, Van Nuys, Riverside, Long Beach and Fresno.

The July 21st quake occurred on the White Wolf fault which was first recognized about fifty years ago. The known length of this fault is about thirty miles.

The epicenter of the main quake was approximately at Wheeler Ridge.

The main shock lasted twenty-five seconds.

The quake struck at 3:52 a.m. (P.S.T.) on July 21, 1952.

Instrumental records indicate that this earthquake was of shallow origin, the focus being at a depth of about ten miles. The magnitude reported by the California Institute of Technology Seismological Laboratory was 7.5 on the Richter Magnitude Scale. The strongest shock ever recorded occurred in Tibet about three years ago, and its magnitude was 8.6. The quake movement has been described as rolling rather than a sharp shock, moving in a north or northeasterly direction.

The loss suffered by farmers due to the quake has been estimated at 30 million dollars. This is probably the first time in U.S. history that agriculture has been the principal victim of earthquake damage.

Cotton rows were offset as much as three feet in some instances. One earth crack was at least five feet deep and five feet across.

Many reports of changes in volume of flow of springs and surface streams were reported, both increases and decreases.

A portion of East Levee, bounding part of Buena Vista Lake, slumped vertically approximately two feet during the quake.

(Historic Kern, March, 1954)

Kern's Giant Grapevine
by Lester McDonald

Far out in the southwest corner of Kern County, unremembered except by a few old residents, stands one of our country's most amazing attractions, the Emerson Grapevine. In 1914 a picture of it appeared in the Davis Commercial Encyclopedia of the Pacific Southwest, with a caption beneath proclaiming it as the "World's Largest Grapevine."

However, I had never heard of it until a few weeks ago when Dick Bailey showed me a newspaper picture of the vine which he had exhumed from an old scrapbook. The yellowed clipping had no date, and we naturally wondered if the old vine was still in existence.

After a few inquiries we learned that the Emerson Ranch on which it was said to be was up in the Paleto (razor-back) Hills beyond Maricopa. Armed with our clipping we set out for the West Side, wondering a bit if we weren't off on a wild goose chase. If the vine was as big as it was supposed to be, why didn't everyone already know about it?

We drove south to the Maricopa Highway, then west through the town of Maricopa and up to the top of Grocer's Grade on the route to Cuyama. Pausing at the service station there for further information, we swung south onto the excellent Mt. Pinos Road for another three miles. From this point on the highway we saw the outline of an old ranch house, standing about a quarter of a mile up a little valley to our left. The dirt wheel tracks leading around the shoulder of the slope didn't look too promising but we chanced it. Bouncing along the ruts we were suddenly pulled up short by a locked gate. The proverbial man with a shotgun was not in sight so we clambered over and approached the house. A closer view showed it to be unoccupied. But where was the grapevine?

Turning a corner of the house at a brisk walk we almost walked into it. Not only was it there but it was still growing! A number of green-leaved tendrils branching out from the old growth gave proof of this.

We counted sixteen stout poles supporting the thick roof-like mass which extends over a space roughly square in shape. Pacing it off, we estimated the vine covers at least forty feet on a side. Later we learned it had once measured 110 feet per side. Simple multiplication reveals that the vine once blanketed over 12,000 square feet.

The enormous girth of the "trunk" is also difficult to believe without seeing it. Using a piece of rope we circled the largest section, and employing our known heights as a comparative figure, we found it to be at least nine feet in circumference. This "trunk" is about twelve feet tall.

A few days after our trip of "rediscovery," we secured the full story of the vine's genesis from Mrs. Josephine Bush, who resides in East Bakersfield.

According to Mrs. Bush, her father, Edward Simpson Emerson, came to Kern County in 1886 and settled near what is now called Paleto Springs. A native of Missouri, he lived for a time in Mexico. Later he moved to Sonoma County in California where he married Julia Dunbar. He then resided in San Luis Obispo County for eighteen years before moving to Kern.

In 1890 the family moved to higher and better ground overlooking Cuyama Valley, where at an altitude of 4,000 feet he ran cattle and raised wheat and turkeys. The lumber for their home was freighted in from Santa Margarita. There were seven sons and two daughters.

In those days it was a three-day roundtrip to Bakersfield by wagon. On one of those trips in 1892 Mr. Emerson stopped at the ranch of his friend, John White, west of the old Panama settlement where he was given some Madeira grapevine cuttings. On his return home these were planted by Mrs. Emerson. But despite her constant care, all but two died. However, these two entwined themselves about each other and within a few years had grown into the giant plant previously described.

A few years ago the ranch was sold to the J. B. Hudson family. Today the surrounding acres are farmed but the old house stands empty. We particularly noticed the sturdy brick chimney, still intact after all these years. This is noteworthy since the house stands almost atop the well-known San Andreas earthquake fault.

Too long neglected, the "World's Largest Grapevine" will once again receive the widespread recognition it so richly deserves.

(*Historic Kern*, March, 1954)

The Mighty Grizzly Bear
by Mary Kay Boyd

Doubtless more accounts of violent encounters with the giant grizzly bears have been told than any other of the wild animals of Kern County. The "bearest" details of such an incident were recorded on the trunk of an oak tree at the site later selected for Fort Tejon, in the Tehachapi Mountains. The carved inscription simply stated that Peter Lebec was killed by "an X bear" in 1837. Extensive research has not shed any conclusive light on the career of the victim—who he was and why he was in the locale of the tragedy.

After Fort Tejon was founded in the early 1850s, the hunting of grizzly bears was a popular sport with the officers and men at this military post. Moreover, the bears, which relished acorns, were especially abundant in the groves of giant oak trees in this sector of the Tehachapi Mountains. According to one hunter, the bear paws, when cooked in the ground under a camp fire, were a rare delicacy.

William W. Hudson, a rancher who lived in the vicinity of Fort Tejon, told the story of an Irishman's encounter with a grizzly bear in 1875. The recently employed Irishman knew enough about the animals to be apprehensive about them. The two men were rounding up mules at dusk when they passed through a grove of oak trees. Hudson saw a grizzly bear and climbed a nearby oak tree, but the Irishman was unaware of the bear until it reared up directly in front of him. As he started to climb two successive trees, bear cubs dropped to the ground. With his hair on end, the Irishman shouted, "Howly Moses, it's rainin' grizzlies."

In 1870 John W. Searles, for whom Searles Lake was named, went on a hunting trip on the Liebre Ranch, in the Tehachapi Mountains. He trailed a grizzly bear into a thicket, but because of the denseness of the chaparral, it took some time to assume a good shooting position. His first shot brought the bear down, but soon it was on its feet and ready to attack Searles. Unfortunately his gun malfunctioned, and the defenseless hunter was felled by the bear, which smashed his jaw and exposed his wind-pipe and jugular vein. Also his shoulder was broken by a second blow, and after taking a final swipe at his victim the bear walked away from the half-conscious Searles, whose companions took him for medical help in Los Angeles.

In 1893 "Old Pinto," a grizzly bear who for a dozen years had been a menace to the ranchers of San Emigdio Canyon in the Tehachapi Mountains, was killed. The bear had a special fondness for sheep, having killed a presumed one thousand of these defenseless animals. When the ranchers undertook to dispose of this grizzly bear, four determined hunters and many rifle shots proved too much for "Old Pinto." He measured eight feet in length and four feet in height, and his weight was estimated to be upward of one thousand pounds.

(*Historic Kern*, September, 1975)

Pacific Coast Field Trials
by Nina Caspari

Sportsmen from San Francisco, Los Angeles, Sacramento and other California cities flocked to Bakersfield in January for more than thirty years to take part in the Pacific Coast Field Trials. The sponsoring Pacific Coast Field Trials Club held its first meets near Sacramento in the early 1880s, but within two years the event was moved to Bakersfield. Around Bakersfield quail were plentiful, and after the first frosts the ground cover was reduced enough to afford the dogs an opportunity to exhibit their field-worthiness. The

The Pacific Coast Field Trials were held annually near Bakersfield, beginning in the 1880s, for more than thirty years.

members of the club were the elite of the state, and their dogs were the very finest. Some of the sportsmen came to Bakersfield in private railroad cars. When the field trials took place in January Bakersfield's hotels filled, and the town took on a fun atmosphere.

The field trials usually lasted four or five days, and the schedule of events included the derby, a race for puppies, the all-age stake, the membership stake, and the championship stake for winners in the other events. The newspapers carried glowing descriptions of the dogs, events, and unusual incidents. The readers were assured that they did not have to know the fine points of the field trials to enjoy them.

In January, 1890 a "ladies' day" was held, and "a goodly number of society leaders followed the chase all morning." At midday they spread a bountiful lunch and "all feasted merrily." A number of ladies sang, to the delight of the sportsmen. An appreciative, gray haired judge exclaimed, "I shall always vote for field trials in Bakersfield even when there is nothing but wire fences and jack rabbits." "Ladies' Day" continued to be a part of the field trials program, and they proved to be ardent devotees of the sport.

The thirty-first annual field trials event, held in January, 1915, was covered by Associated Press, and the news from Bakersfield was featured in the metropolitan dailies. Through the years the dedicated planning and wise selection of excellent terrain by the Bakersfield hosts helped assure that the field trials would be held in Kern County. Besides the sporting nature of the event, the field trials contributed much to the social life of early-day Bakersfield.

(*Historic Kern*, December, 1975)

A Wonderful Exhibition of Horse Breaking
from the *Bakersfield Morning Echo*, October 17, 1903

William Mullen, the horse training evangelist, gave an exhibition of his skill last night on I Street near the post office. A bronco from the Tejon ranch, which had been caught up to break and subsequently turned out because it was sulky and vicious, was the subject, and Mr. Mullen subjected it to treatment, before he had finished, which would frighten the soberest family carriage horse in town out of its seven senses. The climax of the exhibition was reached when the animal stood calmly and without a tremor while a half dozen bunches of firecrackers were exploded about its feet. It was a remarkable exhibition and those who witnessed it had extreme difficulty in believing that the horse was fresh from the lonesome canyons of the Tejon ranch.

After the horse-breaking exhibition Mr. Mullen conducted an evangelistic meeting.

(*Historic Kern*, March, 1978)

Ostriches, Unlimited
by Richard C. Bailey

Many persons will be genuinely amazed to learn that ostriches were first brought into Kern County from Arizona about 1907 by Mrs. William Tracy of Buttonwillow. She can thus be considered our pioneer in this unique industry. Until his death several years ago, "Phoenix," sole survivor of the Tracy troop of 174 birds, was a familiar sight stalking gravely about the ranchhouse yard. At one period there were over 500 specimens in the county, most of them owned by the Tejon Ranch.

The modern business of raising ostriches for their plumes began in South Africa during the 1860s. A Kaffir chief presented six pairs of superb birds to Sir Walter Currie, commandant of the mounted police at Grahamston, Cape Colony. The plumes grown in captivity far surpassed those produced in the wild state, and from this incident a flourishing industry began.

Two hundred ostriches were shipped to New York in 1882 by an enterprising businessman. Of the original group shipped, over 50 percent died during the voyage, and on the subsequent trip to San Francisco, only twenty-two survived. Their eventual destination was Anaheim in Southern California where they found a congenial home.

The next four years saw a total of 100 more birds imported from Africa. Forty-four of these, brought over by Edwin Cawston, were destined to become the ancestors of 75 percent of the ostriches now in America.

According to one account, the last shipment was made from Africa in 1901. A $500 export fee on each bird probably put a damper on further shipments to America.

In 1888 ostrich raising began in Arizona when Josiah Harbert and Newt Clanton purchased a breeding pair and twelve chicks from a Southern California farm. Ten years later their troop had increased to ninety-nine birds. Other ostrich farms began to spring up in the state.

During the interview for this feature, Mrs. Tracy was asked how she happened to get the idea of ostrich raising.

She explained, "I was reading a short article about ostriches in Arizona, and I said to myself, 'That's what I want to do.' So I tried to buy a pair from Cawston's and elsewhere in California, but no one would sell us any. I wrote to several farms in Arizona and finally heard from one that said they would part with one pair of young ones. But even they didn't seem too eager to sell them.

"When I received their letter, I asked my husband to go over to Arizona and buy the pair as I wished to go into the ostrich raising business. Mr. Tracy was a man who was never surprised at anything I might say or do, so he bought them! On the way back, one of the chicks died from an injury. To save me from disappointment, he returned and purchased another to replace the dead bird. At $500 per bird, this initial investment was pretty large, especially as I didn't at the time know anything about ostriches. It took me about twenty years to learn the ostrich business, and at the end of the period the demand for ostrich plumes had ended."

During the interview Mrs. Tracy was asked the obvious question, "Did you ever see an ostrich hide his head in the sand?" Mrs. Tracy and her sons Cecil and Darrell looked at each other and smiled. All concurred they had never seen this performed by a captive bird, although they didn't feel qualified to speak about the bird's actions in the wild state.

Established in 1862, the Tracy Stock and Ostrich Farm at one time comprised 2,240 acres. However, it is now around 1,500 acres.

The Tejon Ranch south of Bakersfield along Highway 99 was also an early site of ostrich farming. Perry Sprague, former boss of water and fences for the company, remembers the ostriches with mixed emotions.

Upon his release from the armed forced at the close of the first World War, Sprague was offered a job by the Tejon Ranch. His duties included the care of 186 ostriches. This was in September of 1919.

Like the Tracy family, Mr. Sprague never saw an ostrich hide its head in Tejon's sand, dirt or alkali.

He was asked what an ostrich would eat. "Anything a cow will," was the reply.

"But, what about those stories of ostriches eating tin cans, bottles, and similar stuff?"

"Nothing to it," answered Mr. Sprague. "Of course they will swallow sharp pebbles and shiny objects, since like a chicken they require help in grinding up their food." This checked with Mrs. Tracy's story of how a crated ostrich had nipped the diamond setting from her ring!

Curiosity arose about the birds' nature. Were they easy to handle? Did they ever attack humans? And if so, in what manner?

Perry Sprague took great relish in relating how a "tough" Marine veteran of World War I had been chased out of a field by an infuriated male that he had foolishly struck.

"If he hadn't climbed in between the horses of his plow team the ostrich would undoubtedly have killed him. Those big Nubians often weigh 350 pounds, and when about to strike they rear up to a height of ten to twelve feet. They kick forward and down with terrific force. I've seen them shear off 1¼-by-6-inch corral boards with a single stroke. You can imagine what that would do to a man!"

Cecil and Darrell Tracy had related how they had been forced to shoot a pursuing bird on one occasion—or face the consequences. Raising ostriches was beginning to shape up as a rugged occupation.

"What about their speed?" Mr. Sprague was asked. "Can they keep up with a horse?"

Recalling a humorous circumstance, he replied, "Frankly, I don't know just how fast they can run, but I chased a Nubian for forty miles one day with a car that would do slightly over fifty miles per hour. He could run faster than that car could go at top speed.

"As for matching a horse! Why, on one occasion I saw a fast horse with a rider easily overtaken. Then every few strides the ostrich would leap into the air and try to kick the fellow out of the saddle. Chased him a mile and a half clear into Rose Station before the bird would give up!"

During her ostrich-raising days, Mrs. Tracy handled every phase of the business, from raising chicks to the preparation of the plumes for consumer use.

"We would pluck young birds at the age of six months, then every eight months thereafter. The average crop was a pound and a half of feathers per bird," Mrs. Tracy related. "A pound and a half of feathers would be worth thirty to fifty dollars in the 'raw' state, depending on the quality. We plucked only wing feathers, never those in the tail."

Remembering their kicking ability, she was asked how they got the birds to stand still long enough to be plucked.

Mrs. Tracy explained that the birds were first caught, then blindfolded in a special pen where the plucking, or clipping, was performed. This operation causes no pain to the bird.

It was learned also that female ostriches in captivity lay an egg every other day until a clutch of twelve to twenty eggs have been deposited. The male and female then take turns sitting on the nest. The male invariably takes the night shift from 5 p.m. to 8 a.m., and the female the day. The incubation period is six weeks. One egg will weigh three and a half pounds. Tasting like duck eggs and scrambled, it will feed a dozen hungry people.

Young birds shoot up about a foot per month, according to Mrs. Tracy, and reach their full growth in six to eight months. A wise rancher never feeds his ostriches too much as this tends to make them belligerent. However, ostriches are afraid of dogs and a dangled rope, but will fight coyotes to protect their young.

It was a surprise to learn there are three varieties of ostriches raised for their plumes: the West Coast, South African and the Nubian. These last are the largest and finest-plumaged—and fiercest of the "camel-birds."

A number of Mrs. Tracy's troop were at Hart Memorial Park on the Kern River for several years. The rest were variously disposed of.

Mr. Sprague related the last forty-seven birds on the Tejon were sold to a carnival in 1924, leaving the ranch's 160 acre ostrich farm sadly deserted. The ranch employees, however, were probably not left too unhappy by their departure.

Fashion authorities are predicting the return of ostrich plumes to popularity, so who knows, perhaps Kern County will again become the center of a unique industry.

(*Historic Kern*, March, 1957)

The Buena Vista Mouse Plague
by Richard C. Bailey

"Fabled Pied Piper Needed In Fields"—This was the humorous sub-head that greeted readers of the Taft, California *Daily Midway Driller* on Saturday, December 4, 1926. It was the harbinger of probably the greatest mouse "plague" in American history.

In 1926 Taft was a small oil community of 5,000 persons situated in the southwestern corner of the San Joaquin Valley at the foot of the Coast Range in Kern County. A short distance to the east lay the amazingly fertile 30,000 acre dry bed of Buena Vista Lake of which 11,000 acres were planted to milo maize and barley.

Suddenly without warning on November 24, a vast horde of squealing scurrying mice issued from the lake bottom maize fields and swarmed over the headquarters community of the Honolulu Oil Company three miles distant. They crowded into fence rows and doorways, pushed into barns and sheds, even forcing their way into the walls of dwellings. Nearby leases and pumping plants were similarly swarmed under. To the people concerned the invasion was scarcely a joke. Mice even invaded beds and nibbled the hair of horrified sleepers.

Since these oil establishments were rather isolated and sparsely populated, the mouse onslaught received little attention and no press notices until December 4. But by that date the citizens of Taft, Taft Heights and South Taft were beginning to hear the patter of numerous little feet. The Taft *Daily Midway Driller* remarked,

"There is a considerable demand for mouse traps, cheese and pussy cats."

On December 6 the mice really hit the publicity jackpot. The *Daily Midway Driller* headlined the activities of the rampaging rodents, and told of the establishment on "Pelican Island" in the Buena Vista Lake basin of a twenty-five-man "poison crew" under the direction of a federal rodent control commissioner named— very appropriately—Piper!

Two days later the paper ran the sub-head, "Why Mice Leave Home Is Question Before Business Men." Through local groups several hundred pounds of poisoned grain were distributed to curb the mice, and everyone thought all was over but the shouting. A reporter kiddingly threatened, "Mr. Mouse and family, look out!" There was no comment from the mice. They were too busy traveling.

On December 15 the mouse battlers spent an entire day plowing a furrow several miles long between Taft and the lake basin. Vast quantities of poisoned grain were then distributed along its entire length. Citizens were told the commissioners had "entered the 'trenches' on Monday with weapons which are believed superior to those possessed by the 'enemy.'"

The "war" between Piper and the mice continued, but developments were unknown to the concerned residents until the neighboring *Bakersfield Californian* announced briefly on December 29, "Field Mice Curbed By Poisoned Grain." Mr. Mouse, it seemed, was really "biting the dust." But the worst was still to come.

On January 6 the *Daily Midway Driller* bleakly announced "Mice Start New Move From Lake." This time the attack centered on Ford City, a Taft suburb. Reports had it that the mice were "moving in, bag and baggage." A number of women-folk moved out.

On the same date additional swarms were reported on the Taft-Bakersfield Highway where the road skirts the northern margin of Buena Vista Lake. One newspaper account stated, "Of the thousands, half are dead as the result of being run over by automobiles, while the other half are hanging around their departed mates presumably." Sightseers by the hundreds flocked to the grisly site.

Six days later the mice were still on the move, toward oil leases in

Elk Hills and Buena Vista Hills, while other hordes were scurrying northward over the barren slopes toward Fellows and McKittrick. Oil company crews were rushed into the breach to defend their companies' property and supplies. The mice, not in the least daunted, kept coming, chewing through the sides of wooden storehouses in their path. They spoiled as much as they ate.

The same day a sheep was reported killed by mice which then proceeded to devour the entire carcass down to the bones. In another instance, an entire sheepskin hanging on a fence was consumed in one day by the ravenous mites.

E. Raymond Hall, zoologist at the University of California, after a two-day survey of the area, declared the Buena Vista mouse plague was "the strangest occurrence of its kind in the history of the United States." He also said that, according to mathematical calculations, one pair of mice "could be responsible for 16,146 others in a year's time."

The only hopeful news at this point were reports of the appearance of an increasing number of hawks and owls in the infested areas. Thousands of waterfowl were also said to be interrupting their migrations to swoop down on the tiny Myrmidons.

You might well be wondering what the cats of the west side communities were doing all this time. Well, after a few days of gorging themselves on choice squeakers, the pussies absolutely refused to consider any more mice. As protectors of the family hearth the cats were a complete washout. Offers of "surplus" felines by sympathetic mouse-free communities were firmly rejected with thanks by Westsiders.

Poison, mouse traps, man-wielded clubs, and cats were instrumental in shortening the days of many mice, but a contagious mouse disease probably did more than anything to end the invasions. At least some investigators were of this opinion. At any rate, the plague finally petered out. By Valentine's Day Mr. Mouse had hoisted the white flag.

Investigations disclosed the presence of three kinds of rodents in the exodus—house, field, and meadow mice, with the house mice far in the lead as to numbers. Final estimates revealed that between thirty and one hundred million mice had swarmed out of the Buena

Vista Lake basin after the beginning of the "plague" late in November until its subsidence around the middle of February.

An article in the *Scientific American* for May, 1927, stated that poison had accounted for five million mice. The use of poison chlorine gas on the "enemy" had been suggested by the army chief of chemical warfare, but this expedient was not resorted to.

According to the U.S. Biological Survey, there are thirty-eight states liable to mouse invasions. So, unless you happen to live in Kentucky, Tennessee, Oklahoma, Arkansas, or reside in one of the states along the Gulf of Mexico, you'd better look out—a little mouse may get you!

(*Historic Kern*, September, 1950)

Index

A. Brown Company, 33, 58, 176
A. Brown Mill, 59
Adams, A. B., 39
Ah Ming Company, 240
air meets, 75-76
Allen, Bryan, 79
Allen, Gabriel, 217
Allen's Camp. *See* Caliente
Alverson, Labon, 10, 15
Amy and Ardizzi, 201
Andrews, E. P. S., 162-63
Andrews, George, 182
Ardizzi, Ben, 201
Ardizzi-Olcese Store, 247
Arlington Hotel, 129, 239
Arms, Hillman, 75
Arnold, Murray, 20
Arvin, 225-30
Arvin Boosters' Club, 228-29
Arvin High School, 229
Arvin Tiller, 229
Asphalto. *See* McKittrick
Association of Brotherly Co-operators, 221
attorneys, 15, 43-45, 47
automobiles, 18, 44, 68, 73, 75, 163, 182-83, 198
aviation, 49, 74-79, 216

Bacon, George, 39
Bailey, Richard, 208
Baker, Charlotte E., 10
Baker, Ellen M., 10, 12
Baker, Johnnie, 39
Baker, Mary, 10
Baker, Mary Featherstone, 10
Baker, Nellie, 10
Baker, Thomas, 9, 10, 12, 13, 14, 24, 25, 72, 106, 169, 171, 182
Baker, Thomas A., 10
Baker Grade, 12, 72, 182
Bakersfield, 10, 12, 13, 14, 15, 18, 19, 22, 25, 26, 27, 28, 29, 35, 36, 43, 44, 45, 49, 61, 66, 67, 68, 72, 73, 74, 75-78, 82, 90, 93, 105, 106, 115-22, 126, 145, 155, 159, 162, 163, 171, 182, 184, 187, 190, 191, 192, 193, 194, 196-97, 198, 199, 200, 201, 202, 204, 209, 211, 217, 218, 232, 237, 242-45, 252, 254, 256
Bakersfield and Kern Electric Railway Company, 67
Bakersfield Californian, 46
Bakersfield City Council, 47
Bakersfield Courier, 14-15, 191, 194
Bakersfield Courier-Californian, 194
Bakersfield Gas and Electric Light Company, 204
Bakersfield Lodge No. 224, F. & A.M., 27
Bakersfield Sandstone Brick Company, 245
Bakersfield Southern Californian, 15, 190, 191, 192, 197
Bakersfield Town Hall, 27
Bakersfield Water Company, 204
Ballin, Fred A., 136, 137
Baptist church, 124
Basques, 105
Baughman, Cliff, 209
Beachy, Lincoln, 78
Beale, C. N., 67
Beale, Edward F., 3, 4, 6, 7, 8, 9, 13, 56, 57, 85, 170, 209
Beale, Mary Edwards, 6, 209
Beale, Truxtun, 9, 209
Beale Clock Tower, 9, 209, 210
Beale Hotel, 15
Beale Memorial Library, 27
Beale Park, 9
Bear Mountain Boosters' Club. *See* Arvin Boosters' Club
Beardsley, L. A., 163
Beatty, Charles, 69
Beatty, Iris, 69
Bedinger, Julia, 40
Bego, Alex, 19-21
Bella Union Hotel, 169
Bena, 72, 185
Benettina's Saloon, 157
Bennett, Charles, 35
Bennett, Inez. *See* Siemon, Inez
Benson, M. J., 201
Bequette, Henry D., 169, 188
Bermudez, A. A., 162
Berry, J. W., 163

Bigler, Ed, 24
Binnix, Thomas H., 169
Bishop, Samuel A., 169, 188
Blaisdell Opera House, 234
Blodget, Hugh A., 66, 244
Bodfish, 30, 166
Bodfish, George H., 175
Bohna, Christian, 10
Borden, Gail, 143
Boron, 159
Boswell, Clarence, 125
Boust, E. J., 230, 231, 232, 235, 236
Boust City, 235, 236
Bowen, Anderson, 123
Bowen, Billy, 59
Bowers, W. R., 163
Bowman, Dave, 140
Bratton, Alexander C., 192
Breckenridge Mountain, 17, 73
Breckenridge Road, 73
Brinkerhoff, Samuel, 85
Brite, John M., 188
Brittain, J. S., 15, 191-92
Britton, John, 43
Brower, Celsus, 206
Brown, Harvey, 10
Brown, Joseph C., 169
Brundage, Benjamin, 23-28, 163
Bryson, B. E., 241
Buckner, Willie, 124
Buena Vista County, 188
Buena Vista Hills, 263
Buena Vista Lake, 29, 30, 83, 90, 230, 231, 232, 235, 239, 251, 261-64
Buena Vista Lake mouse plague, 261-64
Burcham, C. A., 151
Burdette, Henry, 183
Bureau of Reclamation, 216
Burke, Edwin R., 182, 183
Burke, Oliver, 110, 174
Burke Grade, 70
Burnett, Coy, 136, 137
Burnett, Jessie, 38
Bush, Charles W., 170
Bush, Josephine, 252
businessmen, 13, 26, 31, 44, 160, 162, 167, 172, 174, 175, 177, 187, 192-93, 195, 197, 201, 214, 216, 217-18, 223, 226, 228, 234, 235
Butterworth, Mrs. T. A., 38
Buttonwillow, 211, 231, 257

Caldwell, Henry, 123
Caldwell, Joseph, 188
Caliente, 33, 35, 62, 65, 72, 73, 110, 160, 164, 166, 168, 182, 183, 184, 190, 191, 211, 217-20
Caliente Creek, 217, 220
Caliente Hotel, 166
California House, 246
California Water Service Company, 204
Calhoun, Ezekiel E., 169
California Grape Products Company, 215
Calloway Canal, 36
Calm Brothers, 148
Camel Corps, 7, 49, 53-58
Campbell, Francis, 123
Canfield, Charles, 141
Canfield Lease, 154
Cantil, 142, 186
Carr, William B., 93, 95, 96, 211
Castro, Concepcion, 115
Castro, Thomas, 114, 115
Catholic church, 23, 170-71, 197, 216, 229, 235
Central Hotel, 201, 246
Cerro Gordo Freighting Company, 218, 220
Chauvin, Emile, 214
Chee Kung Tong, 116, 118
Chester, George B., 15
Chester, Julius, 19, 191, 192
Chester and Livermore Store, 25, 26
Chico, Jose, 109, 113
Chiles-Walker Party, 50
China Grade, 28, 115, 116, 197
Chinese, 28, 62, 105, 115-22, 160, 193, 195, 196, 197-98, 199, 201, 213-14, 218, 220, 242
Christopherson, Silas, 76, 78
Chumash Indians, 83
churches, 13, 23, 24, 33, 124, 131, 132, 133, 170-71, 197, 216, 226-27, 228, 235
Civil War, 8, 57, 109, 160, 170
Claraville, 107, 110, 159, 169, 171-73, 174
Cochran, John D., 182
Cohn, E., 162
Colby, P. T., 183
Cole, Jesse, 90
Cole, W. N., 241
Collins, A. O., 163
Collins, Henry H., 125
Congregational church, 227, 228
Conner, Ned, 32

Cooley, Spade, 209
Cornwall, J. N., 163
county seat, 26-28, 61, 116, 162, 167, 169, 187, 196
Coy Burnett Field, 139
Coyote Holes, 29
Craig, F. W., 163
Cronin, Dan, 184
Cuddy Valley, 52
Cuen, Ventura, 114
Cumby, Frank, 124
Cummings, Ellen. *See* McCray, Ellen
Curran, James, 128, 242
Curran, Will, 242
Curtis Aviation Team, 75
Cuyama Valley, 251, 252

Dade, Daniel Francis, 170
Davis, Jefferson, 53
Dawson, William, 110, 174
De Forest, Lee, 207
De Guine, C., 143
de la Borde, Claude, 160
Death Valley 49ers, 17, 140
Delano, 99, 199, 211, 212-17
Delano, Columbus, 213
Delano Fruit Company, 215
Delonaga Hot Springs, 69, 70
Democrat Hot Springs, 73
Denker, Andrew H., 169
Di Giorgio Farms Company, 228
Diamond Salt Company, 186
Doherty, William J. 206
Dominguez, Jose Antonio, 84
Doss, Edward W., 13, 14
Doukhobory church, 132
draughts, 30, 33, 177
Druid's Lodge, 246, 247
Drury, J. C., 192-93
Drury, J. S., 239
Drury, W. E., 76
Dugan, John F., 201
Dugan and Ryan, 201
Dumble, E. H., 26
Dumont, Albert, 98
Dunlap, James, 181
Dunlap, John, 59

Earl Fruit Company, 215
earthquakes, 12, 19, 83, 88, 93, 209, 237, 248-51, 253
East Bakersfield, 98, 130, 202

East Indians, 105
Edison, 224
Edison Land and Water Company, 211
Edison Power Development Company, 224
El Camino Viejo, 52, 84
El Dorado Mining District, 172, 174, 175
El Paso Range, 139, 141
Eldon, John, 19
Electric Water Company, 204
electricity, 66, 73, 137, 204, 224, 235
Elk Hills Reserve, 104, 263
Elliott, Frank, 98
Elmer Post Office, 19
Elwood Brothers, 230
Ely, George, 75
Embler, A. B., 215
Emerson, Edward Simpson, 252
Emmons, Edith, 76
Englishmen, 36-41, 105, 130
Episcopal church, 24, 171
Erb, E. J., 76
Eugene Grade, 70
Evans, George S., 108
Ewing, J. Newton, 202
explorations, 2, 7, 16, 50-53, 64, 187

Fages, Pedro, 16, 52, 83, 84
farmers, 13, 49, 62, 81, 102, 104, 105, 115, 125, 126, 169-70, 175-77, 178, 184, 185, 186, 187, 211, 215, 222, 223, 225, 227-28, 229
Fellows, 45, 263
"Fence Law," 14
Ferris, Joe, 75
Filipinos, 105
fire companies, 128, 201, 237, 238, 246-47
fires, 128, 206, 214, 234, 235, 237, 242-48
Fish, H. H., 66
Fisher, George A., 137
Five Dogs Creek, 19
Fletcher, Henry, 124
floods, 12, 26, 128, 142, 214-15, 237-42
flour mills, 12-13, 15, 26, 180, 184
Foothill Citrus Farms Company, 225, 227
Fort Tejon, 7, 51, 53, 56, 57, 108, 111, 112, 169-70, 180, 181, 217, 250, 253
Fourtier, George, 75
Fowler, Thomas, 13, 14
Fox, L. T., 85
Francis, Roy N., 76
Frazier Borate Company, 143, 147

Freeman, James W., 169, 188
freighting, 18, 29, 49, 58-60, 71, 72, 109-10, 141, 145-47, 168, 174, 181, 182, 218, 220, 234
Fremont, John Charles, 17, 50, 51, 70, 85
Frenchmen, 105
Friant-Kern Canal, 216
Funk, John, 86

Galtes, Pablo, 192
Garces, Francisco, 2, 3, 16, 49, 51, 83
Garlock, 159
gas, 135, 137, 204, 235
Geringer Grade, 171
Glenburn. *See* Jewetta
Glennville, 19, 32, 163, 169, 170, 171, 177
Godey, Alexis, 50, 86, 212
gold rush, 6, 10, 17, 22, 81, 139
Goler, 149, 150
Goodale, F. W., 162
Gosford, 223
Gossamer Condor, 49, 79
Grand Hotel, 25, 129
Granite Station, 19-21, 68, 69, 70
Grapevine Pass, 7, 51, 52, 53
Gray, Thomas, 98
Greenhorn Mountains, 17, 29, 32, 58, 59, 70, 160, 170, 177, 180
Grey, George, 61
Grijalva, Jose, 109
Grocer Grade, 251
Grosvenor, Charlotte, 40
Grosvenor, Robert, 40
Grosvenor, Thomas, 40
Grower's Co-op, 215

Hagen, Rudolf, 141, 142
Haggin, J. B., 86, 93, 211
Haggin and Carr, 123, 126
Hall, Harry S., 239
Hall, Malcolm, Sr., 124
Hall, Marcus, 131
Hamilton, Ezra, 18, 19, 72
Hamilton, H. M., 75
Hammel, Henry, 169, 174, 188
Hanning, Cecil H., 33
Hare and Hounds (paper chase), 39
Harmon, Myron E., 180
Harpending, Asbury, 160
Harper, Samuel, 182
Harris, Caroline Payne, 164
Harris Grade, 173

Hart, Martin, 110, 174
Hart, Moses, 110, 174
Havilah, 14, 17, 18, 23, 24, 25, 26, 51, 61, 71, 105, 110, 116, 159, 160-71, 172, 175, 181, 182, 183, 187, 188, 196, 218
Havilah Miner, 82
Havilah Weekly Courier, 13, 14, 170
Hazlum, James, 110, 174
Henley, Beth, 209
Henry, John, 123
Holloway, H. H., 78-79
Home Extension Society, 211
Hood, William, 61, 64
hospitals, 23, 128, 216
Hot Springs Valley, 35, 181
hotels, 13, 15, 18, 19, 25, 44, 59, 69, 129, 130, 155, 166, 169, 191, 193, 201, 206, 228, 239, 242, 246, 256
Houghton, Will, 242, 244
Houston, Henry, 124
Howard, John, 124
Hudnut, Richard, 25
Hudnut Park, 75
Hudson, William W., 253
Humiston, Luther F., 169
Hunt, Clarence, 98
hunting, 90-91, 253-54
Hyde Steam Wagon, 95-96

Indians, 2, 6, 7, 8, 16, 22, 30, 31, 52, 83-85, 88, 101, 106-14, 170, 174, 177-78, 181, 212, 213, 225, 230
Industrial Workers of the World, 96, 98-99
Inyo Stage Line, 182
irrigation, 36, 115, 119, 128, 133, 176-77, 186, 187, 212, 214, 215, 224, 225
Isabella, 74
Isabella Dam, 237
Italians, 105

Jackson, A. R., 66
Jackson, C. D., 66
Jacoby and Company, 13
James Hotel, 191
Jameson, J. W., 137
Japanese, 105
Jastro, Harry, 67
Jastro, Henry A., 15, 36, 46, 102, 244
Jawbone Canyon, 107, 108, 109, 110, 174
Jewett, Charles E., 163
Jewett, Philo D., 12, 82
Jewett, Solomon, 82, 244

Jewetta, 223
Joe Walker Town, 183
Johnson, Jack, 124
Johnson, Johnnie, 33
Jones, Augustus D., 14
Jones, J. P., 183
Jones, William, 111-12, 113
Joyful, 220-22
Juncosa, Domingo, 83

KPMC, 207-9,
Kang Yu-wei, 119
Kay, Gene, 231
Kaye, W. W., 43
Keene (Woodford), 65
Kelso, John W., 174
Kelso Canyon, 109, 113, 171
Kelso Creek, 172, 173, 174
Kelso Valley, 30, 31, 107, 108, 109, 110, 171, 174
Kennedy, William L., 188
Kern, Edward M., 70
Kern Canyon Road, 74
Kern City (East Bakersfield), 43, 44, 67, 147, 200, 201, 245-48
Kern County, 1, 10, 18, 23, 49, 70, 72, 78, 81, 89, 98, 99-101, 102, 105, 123, 124, 125, 135, 157, 159, 160, 162-64, 169-71, 172, 187, 188, 190, 193, 194, 202, 211, 220, 222, 225, 230, 237, 251, 252, 253, 261
Kern County Board of Supervisors, 27, 74, 169, 184, 185, 188
Kern County Courier, 14-15, 191, 197, 198, 200
Kern County Gazette, 192, 194
Kern County Land Company, 36, 46, 86, 93, 102, 124, 133, 204, 211, 212, 240
Kern County Library, Arvin Branch, 229
Kern County Political Committee, 124
Kern County Union High School, 124
Kern County White Citizens Committee, 123
Kern Island, 9, 10, 12, 13, 25, 26, 169, 170, 187
Kern Island Canal, 93, 94, 119
Kern Island Irrigating Company, 202, 204
Kern River, 2, 3, 10, 13, 17, 25, 26, 50, 62, 69, 70, 71, 82, 98, 101, 106, 108, 109, 113, 159, 187, 196, 197, 198, 211, 237, 238-42
Kern River Canyon, 70, 74

Kern River Flour Mill, 26, 93-94, 119
Kern River gold rush, 17, 174
Kern River Oil Field, 155, 158, 230, 232
Kern River Valley, 70, 112, 113, 170
Kern Valley Bank, 244
Kernville, 17, 29, 30, 31, 73, 105, 110, 159, 160, 166, 169, 170, 171, 172, 177, 183, 184, 225
Keyesville, 17, 71, 72, 105, 110, 111-12, 113, 159, 160, 169, 174, 178, 180
Kimberlin, James Monroe, 222, 223
Kimberlina, 222-23
Klipstein, Henry W., 202, 239, 240
Knob Hill Oil Company, 232
Koehn Lake, 186
Kratzmer, August, 129
Kreiser, Ralph, 208
Ku Klux Klan, 99

labor unions, 201
Ladlow, Charles, 215
Lakeview Gusher, 234
land grants, 84, 85, 86, 212
Landers, William, 30, 31, 32, 35
Larkins, Thomas, 143
Last Chance Canyon, 142
Lavers, David, 59, 169
Lavers' Crossing, 169
Learn, Margaret, 28
Lebec, Peter, 253
Lee, John, 109
Lemert, Ralph, 207
Lightner, Abia T., 24, 163, 178, 180
Lightner, Daniel, 184
Lightner, Lavenia. *See* Rankin, Mrs. Walker, Sr.
Lightner, William, 184
Likely, Charles, 58, 59
Lilly, William B., 188
Lin Sen, 119
Lindsay Hotel, 201
Linn's Valley, 59, 169
Linz, Fred, 75
Lions Trail, 181
Littlefield and Philan, 15
Lively, Joseph, 169
Livermore, Horatio P., 93
Livermore and Chester, 13
Livingston, J. C., 33-34
Lockwood Valley, 143
Long Beach Salt Company, 186
Lopez, Jose Jesus, 84, 212

Los Angeles, 12, 18, 22, 33, 51, 56-57, 60, 61, 62, 108, 110, 136, 139, 141, 148, 149, 174, 181, 190, 196, 217, 250
Lum, Sing, 122

McCowan, Barkley, 47
McCray, Alexander, 28
McCray, Charles, 28
McCray, Clinton, 33
McCray, Della, 33
McCray, Ellen, 30-31, 34
McCray, Gladys, 33
McCray, John, 28-32
McCray, John (younger), 33
McCray, May, 31
MacCready, Paul, 79
McCuen, George, 24
McCutcheson, Frank, 176
McDougall, Benjamin G., 206
McFarland, 224
McFarlane Road, 170
McGrann, Cora, 163, 184
McGregor, Donald, 75
McGregor, Henry, 76
McKay, George, 160
McKeadney, Hugh, 183
McKittrick, 45, 157, 158, 211, 231, 263
McLaughlin, Moses A., 109-14, 181
Macking, Fred, 15
Manly, Lewis, 140
Marcel, 185
Maricopa, 45, 211, 231, 251
Marion, A. W., 201
Marsh, William, 188
Martin, Henry, 133
Martin, Pleasant, 123
Martindale, 133
Matlock, W. V., 201
May, Bill, 69
Mays Gusher, 234
Maxson, Sam, 182
Mehrten Brothers, 29
Mennonite church, 133
Merriam, Ella. *See* Smith, Ella
Methodist church, 13, 33, 124, 197, 235
Mexican War, 3, 4, 22, 53
Mexicans, 30, 101, 105, 115, 195, 196
Mexico, 8, 22
Meyer, Daniel, 244
Midway Oil Field, 141, 230, 231, 232, 236
Miller, Gus, 167
Miller, Hannah, 167

Miller, Henry, 94, 129, 239
Miller, John P., 163
Miller and Lux, 211, 231, 235
Mince and Murray, 29, 30
miners, 16, 18, 22, 23, 30, 62, 70-71, 105, 108, 135, 136-39, 143-46, 147-54, 159, 160, 169, 171-75, 178, 183-84, 188
Minter, Monroe, 24
Minter Field, 216
Miramonte Colony, 211
missions, 3, 52, 83, 84, 88, 89
Mitchell, Benjamin T., 160
Mitchell's Hotel, 59
Mojave, 18, 30, 65, 110, 151, 159, 191, 220
Mojave Desert, 16, 51, 65, 150, 159, 172
Molokane church, 132
Monolith, 136
Monolith Portland Cement Company, 136-39
Montano, Dolores, 114
Montgomery Brothers, 10
Mooers, F. M., 148
Moore, Aman, 136
Moore, Payton, 166
Morning Echo (Bakersfield), 19, 46-47
Morris, Johnny, 145
Morris Development Company, 215
Mosley, Robert, 125
Mount Pinos, 251
Muehe, William, 93
Mullen, William, 256
Munckton, Clara, 172
Murphy, J. J., 201, 247
Murphy, Tom, Jr., 75

Nadeau, Remi, 18
National Association for the Advancement of Colored People, 125
Nazarene church, 228
Negroes, 105, 123-31
Neill, John, 35
New York and Clear Creek Mining Company, 24
newspapers, 13, 14, 15, 19, 46-47, 170, 187, 190, 191, 192, 194, 197, 229
Nicoll, John, 24
Noriega Hotel, 201

Oak Creek Canyon, 18
Oak Creek Pass, 51
"Okies," 105

271

Obispo Oil Company, 158
O'Boyle, Thomas J., 201
Odd Fellows' Lodge, 27
Ogden, James, 129
oil, 28, 44, 45, 104, 135, 154-58, 193, 211, 230-36
oil gushers, 234-35
Oil Land Withdrawal Order, 232, 234
Old Town (Tehachapi), 18, 65, 169
Oldfield, Barney, 78
Olds, H. P., 191
Oregon Midway Oil Company, 231, 232
Orloff, Sam, 235
Overland Mail Company, 170
Owens Valley Aqueduct, 142
Oyler, John Franklin, 182
Oyler Canyon Road, 182

Pacific and Atlantic Telegraph Company, 202
Pacific Coast Borax Company, 143
Pacific Coast Field Trials, 254, 256
Pacific Gas and Electric Company, 204
Pacific Telephone and Telegraph Company, 202
Packard, Jeff, 238
Palmer, Robert, 171, 172
Panama, 114, 221
Payne, Howard, 158
Pentecostal church, 228
Perelli-Minetti, A., 215
Perez, Jose, 30
Person, Pop, 124
Peters, Lowell, 38
Petersburg, 169
Peterson, N. P., 24
Pettus Gold and Silver Mining Company, 172, 173
Pifer, Phil, 209
Pinckney, Joe, 125
Pinckney, William Henry, 125-31
Pinckney Brothers, 123, 124
Piute Indians, 225
Piute Mountains, 30, 107, 110, 171, 172, 173, 174
politics, 13, 14, 23, 26-28, 36, 45-47, 124, 125, 169, 188
Porter, David, 53, 54
Portuguese, 105
Poso Creek, 2, 29, 59, 71, 123
post offices, 15, 19, 31, 39, 143, 144, 177, 186, 187, 192, 201, 222, 226, 227, 229

Poulson, Charles, 78
Power Development Company, 204
Power, Transit, and Light Company, 67, 204
Poznoff, Vasili, 132, 133
Presbyterian church, 197, 235
Price, Romeo Fit, 124
Producers' Guaranty Oil Company, 231, 232

Quartzburg, 160
Quinn, Harry, 213, 214

radio, 207-9
railroads, 13, 15, 18, 32, 49, 50-53, 60-66, 72, 74, 110, 116, 120, 128, 130, 133, 141-42, 159, 182, 184, 185, 196, 198, 199, 200, 201, 211, 212-13, 217-20, 223, 224, 228, 232, 238, 239, 241
ranchers, 28, 30, 32, 33, 36, 49, 62, 81, 82, 94, 99-101, 115, 130, 132-33, 169-70, 178, 184-85, 187
Rand, A. A., 23
Randsburg, 129, 148, 150, 152, 153, 159
Rankin, Charles, 35
Rankin, Walker, Jr., 180
Rankin, Walker, Sr., 35, 166, 180, 184
Rankin, Mrs. Walker, Sr., 180
Recreation Park, 75
Red Rock Canyon, 110, 139-43
Reed, H. T., 24
Reed, Mrs. H. T., 24
Reed, Theron, 163, 169, 182
Reed and Thompson, 24
Reese, George, 124
Reid, Alexander, 160, 188
Reinstein, Phillip, 15
remittance men, 37, 130
Requa, Richard, 137
Reynolds, Frank, 24
Rhymes, James J., 169, 188
Ricardo, 141
Richardson, Arvin, 225, 226, 227
Rilcoff, Nicholas J., 132, 133
Riley, Joseph B., 169
Ritz, George, 24
roads, 7, 17, 18, 19, 20, 26, 35, 51, 52, 53, 54, 56, 58-60, 70-74, 84, 107-10, 141, 144-45, 170, 171-72, 173, 176, 177, 181-82, 197-98
Roberts, J. V., 109, 113, 176, 178
Rogers, Dora B., 163

Rogers, John, 140
Rogers, Lewis S., 15, 128
Roper, Fordyce, 93
Rosamond, 18
Rosedale, 36-41, 130, 211
Ross, William B., 169
Ruiz, Francisco, 52
Rumford, Isaac B., 220-22
Russell, B. G., 124
Russell, W. H., 147
Russians, 105, 131-33

Sageland, 107-8, 111, 159, 171-75
Sagely, Redmond B., 169
St. Clair, Leonard P., 204
Saint John Grade, 174
saloons, 13, 15, 19, 20, 24, 44, 45, 46, 160, 193, 197, 201
Saltdale, 186
Sam Yup, 116
San Emigdio Canyon, 83, 84, 88, 89, 212, 254
San Emigdio Pass, 52
San Emigdio Ranch, 84, 85, 86, 212
San Emigdio Village, 212
San Francisco and McKittrick Oil Company, 158
San Joaquin Light and Power Company, 67, 204
Sanders, W. W., 175
San Joaquin Valley, 2, 3, 7, 12, 17, 22, 24, 25, 49, 50, 51, 52, 53, 61, 64, 70, 71-72, 82, 83, 89, 93, 105, 106, 111, 116, 124, 154, 171, 178, 187, 196, 209, 211, 212, 225, 248, 261
Santa Fe Railroad, 128, 232
sawmills, 12, 58-60, 110, 144, 172, 180
Schamblin, Charles, 207
Schamblin, Frank, 207
Schamblin, Leo, 207
schools, 12, 13, 15, 23, 31, 35, 115, 164-69, 170, 184-85, 216, 225-26, 228, 229, 235, 244
Scodie, William, 110
Scott, L. F., 76
Scribner, W. H., 204, 240
Scribner's Water Tower, 244
Searles, John W., 254
Sebastian Indian Reservation, 7, 10, 170
Seventh Day Adventist church, 133, 216
Shafter, 131, 132, 133, 211
Shafter, William R., 201

Shell Oil Company, 158
Shephard, W. R., 39
Sherman, George, 78
Shirley, Wesley W., 25
Siemon, Alfred, 41-47
Siemon, Inez, 42, 43
Sierra National Forest, 107
Sierra Nevada, 50, 51, 57, 70, 74, 82, 139, 142, 152, 171, 174, 217
Simpson, Henry, 123, 124, 128
Sinclair, David A., 169
Singletary, Emory Charles, 85
Smith, David, 181
Smith, Ella, 32
Smith, F. M., 143
Smith, Isaac W., 50
Smith, Jedediah S., 17, 51
Smith, Joe, 26
Smith, L. B., 24
Smith, Thomas, 32, 176
Smyrna, 211
social life, 1, 34, 38-39, 40, 129, 168, 175, 183, 194, 197, 212, 215-16, 234
soldiers, 3, 4, 6, 7, 16, 22, 83, 108-9, 181
South Fork Valley, 29, 30, 35, 169, 171, 173-74, 175-76, 178
Southern Hotel, 25, 130, 155, 206, 242, 244
Southern Pacific Railroad, 13, 18, 26, 28, 34, 43, 60-66, 110, 116, 120, 141-42, 159, 182, 185, 187, 190, 198, 199, 200, 201, 211, 213, 217-20, 222, 223, 224, 232, 234, 238, 239, 241, 247
Spangler brothers, 214
Spencer, Henry, 124, 125
Sprague, Perry, 258, 259-60, 261
stage lines, 18, 19, 29, 61, 68, 71, 72, 73, 141, 160, 162, 166, 170, 175, 182-83, 190-91, 217, 220
stamp mills, 23
Standard Oil Company, 158
Staples, A. T., 226
Stauffer, John, 143
Stauffer Chemical Company, 147, 148
Stevens, Elisha, 21-23
Stevens, Matt, 123, 124
Stinson, Katherine, 78
Stockdale Country Club, 245
street cars, 44, 66-68, 73, 201
Stuart, Thomas B., 169
Sturm, Curt, 208
Suey On Association, 118
Sumner, 28, 60, 62, 66, 187, 211

273

Sumner, J. W., 24
Sumner Street Railroad, 56
Sun Yat-Sen, 119
Sunset-Maricopa Oil Field, 232
Sunset Railroad, 232, 234
Sunset Telephone and Telegraph Company, 202
swamp and overflow lands, 10, 25
Sze Yup, 116, 118

Taft, 45, 99, 158, 211, 230-36, 261, 262
Tailholt. See White River
Tehachapi, 10, 65, 128, 136-39, 220
Tehachapi Creek, 65
Tehachapi High School, 139
Tehachapi Loop, 61, 64-65
Tehachapi Mountains, 2, 3, 50, 51, 61, 72, 78, 253, 254
Tehachapi Pass, 18, 51, 52, 53, 61, 64 107, 110, 218
Tehachapi Valley, 51, 64. 170, 181, 217
Tejon Pass, 7, 17, 18, 51, 52
Tejon Ranch, 8, 9, 57, 184, 256, 257 258, 259
telegraph, 13, 202, 223
Telegraph Stage Company, 175, 217, 220
telephone, 34, 202
television, 207-9
Tevis, Lloyd, 93, 211
Thompson, George, 86
Thompson, V. G., 24
Thompson, Mrs. V. G., 24
Thoms, Amos O., 61
Thorkildsen, Thomas, 143
Tibbett, George, 238, 240
Tiffany, George A., 170
Todhunter, Clinton, 140
Tomlinson, John J., 182
Towne, A. N., 223, 224
Towne, A. N., 223, 224
Tracy, Cecil, 258, 259
Tracy, Darrell, 258, 259
Tracy, Ellen M. Baker, 24
Tracy, Fannie, 257-61
Tracy, Ferdinand A., 12
trappers, 17, 21, 22, 51, 52, 70
Tulamni Yokuts Indians, 230
Tungate, John B., 15
Tyler, Charles E., 202

Underwood, Herbert, 40
Union Cemetery, 15

U.S. Forest Service, 144
U.S. Potash Company, 136

Veeder, C. H., 15
Verdier Hotel, 201
Vessel, Belton, 123
Vessel, Gideon, 123
Vignave, Leopold, 212
Virginia Colony, 202
Visalia, 10, 13, 14, 29, 32, 61, 72, 113, 170, 175, 181, 194, 196

Walkara, 17
Walker, George, 180
Walker, Joseph R., 50, 70, 178
Walker, Will, 123
Walker Basin, 18, 35, 72, 110, 166, 169, 170, 177-85
Walker Pass, 29, 30, 50, 51, 64, 70, 71, 74, 107, 108, 178
Wallace, F. S., 163
Wallace, W. J., 215
Walser, Daniel W., 180
Walt's Station (Oildale), 69
Wannock, Otto, 76
Ward, Johnny, 125
Wasco, 211
Wayne, Henry, 53, 54
Wear, George W., 190-94
Weedpatch, 226, 227
Weick, Charles H., 178
Weill, Alphonse, 245
Weldon, 31, 33, 108, 110, 173, 178
Weldon, William B., 109, 113, 178
Weller, Amos, 39
Wells, Fargo and Company, 182, 247
Weringer, Joseph, 185, 186
Western Salt Company, 186
Western Union Telegraph Company, 202
Whiskey Flat. See Kernville
Whitaker, George M., 201
White River, 2, 31, 59, 213
Whiting, William, 208
Wilkinson, N. R., 27
Williams, Alex, 163
Williams, Hamp, 171, 172, 180, 183
Williams, Nick, 35, 181, 182
Williamson, R. S., 50-53, 64
Willow, Ed, 239-40
Willow Springs, 15-19, 51, 110, 169, 170, 181
Winters, E. W., 124

Wirth, A. C., 176
Withington, Bob, 238
Woila, 106
Wood, Elizabeth, 166, 167
Woodson, Bill, 209
Woody, 59, 185-86
World War I, 125, 228
World War II, 47, 138, 216
Wright, George, 38
Wynn, Dick, 209

Yokuts Indians, 106-7, 225
Young, Ewing, 52
Yowlumne Indians, 106, 107

Zalvidea, Jose M., 83, 88, 89